THE ATHLETE'S GAME PLAN FOR COLLEGE AND CAREER

by Stephen Figler and Howard Figler

with a Foreword by
Senator Bill Bradley

Peterson's Guides
Princeton, New Jersey

Printed in the United States of America.

10 9 8 7 6 5 4 3 2 1

Library of Congress Cataloging in Publication Data

Figler, Stephen K.
    The athlete's game plan for college and career.

    1. College sports—United States. 2. Sports—
Vocational guidance—United States. 3. Student
aspirations—United States. 4. Education, Higher—United
States. 5. Student aid—United States. I. Figler, Howard.
II. Title.
GV347.F53   1984   796'.07'1173   83-22112
ISBN 0—87866—266—9

For other Peterson's publications of interest, please see the annotated book list at the back of the volume.

To Mom and Jack,
especially for the gift of their values.

ACKNOWLEDGMENTS

We would like to voice our appreciation to Tom Griffith and Len Wycosky of the California State University at Sacramento Advising Center for access to materials and for their valuable insights. Sandra Grundfest and Kathleen Peterson significantly improved our efforts with their astute editorial commentary, while Jeanne Drewsen provided welcome enthusiasm and helped immeasurably by watching over our interests. Information about National Football League players and about major league baseball players was provided by Pete Abitante and Vincent Nauss, respectively. Data concerning National Basketball Association players were compiled by Dan Sharf and Dr. Carl Ojala of Eastern Michigan University. Thanks, also, to those student-athletes who expressed feelings and perceptions about their athletic and post-collegiate experience, permitting us to relate their thoughts for the reader's greater understanding. This list includes Jack Collins, Mike Cotten, Fran Englese, Phil Gayle, Steve Hoffman, and Dean Wurzberger. Finally, Jill has earned special appreciation and love for putting up with a couple of brothers who sometimes get crazy.

CONTENTS

PART I
GAME PLAN FOR CHOOSING A COLLEGE

PART II
GAME PLAN FOR WINNING IN COLLEGE

PART III
GAME PLAN FOR A SUCCESSFUL CAREER

FOREWORD BY SENATOR BILL BRADLEY

As they near graduation each year, countless high school athletes naturally have high hopes of going on to intercollegiate competition. After entering college, many learn that they don't have enough talent. But for those who are blessed with exceptional athletic ability, there is an immediate challenge: how to handle the simultaneous pressures of competition in the classroom and on the playing field.

As statistics and news reports reveal, these pressures too often result in failure—academic, athletic, or both. Most of the tragedies can be averted if prospective student-athletes have proper preparation for the unique problems facing them and the extraordinary demands placed upon them.

I remember how hard it was for me to adjust during the first year I spent at Princeton University. When I was on the freshman basketball team, we practiced daily in the gym from about 4:30 PM until 7:30 at night. After the basketball season ended, I decided to play baseball, too. Halfway through that second semester, I discovered that my grades had dropped. Reluctantly, I gave up baseball and began going to the library every day, studying from 5 or 6 PM until midnight. By the end of the year, my grades came up. That gave me great confidence. I knew then that I could compete in academics as well as athletics.

So I urge all collegiate athletes to give top priority to getting the finest education that they can. That is their prime responsibility to themselves. Nothing is more important during their years in school, or for later success, and the sooner they know that, the better.

Similarly, student-athletes should have realistic expectations—recognizing that their future in sports is uncertain and that, even if they become professionals, the life of a pro is short. Only 2 of every 100 college basketball players make it into the pros, and the average pro-football career spans only 3 years.

Thus, it is essential for even the best of collegiate athletes to fully develop all their scholastic skills and prepare for life outside of sport. They must do their class work with as much discipline and effort as they bring to athletic activities. For example, any basketball players who can concentrate inside a crowded arena and put in two game-winning foul shots also can study with intensity for a few hours each day. The trick is to use time well.

But student-athletes also should develop nonsports interests and be involved in various facets of campus life. This will help them gain new experiences and perspectives needed to make sound decisions. As the author D.H. Lawrence once said, Americans always say what we are not, but we are never really free until we decide what we positively want to be.

To me, that means life is a series of choices. We have discretion in making those choices, and in determining what we become.

As I was finishing high school, for instance, I was encouraged to go to a certain university, and I made plans to attend that school. But then I changed my mind and instead went to Princeton. When I earned my degree there, people advised me to play professional basketball. But I wanted some time to read, to study economics, to travel, and to gain perspective on myself and life. So I applied for a Rhodes Scholarship to go abroad to Oxford University. When I completed my studies there, people said I should attend law school. But I decided to play pro basketball. When my playing days ended ten years later, some people urged me to campaign for election to a position in local government. But I chose to run for a seat in the U.S. Senate.

The point is that all individuals have to decide what is best for themselves if they want to try to control their future. Because of the special abilities they have, athletes have many educational and career opportunities open to them.

Long before they go off to college, most athletes experience that satisfying feeling which comes after putting forth an effort in sports and succeeding. But if they are not ready to give as much for academic excellence by the time they enroll in college, they will not survive.

This is not a new problem. Everybody has heard about it. But it's not going away, and it may be getting worse instead of better.

By writing this book, Stephen and Howard Figler have made a major new attempt to focus attention on the situation. I hope *The Athlete's Game Plan for College and Career* proves to be an important source of help to many student-athletes.

BILL BRADLEY
U.S. Senator, New Jersey

PREFACE:
HOW THIS BOOK
WILL HELP YOU

For most college students, academic studies and career preparation are the highest priorities. For student-athletes, however, athletics often nudges other priorities aside. Although sometimes this is the fault of coaches and frequently it comes from public pressure, student-athletes themselves often must share in the blame for neglecting the very important sides of their lives that reach beyond athletics. We have written *The Athlete's Game Plan for College and Career* to help every student-athlete, whether in college or planning to attend college, achieve balance among sports, academics, and career preparation, without sacrificing any of them.

Specifically, *The Athlete's Game Plan for College and Career* will help you in several ways. While you are still in high school, it will help you make an informed choice among colleges, whether or not you are being recruited as an athlete. If recruiters *are* after you, it will help you to evaluate them and avoid potential problems. For those who aspire to professional sports, it presents hard data on which schools contribute the greatest numbers of pro athletes in each sport, and what your chances for achieving pro status really are.

As a college student, you will appreciate the presentation and explanation of the complicated rules that you will have to follow to stay eligible for varsity sports without jeopardizing your athletic career or the team's good name. Of greatest importance, however, are the advice on how to get the benefits you deserve as a college athlete and the specific guidelines we offer for coping with both academic and athletic demands.

The Athlete's Game Plan for College and Career will also be helpful in career planning. It explains how the specific skills you develop in sports will help in your future career, offers career suggestions both in and out of sports, and describes how to go about looking for a job.

In short, *The Athlete's Game Plan for College and Career* helps you choose the right college for you, advises you on how to get through college with the best athletic and educational experiences, and helps you plan for your career after college. With its help, you will earn your degree and will take pride in the achievement of both your academic and athletic goals.

To benefit from *The Athlete's Game Plan for College and Career,* you need not read it from beginning to end, nor should you necessarily read it all at one time. The book offers helpful information for the student-athlete from high school through college graduation, so pertinent chapters may be read at the appropriate time during that entire period of your life. It is intended to be your companion and reference guide throughout all phases of your college career.

STEPHEN FIGLER
Sacramento, California

HOWARD FIGLER
Austin, Texas

INTRODUCTION:

COLLEGE ATHLETES

ARE SPECIAL

In This Section...

Why College Athletes Are Special

The Price You Pay For Being Special

Having the Right Attitude About Yourself

The ABCs of Being a Student-Athlete

As a college athlete, or as someone who has a realistic goal of becoming a college athlete, you already compete with the elite in your sport. Among the many people who would like to compete at your level, very few have made it. Your special status as an accomplished athlete is recognized by students and faculty and, in many cases, by the community as well. You enjoy the attention and feel you deserve it because of the hard work that it takes to be an athlete. But you probably have found—or will shortly find—that there are special problems associated with being an athlete in college. How can you do well in schoolwork while pursuing your sport full-time? How do you develop a career plan to help you succeed after your playing days end? Can you prevent athletics from hampering both your schoolwork and your career goals?

Athletes are treated specially in college. This select treatment helps to slice through much of the red tape and many of the hassles that non-athletes have to contend with. But the sword cuts both ways, because athletes have to put up with special demands that other students don't have to face. The often privileged status of an athlete is accompanied by an obligation to the school most other students don't have to bear. The athlete pays a price for the high status, recognition, and occasional material comforts. Because you are a representative of the school and have obligations to your teammates and coaches, someone else determines where you will spend a good part of your time and energy.

Having special status thus creates problems for some athletes. Some people even see athletics and college academics as directly in conflict with each other. But the student-athlete can succeed at both sports and schooling, without doing injustice to either. *The Athlete's Game Plan for College and Career* will help you learn how to prosper in both athletics and academics. By learning to anticipate problems, you can develop strategies to counter them. Athletics and academics can function as teammates rather than as opponents in your life, if you know the potential trouble spots and learn how to handle or avoid them. The student-athletes who achieve maximum success in their lives are those who learn to make the most of their special status, not just in athletics but in their pursuit of educational and career goals as well.

During the past ten years, women's collegiate sports have grown in importance, and the differences between how men and women athletes are seen and treated are rapidly narrowing. Women now have largely the same opportunities and benefits in college sports that men have enjoyed for over a century. (This is a result of law—Title IX of the 1972 Education Amendments—and growing public acceptance of women's sports.) Spectator appeal and pressure from fans and the press generally haven't yet reached the levels that exist in men's sports, though the general trend seems to be moving in that direction. As female sports competition continues to grow, women athletes will have to take the bad with the good, including the many problems that plague men's college athletics and male student-athletes. In this guide, we will consider the needs, goals, and problems of men and women athletes to be similar; only when there are clear differences will we treat them separately.

WHY COLLEGE ATHLETES ARE SPECIAL

It's not enough just to know that you are special. In order to make the most of this status, to keep on top of the situation, it's important to understand where and why your role as student-athlete makes you special.

Selection

When athletes are given a scholarship or even when they are recruited without getting a scholarship, they have special status from the first day they arrive on campus, before doing anything as a student. Even "walk-on" athletes (those who haven't been recruited) are treated differently than other students, simply because they are athletes. Athletes are special because, in a sense, they are working for the college. Whether or not the athlete is paid directly (in the form of a scholarship), he or she represents the school by performing on an intercollegiate athletic team. Football and basketball players often serve a significant public relations function for their college, but even athletes in minor sports serve this same function in a smaller way. Since the college benefits from your efforts as an athlete, those who run the school often feel some obligation to take care of you. Because athletes must maintain a tight schedule, many colleges give them priority in getting into classes of choice, even during their first term on campus. Athletes often get special meals and special treatment at the health center. And because of their team commitments for games and travel, athletes are often given the "privilege" of missing more classes than nonathletes and taking exams at different times. A growing number of schools even have special advising, counseling, and tutoring programs for athletes.

Visibility

Athletes are the most visible of all college students, meaning that most people on a campus know who the athletes are. The student grapevine identifies which students are athletes, and athletes often can't escape this identity, even if they might want to. Besides their often obvious physical appearance as athletes (who typically are larger, stronger, or just in better shape than most students), athletes are seen in contests and may even have their names and accomplishments appear in the school or public press. The college administration considers its athletes as probably the most visible representatives of the school to the public. Who besides other scientists knows what accomplishments or failures occur in the chemistry or biology department? But the public is kept well aware of the successes and failures of the school's athletic teams.

Time Commitment

The amount of time athletes devote to their sport (and thus to the school's benefit) sets them apart from other students. Student government leaders, those who work on school publications, and those in drama or band also spend considerable time on activities that benefit the college, but they seldom spend as much time on these activities as athletes do in their sport. Besides, they can often determine for themselves how much or how little time to devote to their extracurricular activity, while athletes have no choice, beyond whether or not to compete at all. Once an athlete decides to compete, the coach demands of athletes as much time as the coach wants and needs. This demand of time is in itself enough to put athletes in a special category, and it often causes some very significant problems for college competitors.

Prestige

Many people are in awe of college athletes. The list of these people is long and includes local fans, other students (although not all of them, as you'll find out), some faculty and administrators, and certainly the well-heeled businessmen and alumni who give so much money to support college teams. Being the center of all this attention, athletes are often put on a pedestal, especially if they do well and bring fame to their school.

Money

From the smallest college to the biggest of big-time universities, a great deal of money is invested in intercollegiate sports and thus in athletes. No other student activity requires as much investment. While more than $1-million may be spent on the football team of a major university each year (at least 20 schools spend over $100,000 annually for their head coach alone), maintaining a small-time golf team, with only one coach and fewer than ten athletes, still will cost a college several thousand dollars. For many schools, those few thousand dollars represent a large investment, which means that even those few golfers are special to the college.

Pro Potential

Herschel Walker was obviously considered to be someone special on the campus at Athens, Georgia. His size, his ability, and the fame and fortune he was bringing to the university all made him special. But Herschel was also special because everyone knew that here was a person who would become a millionaire the same day he decided he wanted a paying job. Herschel Walker would be promised more money that day than any of his teachers or even his coaches would earn in their entire lives.

Herschel Walker's sports career is merely a recent outstanding example of the quick fortunes awaiting top college athletes in certain sports. The tantalizing possibility of achieving millionaire status overnight puts top-performing college athletes into a special category. Sometimes, the fame and fortune supposedly awaiting top-level athletes leads fans, faculty, administrators, alumni, and even fellow students to give them special privileges and treatment. This inevitably sets these athletes apart. And many fall into the trap of expecting—or even demanding—special treatment.

The availability of lucrative careers in professional sports is one of the few areas in which there remains a significant difference between men's and women's sports. Currently, the only major professional athletic careers open to women are in tennis and golf. (The professional opportunities available in track and field, gymnastics, skiing, and several other individual sports are limited to only a small handful of athletes.) Women's professional softball and basketball disappeared after a few years, though they may reemerge. While the variety of professional sports opportunities is greater for men, we hesitate to say that men have a greater chance of becoming professional athletes. In part, this is because there are so many more male athletes hoping to become professionals.

THE PRICE YOU PAY FOR BEING SPECIAL

You may thrive on the special consideration and treatment you receive as an athlete. It feels good to be wanted, respected, given favors, and generally treated as someone special. The problem is that this sort of treatment can blind you to the fact that you may be travelling a short street with a dead end.

You ought to think of yourself as "employed" in college athletics if you have been chosen to participate on a team, even if you are not paid through a scholarship. Whether or not you are awarded a scholarship, you are still expected to "do your job." This role brings with it certain problems that make it difficult to function as a normal student. Athletes' special problems, while largely invisible to the public and sometimes ignored by the college, are very real to the athletes. We'll give brief explanations of some of these problems here. Later chapters consider these problems more fully and provide strategies and answers to deal with them.

Eligibility

Every college student—athlete or not—must maintain a minimally acceptable grade-point average to remain in good academic standing. The penalty for falling below this level is probation and eventually disqualification from school, if the deficient GPA is not corrected. In addition, students on an athletic scholarship or grant must take a certain minimum number of units to be eligible to participate in team play. This is only one of the many eligibility rules that athletes must concern themselves with.

Few students other than athletes are likely to be influenced by school employees (such as coaches) to curtail their academic duties in favor of some other activity. Coaches have been known to suggest and even to order their athletes to take only the minimum 12 units needed to remain eligible. This leaves more time for athletics and team commitments, but it makes the eligibility issue a constant problem for many athletes. As an athlete, you might be tempted to take the least difficult or most convenient minimum number of course hours you can find, rather than challenging yourself with more substantial and meaningful classes. Focusing on minimum eligibility instead of on academic progress toward a degree can detract from the quality of your educational program and lead to unforeseen problems when graduation finally does draw near.

Time Pressures

College athletes often find they spend twice the amount of time training and competing in sports as they did in high school, while at the same time the requirements of schoolwork in college have also doubled. This presents a problem if your coach makes additional demands on your time—or if you make these demands on yourself.

College athletes are required to be full-time students progressing toward a degree. This is a full-time job and rightly is your primary responsibility as a college student. But in many cases, the training, travelling, and competitive demands on athletes amount to a second full-time job. In order to handle both jobs, you must learn how to manage time extremely well—in fact, better than most students who are only students. Being a college athlete means not only training hard and performing well in your sport but giving enough time and attention to schoolwork. Time management skills are needed to cope with this problem, for if you take on too much, it can bring an early end to your athletic involvement, or even to your education.

Financial Problems

College athletes often have special financial needs, not because they require any more money than nonathletes, but because they rarely have the time, much less the energy, to earn money from a part-time job. It's tough enough to do well in two full-time jobs (sports and schoolwork), without adding a part-time job.

Many athletes receive an athletic grant, an academic scholarship, or a loan or grant based on need. But even the best financial aid package is designed to cover basic educational and living expenses only. Little, if anything, is left over for daily expenses, clothes, and entertainment. Sports boosters, and even coaches, may offer to help athletes with their financial difficulties, and the athlete presented with such an offer may be tempted to accept the extra aid. But doing so may only lead to far more serious problems, such as loss of amateur standing and penalties to the school's athletic program.

Personal Pressures

Coaches and teammates exert pressure on you to be committed and to do well in your sport. Pressure also may come from fans within the school and from boosters. In some sports (not always limited to major sports), the media bring added pressure. Even when your particular public—your group of fans—is small and the press couldn't care less, you are likely to feel some pressure to please them. But the most consistent and maybe even the heaviest source of pressure bearing on college athletes comes from within themselves. Even when athletes have done well personally, they often feel as if they bear some guilt when the team doesn't win. There is always "something more" they could have done to bring victory. This is a special pressure known to all athletes and felt by very few outside of sports.

Academic Progress

It may seem strange to single out athletes as having problems in making academic progress. Isn't this a problem for all students? It is, but the problem takes on special dimensions for athletes. Identifying a major field of study and maintaining progress toward a degree are two sides of the same need: gaining an interesting and useful education. In addition to the personal and time pressures just discussed, some people have foolish and degrading beliefs that athletes are not suited to some academic majors. This may lead athletes who haven't yet identified a strong interest in a field of study to select an easier major than they otherwise might choose, or simply to pick one (such as physical education or recreation) that is often identified with athletes.

Athletes may eliminate a preferred major and career direction because it conflicts with the sports side of their life. Or, they might proceed toward a degree at a slower pace than other students, again, because of athletic commitments. None of these problems relating to academic progress necessarily result from being a college athlete, yet the fact that each occurs illustrates the need athletes have for special guidance.

Career Selection

The intensity with which college athletes compete in their sport and the consuming part it plays in their lives seem to inhibit many athletes from planning for life after college. Too often, athletes don't take the time and effort to do any active, future-oriented career planning. Why struggle with the future when the present is so much fun and so rewarding? And, of course, there is that legion of college athletes whose planning for the future begins and ends with their dreams of a career in professional sports.

HAVE THE RIGHT ATTITUDE ABOUT YOURSELF

Each of the problems of being a student-athlete mentioned above is dealt with in later chapters. Tricky recruiters, bad advisors, difficult-to-approach or exploitive coaches, peer influence, college and eligibility regulations, educational choices, competition for careers, and a host of other problems all are given attention.

In the advice and recommendations *The Athlete's Game Plan for College and Career* offers, you will detect three guiding principles. Keep them in mind as you travel the student-athlete road:

Respect yourself as an athlete. Participation in sports gives you universal benefits, regardless of your particular sport, area of study, or intended future career. The discipline, mental skills, emotional control, and sense of teamwork you develop in athletics all will enhance your personal maturity and thus your prospects as a student and career professional. Few students work as hard and as productively as the student-athlete. Be happy with your efforts and translate them into future gains.

"When in Rome, ... :" You are a student, so be a good one. You are as much a student as you are an athlete; you *must* embrace that view in order to reap the fullest education available to you. Not all students are good students. Observe those who make it their business to gain all they can from the college and its faculty. They are getting their money's worth. Imitate the good students. Find out how they discover where the good classes are and how they pinpoint the superior professors. The labor market believes so strongly in the worth of bright and productive college graduates that it gives them most of the best jobs available and promotes them to positions of leadership. Make sure you are in the front row when the good stuff is handed out.

"Ceci [Hopp of Stanford] won the 3,000-meter event in the inaugural NCAA women's track meet. [Since then], she [has been] running, swimming, and weight-lifting five hours a day in preparation for the 1984 Olympics. Although she looks forward to the Olympics, Ceci is emphatic about trying to 'keep that goal in perspective. If I fail in one respect, I don't want to feel that I have failed overall.' "

[*The Stanford Magazine,* Summer 1983.]

You're only a dumb jock if you think you are. If you let people give you bad advice and you accept a major field or a job offer because you think there is nothing else you can do, you are cultivating a dumb jock myth inside yourself. Athletes have intelligence, drive, and commitment. You can translate these qualities into career success if you *believe* you possess them. Athletes are smart, alert, and motivated. They could never have survived training and competition without these virtues.

Career success, as well as athletic success, is only attainable when you believe in your own abilities. This belief leads to assertiveness, self-confidence, the capacity to see what you want to accomplish (whether a drive to the hoop or a partnership in a CPA firm), and the initiative to mobilize yourself toward your goal. Through their sports involvement, jocks know that direct application of skill and determination pays off handsomely. And that ain't dumb.

In order to successfully handle the dual roles of student and athlete, you must anticipate the problems that may frustrate your goals. Some of the specific problems you may encounter include:

- Being deceived by college recruiters and thus making a poor choice of college.
- Misunderstanding or being misled by eligibility rules.
- Allowing yourself to be misdirected in your academic goals (i.e., taking the easy route).
- Overlooking legitimate sources of money to help you complete your degree.
- Overlooking graduation requirements.
- Having your progress slowed by bad advice about courses and academic programs available to you.
- Lacking a career goal to pursue after your competitive athletic days end.
- Not knowing the best way to look for a job (possibly because you expected someone to hand you one).
- Being shortchanged on career skills you could have been acquiring during college (because you were too busy with sports).

THE ABCs OF BEING A STUDENT-ATHLETE

The above problems and others like them can be avoided only if you look upon your college years as an integrated package of athletics,

> *Some college officials "think of their athletes as if they were disposable razor blades. They give them uniforms, schedule games for them, and sell tickets so they can make money and paint their gym or buy nice new desks for the athletic department, and when the kids are used up they simply throw them away, with no conscience. ... The world is full of people who are only too ready to think you're a fool, just because you're a jock."*
>
> —Comments of a news editor who covers college sports
> [Joe Hamelin. *Sacramento Bee*, June 13, 1983.]

education, and career preparation. Problems often occur because athletes allow their sports to dominate them, to the neglect of education and career. We call looking at the overall picture of your life in college the ABCs of being a student-athlete.

A is for Athlete

College athletes not only *want* to compete but they have a *need* for competition, so much so that they often are willing to sacrifice what nonathletes take for granted in life: leisure time, extra money from a part-time job, a full social life, a body free from pain, time for studies, and even privacy. Competing in their sport is more important to athletes than any or all of these other aspects of college life. Many athletes don't even weigh the value of competing on a team against the loss of these other things. No contest! This is often as true of the small-college athlete in a minor sport as it is of the big-time football or basketball player. We are describing *desire*—the desire of a person to compete and be known as an athlete. The desire to be an athlete may be the single most important motivation currently in your life.

Although college athletes give up much of what other students take for granted, they receive a lot in return. In addition to the sheer pleasure of competing, athletes often gain respect and maybe even adulation, a strong and attractive body, the opportunity to travel, practice in operating under pressure, helpful personal contacts, the possibility of fame, and even a slim chance at fortune. In other words, participation in athletics can enrich your life immensely, and you can have a heck of a good time in the process.

B is for the Other Benefits College Can Bring

The important benefits of your years in college are *not* the credits and grades you get on a transcript. The real and meaningful benefits come from the things you do in the classroom, your discussions with other students between classes, your efforts and accomplishments outside of the classroom (in addition to athletics), your interaction with faculty and college staff, your development of good reading and study habits and the habit of critical thinking, and your gaining an appreciation for knowledge and what it can do. Although it's easy to aim primarily for credits and grades (the system's tangible, measurable goals), these are only symbols of what you were supposed to have learned and how you are supposed to have grown.

You may find ways of getting good grades and piling up credits in easy courses without really learning much of value. (Even the best schools have Mickey Mouse courses.) But earning credits in this way is like winning an athletic contest against some poor, underpowered opponent; there isn't much value or satisfaction in either. In fact, it's a waste of your time and effort compared to what you could be doing. The choice is yours. You can miss out on most of the potential for learning and personal growth simply by doing only what is necessary to stay eligible for sports; or you can take the tougher, more rewarding road and try to get all of the benefits that college has to offer.

Even if they know this, some college athletes still feel that there is reward enough in just being an athlete, and that it is just too much hassle to get wrapped up in schoolwork. But treating schoolwork that way will not only hurt your grades, academic progress, and career preparation, it could also hinder your athletic progress. Coaches often point out that how you practice is how you will play, meaning that practice is the time for building good habits, which can then later be called on during the pressure of competition. Habits built in school-work carry over into athletics, and habits built in athletics should carry over into schoolwork. Athletes who get into the habit of taking the easy way in schoolwork will probably do the same in athletics. They may be able to fool the coach, but their teammates know who isn't going all out.

The direct and indirect benefits of college can, if you let them, take you far beyond what is gained by just being an athlete. These benefits include:

- Development or improvement of work habits
- Practice and direction in solving problems
- Development of your ability to think critically and make informed decisions
- Broader knowledge and appreciation of the world
- Greater understanding of your place in the world

- Knowledge of specific new subjects
- Useful and enjoyable lifetime personal contacts
- An interesting career direction

All of these benefits and more come from putting time and effort into being a student as well as being an athlete. They are the real fruits of a college education, which all college students, including athletes, should take with them when they graduate. You should not be satisfied with less.

C is for the Career You Are Approaching

Career—the word almost shimmers: that future which always seemed so distant, but is now around the next bend or two. You wouldn't be the first person to quake at the thought of it. Meet someone new and what does he or she usually want to know immediately after your name? What you do (or plan to do) for a living; what career you are in or studying for. You may not feel ready to be put into a category, defined by a line of work, but the world seems to want it that way.

Maybe you aren't yet too concerned about a career because it seems far off in the future, two or more years down the road. But you know the time will eventually come when you have to face the necessity of choosing a new direction in your life. The closer it gets, the harder it is to face, unless you have a plan to help you find a career direction or you seek out people trained to help in this area.

In some cases, a college education can lead you directly into a career. Engineering, computer science, and accounting are some popular examples. (We are talking here about a college education giving you the specific skills necessary for direct entry into a job, *not necessarily* the availability of those jobs.) In other cases, a college education cultivates universal skills which you may then have to mold in your own way. English, history, mathematics, and psychology are some examples. But in all cases, your experience in college should help you grow to the point that a career of your choosing is within reach. This obviously won't be the case if you spend your years in college being an "eligibility major," a term for those who take only enough units to stay eligible for sports.

Your initial career choice may have something to do with your experience and interest in sports. But the choice you make will more than likely be at least as influenced by your other skills, interests, and nonsports experiences. This combination of what you gain from sports and what you learn from schoolwork and the other sides of college life should give you skills, contacts, and a widening vista of interests, so that you are more likely to make a wise and informed career choice.

Remember the ABCs of the college athlete's life. You are best served, now and in the long run, by taking care of each of these three concerns. Coaches, fans, and even some teammates may want you to emphasize the athletic part at the expense of the benefits of a college education and your future career. At colleges where athletics are at odds with these other concerns, athletes are being exploited. You are the best one—at some schools, the only one—to make sure that it doesn't happen to you. You should gain more from college than just a few years as "someone special." You deserve more lasting educational benefits and at least a healthy start toward an interesting, worthwhile career.

Don't expect college to provide these educational and career benefits automatically. College officials—coaches, professors, advisors, and counselors—may not follow the progress of your education very closely. (Eligibility, yes; progress, no.) They may claim in public that they care about how well their athletes do in the classroom, and they may even monitor your progress toward graduation; but you can't count on these individuals to know and care whether you are learning very much that will help in your life after college.

A diet of easy courses means you've lost out on a worthwhile education. When you cannot get or hold a decent job later because you cannot read and write effectively, speak well, or solve problems efficiently, the employer will not be sympathetic to the excuse that you were busy being an athlete in college.

What if you eventually get a degree? Does that automatically mean that you are educated? A combination of academic concessions, easy courses, and low grading standards for athletes could mean that you might accumulate enough credits to receive a college degree, even if you have learned little or nothing of value in the process. It is up to you to *earn* your education. Once you receive an empty education, it will be far harder to obtain a useful one. Other colleges may not want you. Besides, you will probably be tired of being a student by then, anyway. We want you to get a quality education now, while the getting is still good.

These are the ABCs—the basic and most important elements of the athlete's years in college. If you leave college having had a good athletic experience, having earned a good and useful education, and with a promising career direction in mind, you've done well and the college has done well by you. If you miss out on one or two of these elements, you've been cheated—or you've cheated yourself.

Sports experience and a good education can complement one another so well that during your entire lifetime you will reap the benefits of the effort you put into each. Effort put into your education may not be as exciting and immediately rewarding as the effort put into your sport. But long after the shouting and applause have faded, you will remember, appreciate, and use a well-earned college education. The quality of your education—measured more by what you put into it than by the school you attended—will affect everything you do, including your career development and your relationships with people.

One of the hardest things that any athlete has to face is the end of his or her career in active, high-level competition. The trip from star status to has-been takes only a moment. Many former athletes have called it a kind of death. The best way to beat that "death" is to prepare for a life after athletics and college. You, the athlete, can prepare for your next life in the work world by paying attention to your schoolwork and career development while you are in college living it up as an athlete. That first step beyond college is a long and steep one, and there are far fewer people around willing to help an ex-athlete than there were in the days when that same athlete had eligibility remaining. That is one of the harder facts of life that athletes must learn to accept.

We believe strongly that it is possible to have a satisfying collegiate athletic career while obtaining a serious and useful education. But if you are just going through the motions in college, there is no guarantee that this will happen. In fact, because the pressures on an athlete to perform are so enormous, it is considerably more likely that a quality education will remain beyond your reach, unless you learn how to make the system work in your favor. You must learn to fight the pressures that will entice you to commit yourself primarily to athletics—to being an eligibility major. You must strive to be successful in both sides of the student-athlete role. There are many obstacles to your getting the maximum benefit from this dual role. *The Athlete's Game Plan for College and Career* will identify these problems and offer solutions, to help you have a good athletic experience while obtaining the education that will benefit you in your career and throughout your life.

PART I

GAME PLAN FOR CHOOSING A COLLEGE

Coaches and athletes use game plans to achieve a very clear goal: to win the contest. Their game plan shows them how to stay on the path to their goal and what alternative paths to take if something interferes. Deciding about which college will be the best for you is an extremely important decision in your life; it should not be made quickly or lightly. A bad decision can hinder you in many ways, waste your time, effort, and money, ruin your athletic experience, sour you on education, and generally foul your progress toward becoming a success. A good decision, on the other hand, can make life enjoyable in each of these areas.

Student-athletes can and should adopt a game plan to help improve their chances of making a good choice among colleges. Unfortunately, too many athletes tie their future to a particular school simply because it is close to home, is cheap, or has expressed interest in recruiting them, or because a friend or family member went there. Choosing a college simply for one or two of these reasons would be like a coach entering a contest without knowing the rules, what the contest will cost or how to pay for it, or what the relative strengths and weaknesses of the opposition are. That is no way to expect to win.

Making the *right* choice for you among the hundreds of possible colleges is not an easy task, but you are more likely to make a good choice by focusing on the following elements, covered in Part I, as the basis of your college selection game plan:

1. Consciously determine which personal, academic, and athletic factors are most important to you in a college, and find out what each of the colleges you are interested in is looking for in its students.

2. Have a clear view of where the potential professional athletes in your sport go to college. If you have no plans for entering the pros, you may even want to avoid these schools, since you won't want to be competing with pro-caliber players for a spot on the team.

3. Understand the "sales techniques" that recruiters use and know what they (and you) may and may not do, so as to ensure that you don't get into trouble with agencies that govern college sports.

4. Learn about the pros and cons of athletic scholarships and how to obtain other forms of financial aid.

Game plans need not be elaborate; in fact, some of the best game plans are very simple. To be useful and effective, though, they must cover the important areas of concern. The elements we've just listed should be the primary ingredients in your game plan for selecting a college. Armed with knowledge in these four areas, you will be better able to make the best decision about where to go to college. You will also have a better idea of what to expect from your college—both academically and athletically—and what your college will expect from you.

1

SELECTING

YOUR COLLEGE

In This Chapter . . .

The Selection Process Used by Colleges

Special Admissions Considerations for Athletes

What to Look For in a College

Athletics as a Factor in Selecting Your School

Strategies for Making the Best Choice

Should You Go to a Two-Year College?

When the time comes to begin seriously thinking about which college to attend, many athletes think mainly of athletics-related reasons for attending particular colleges. That's natural for someone whose life has been filled with athletics. But while it may be natural, it isn't smart, because athletics-related factors are less predictable and stable than any other factor worth considering when selecting your college. The coach to whom you want to commit four years of your life may not be around for your entire collegiate career. Coaching is one of the least stable of all professions. Coaches get fired because they are losing, or they move on to better coaching jobs because they are winning. The pressures of their job are so intense that increasing numbers of coaches are becoming burned out and quitting the profession while still young. Even coaches who stay at your college during your entire time there may not turn out to be as wonderful as they may have seemed while you were being recruited.

Are you attracted to a particular college primarily because it needs someone like you to fill a position or event? Are you overlooking some negative aspects of this college at the expense of other schools that may be all-around better choices but that don't need your athletic talents so "desperately"? No matter what coaches tell you, they are not banking entirely on you to fill that spot on the team. What will you do if someone better shows up to play your position or compete in your event? What if you get injured badly enough that you can't compete? These things could happen at any time, including your freshman year. You might be on the sideline or off the team entirely. Not happy things to think about, but they happen to many athletes and could happen to you. The important point is where it leaves you in terms of your college education. You won't want to be at a school that satisfies only your sports needs, *especially* if that part of your life falls apart.

Athletes don't concern themselves with a college's financial problems. They figure that, somehow, the school will have the money to field their team, especially if the school went to the trouble and expense to recruit them. But in these days of financial problems, many colleges are dropping some intercollegiate sports or downgrading them to club status. This can happen even when coaches project great athletic success for their school's teams. The University of Baltimore in 1979 upgraded its athletic program from Division II to Division I, the top level of NCAA competition. Only four years later, it was announced that the entire intercollegiate athletic program was being dropped. If this happened in your sport, would you still be happy at your college? Would it fit your other needs?

In order to make a good choice of colleges, you have to make a thorough investigation of all the factors that could affect the success and enjoyment of your college life. You must consider other factors in addition to sports when selecting your college. Keep sports high on the list, certainly, but try to imagine how you would feel about spending your college years at each school on your list if you *didn't* compete on the team.

THE SELECTION PROCESS USED BY COLLEGES

The college selection process is a two-way street, and it's important that students keep this in mind as they weigh what they *think* will be their options. Before examining the factors you should consider in selecting a college, let's discuss what determines whether a school will want you as a student.

Open vs. Selective Admissions

In terms of what a student has to do to get admitted to a college, schools fall into two broad categories: those with an open admissions policy and those that maintain selective admissions standards. Contrary to what the name implies, open admissions colleges do not accept any and all applicants. Instead, open admissions schools establish a set of minimal standards to ensure that each student admitted is able to do college-level work. A high school diploma or the equivalent is one such minimal standard required for admission to an open admission college. At some such colleges, however, you may be able to substitute for the high school diploma a certain minimum number of units that have been taken at a junior or community college. In California, for example, a student can enroll at a public community college without ever having graduated from high school. If he or she accumulates 56 college-level credits at the community college, the California State University system must then accept this student into a bachelor's degree program without any further admissions screening.

Some selective admissions schools use what is called an eligibility index to decide which students to admit. The eligibility index is often a combination of your high school GPA and your score on one of the two standard college entrance tests, the SAT or the ACT If your index number is above the minimum set for that year, you are admissible. If your high school GPA is high enough (some colleges set the limit at 3.2 or better), your SAT or ACT scores may not be weighed as heavily in the admissions decision. On the other hand, if your high school GPA is below a certain level (usually 2.0 is the minimum acceptable level), even an extremely high score on the SAT or ACT wouldn't be enough to get you admitted. If that were the case, your best bet would be to go to an open admission community college for at least a year and improve your grades, so that these college credits and GPA would become the basis for admission to the four-year college you want instead of your high school record.

Many selective colleges want much more evidence of a prospective student's ability to achieve a bachelor's degree than merely those factors considered in an eligibility index. How selective each college is depends on many considerations, including the number of applications that are received each year. This means that you might be rejected from a particular school one year yet be admitted another year, when the college has received fewer applications and has more space.

Some college applicants don't receive an immediate acceptance but are put on a waiting list, which can be frustrating. Colleges have waiting lists because each year officials have to estimate how many applicants who have been admitted will actually enroll. Underestimating will cause crowding, while overestimating will cost the college money in unused space. If you are on a waiting list, you might not know until late summer whether you've been admitted to a particular college for the following fall term. Athletes whom a coach is particularly keen on recruiting are sometimes given priority on the waiting

5

list and may be admitted at the last moment. But don't count on this happening, or you might wind up out of luck and out of school when the term begins.

Factors Used in Selective Admissions

Following is a list of factors that selective colleges are likely to use in choosing their students. The list is generally in order of importance, although each school has its own system of weighting these factors.

Grade-point average. The more selective the college, the higher your GPA must be, usually excluding physical education courses. To be accepted at such highly competitive colleges as those in the Ivy League, Northwestern, Stanford, Rice, or Case Western, for example, you should have a 3.5–4.0 high school GPA and will have to be very strong in some other areas, such as student government or other extracurricular activities.

SAT or ACT scores. These standard admission test scores are required at most colleges. They are only estimates of a student's ability, yet these tests help admissions officers to compare students from various high school environments, thus helping to overcome the problem of comparing GPAs earned at different schools.

Letters of recommendation. Personal recommendations are required for college admissions less often than they used to be, but at schools where they are asked for, treat them as very important. Make a list of people you feel can best recommend you to your preferred colleges. This list might include teachers, coaches, other school officials, alumni of the college you are applying to, and employers. They all should be people who know you and know your capabilities. Admissions people tend to devalue letters from family doctors, clerics, and elected officials. If you don't include letters from teachers or coaches, admissions officers will wonder why. Most important, ask only people who you know will have a good opinion of you. Evaluators expect to read glowing recommendations and will look for any hint of weakness. Lukewarm comments that suggest you are "good but not great" can hurt your chances. Before directly asking the people on your list to write a letter or fill in the recommendation form on your behalf, ask if they would feel comfortable recommending you. If there is any hesitation, thank the individual and move down your list to someone else.

The essay. On many college applications you are asked to write a brief, informal essay about yourself or else to elaborate on a particular topic (e.g., the meaning of a college education; why you want to come to the college; what you want to be doing in ten years). Essay questions such as these are included as part of the application for two reasons: to provide admissions officers with a sample of your writing ability and to give them an insight into your interests and motivations. The essay should be taken seriously and labored over. It projects an image of you that admissions officers cannot obtain from the rest of the application (which amounts to a listing of biographical information). The effort you put into the essay shows how much you care about attending the college. How much it counts relative to other factors varies from one school to the next, but if an essay is required, the admissions staff intends to read it.

Extracurricular activities. This is where your sports background can impress admissions officers. Be sure to include nonsports activities, such as school publications or clubs, and especially include positions of leadership you've held. But do not overload the list and certainly don't pad it with false or misleading information. Listing too many activities could suggest that you haven't been serious enough about the academic side of high school.

Legacies, "legs," or who you know. At some schools, especially private colleges, having a close family member who graduated from that college will automatically provide you with preferential consideration. (A parent or older brother or sister who is an alumnus gives you one "leg," two give you two "legs," etc.) The more "legs" you have, the better, since schools benefit by establishing a tradition within families. Especially if a family member was successful at the college, admissions people assume that you also are likely to be successful. They also know that when many family members go to the same college they tend to donate money to it.

The interview. Not all schools require an interview, especially for applicants who live at a great distance. We strongly suggest, however, that you visit any campus where you might be committing yourself

---

"High school graduates who are excellent athletes as well as outstanding students reveal a degree of maturity and strength of character that distinguish them and make their presence on campus worthwhile."

—Fred Hargadon, Dean of Admissions, Stanford University
[*The Stanford Observer*, November 1981.]

7

to spend two or more years of your life. While visiting, speak with a number of different people, more than just to say "Howdy." We'll discuss whom you should talk with and what to ask later in this chapter.

SPECIAL ADMISSIONS CONSIDERATIONS FOR ATHLETES

In some cases, being a prospective star athlete may weigh more heavily than any or all of the above selection factors. Athletic ability could get you into a school where you otherwise might not have been admitted. Those who make decisions about who will be admitted to a college may take into account the needs of coaches for particular players, even if some of those players do not have as much potential for academic success as other students being considered. People who make such admissions decisions may be fans of the school's teams, or they may be influenced by pressure from the athletic department, athletic boosters, or other school administrators.

Athletes admitted to college who are unqualified to do college-level schoolwork are often shunted into special tutoring programs, the Economic Opportunity Program (EOP), or other special admissions programs. In spite of the help such programs may offer, being in the situation could put you in over your head if you are unable to keep up with the other students. It is particularly difficult to catch up with other students if you have to practice or compete in your sport nearly every day. Being admitted to a college mainly because you are needed as an athlete not only could hurt your academic progress but could put you at greater risk of losing eligibility for sports. An unqualified student admitted to a school primarily for his or her athletic ability usually pays a heavy price in the end.

We strongly suggest that you only consider colleges to which you would be admitted even if you were not an athlete. Only in this way can you feel secure that the admissions officers have judged you to be capable and likely to succeed at their college. (Whether or not you actually succeed, of course, is up to you. Those responsible for admissions only judge whether you have the ability.)

WHAT TO LOOK FOR IN A COLLEGE

The sports environment at any college on your list of possible choices will probably be as important to you as any other factor. But even if your motivation for going to college is mainly to continue competing in your sport, sooner or later you will probably come to realize how important a good education is.

A variety of factors should enter into your decision about which college to choose, including: location of the college, size of the student body, net cost to you or your parents, orientation of the educational environment, options for majors, and housing and social life considerations—all in addition to those very important sports-related factors. Let's examine each of these factors separately.

Location of the College

When considering how well a school's location suits you, think about the climate, the size of the surrounding population, and the proximity of the campus to home and friends and to the area where you eventually might like to begin your career. Even though some of these concerns may seem important to you now and others may not, each deserves your consideration.

Climate. We often take climate for granted, but scientists have shown that climate can severely affect our moods and the efficiency of our performance. If cold weather, snow, or frequent rain bothers you now, don't assume that you will be able to overcome that reaction when you go off to college. Some people get depressed when trees become bare and the cold of winter sets in; others are depressed by the day-in, day-out sameness of a lack of seasonal changes. If you are severely bothered by hay fever, think carefully before selecting a college in an agricultural area. If hot, dry weather makes your skin crawl, think twice about a school in the Southwest. How people react to climate is *not* a matter of maturation or will power.

Urban or rural setting. If you've been raised in the city, do you think you could feel comfortable spending most of four or five years in a town with a slow pace, where everybody knows everything about you, and there is little or no nightlife? If you've been raised in the country, could you feel at home in a fast-paced urban setting, where noise and commotion never seem to stop and no one seems to know or care about you? Maybe on your campus visit you liked the life-style because it was a change from what you were used to. But can you see yourself liking it when it becomes your daily life?

Closeness to family and friends. You may feel very anxious at the thought of moving away from family and friends to attend college. Or, on the contrary, you may feel that college is the opportunity to set yourself free and expand your horizons. No matter which way you feel, it will probably become less important once you are settled into school. Contact with family members is usually possible in some form if and when you really need them. You may drift apart from old friends, but that is in the natural order of growing up. The easiest time of your life to make new friends is during college, especially if you just let it happen.

If you go to a college located within a 2- or 3-hour drive of your home, you will probably see your family and old friends fairly often, possibly every week, especially during your first year at college. If school is as much as 6 to 8 hours from home, you would perhaps see family and friends three or four times each term, or possibly more if they want to see you compete. If school is much more than 8 hours from home, don't expect to see family and old friends other than during the holidays and rare weekends, unless they are especially motivated to see you compete.

It's hard to tell before you try it whether being apart from family and friends would be an emotional hardship or would give welcome freedom and more of a chance for you to grow in your own direction. But even though you can't predict how you will react to being separated from your parents once you are settled into college life, your feelings on this issue should still be considered in your choice of schools. Make sure you discuss with your parents how all of you feel about being close or distant. Too often this is an issue that gets overlooked or hidden because we don't want to hurt others' feelings. Discussing this openly as one element in your college choice can help to overcome later worry and problems.

Future job. You may feel that it's too soon to be thinking about where you want to work after graduation when you are only at the point of selecting your college. You may have little or no idea of what you want to major in yet, much less what specific career and job you'll be seeking upon graduation. But you should realize that the reputation you earn and most of the contacts and associations you will be making will be most useful in the general location of your college and less useful the farther away from school that you begin your career.

Size of the Student Body

Some people feel very comfortable among large herds of people, while others feel intimidated by crowds. Some students work and grow best with the intensive personal attention from teachers and advisors that is more likely to occur at a small college, while others value more highly the range of resources, both educational and recreational, that tends to exist at big universities. As with climate, don't assume that you can adjust to and thrive in any environment, because that environment will be there every day, all day. Also, remember that more people on campus does not necessarily mean more friends on campus. In fact,

10

the opposite is often true. In large cities, large universities, large dormitories, and large classrooms, students see lots of people but tend to interact with and become friendly with few. In smaller settings, students often have more chances to interact one-on-one and become friends with a larger number of people.

Net Cost of Your Education

The cost of going to college is clearly an important factor in determining which school you finally choose. Inflation has doubled the cost of a college education over the last decade. Tuition and room and board expenses have risen between 11 percent and 16 percent each year, and costs are likely to continue rising. In 1983–84, expenses for one year in college, including tuition and fees, room and board, transportation, books and supplies, and personal expenses, were estimated to average $3868 at two-year public colleges and $8440 at four-year private colleges nationwide. Students who want to attend a public college in a state other than the one in which they live and their family pays taxes can expect their annual tuition costs to be up to $3000 more than those of residents of that state. With the much higher cost of tuition at private colleges, a single year at the nation's most expensive schools, such as Amherst, MIT, Princeton, Harvard/ Radcliffe, Stanford, Brown, or Cornell, can cost well in excess of $13,000.

The net cost of your education is the money you or your parents have to spend after deducting any scholarship, grant, or work-study income you will receive. It includes your anticipated outlays for tuition, college fees, books and study materials, room and board, transportation to and from home, clothes, entertainment, and other miscellaneous expenses. Most college catalogs include an estimate of student expenses at their school; these figures often are broken down separately for in-state and out-of-state students and according to the living and meal arrangements that are available. We recommend strongly that you look carefully at the dollar-by-dollar breakdown of expenses in the catalog of each college you are considering.

If you were not offered an athletic scholarship or some other monetary grant or tuition waiver, cost may be the most important factor in determining which college you will select. If cost is a major problem, your choice might be limited to local schools so that you can live at home. An alternative that many college students take to cut costs is to attend a local two-year college for a year or two before heading off to the four-year college of their choice. In recent years, some highly selective colleges have increased the number of transfer students they

11

will accept because they realize that the cost of a four-year education at their school has gone beyond the reach of many families.

To help defray the cost of their education, roughly half of the students at four-year colleges across the nation receive some financial aid, work part-time, or both, but the numbers vary widely from school to school. Loans can be a college student's salvation, although paying back the principal and interest may prove to be a burden long after you graduate. Work-study programs provide a means of gaining income, but you must spend time and energy earning it. Chapter 4 provides more information on what sorts of financial help you can get for college.

Liberal Arts or Career-Oriented Focus

A liberal arts education is a broadly based academic program that focuses on understanding our world and cultural heritage. Improvement of writing, thinking, and analytic skills forms the focus of a liberal arts education. Few courses that a liberal arts major takes (e.g., Critical Thinking, Twentieth-Century Literature, the Culture of Classical Greece) will apply directly to a specific career, although the skills fostered by liberal arts study serve well in many occupations.

A technical or career-oriented program is more narrowly focused, emphasizing knowledge needed to do well in a particular career or profession. Many of the courses taken in a career-oriented program will focus on information and skills needed in a particular line of work (e.g., corporate accounting, magazine writing, reinforced concrete design, teaching the retarded).

Some liberal arts colleges also provide training that is career oriented, with programs in education, journalism, business, and similar employment areas, while many technical institutes also offer liberal arts majors. To confuse the issue a little further for the moment, many career-oriented programs also require general education or core courses in thinking skills, communication skills, and the humanities.

The point is not what you can study where, but where you will be most comfortable studying what you want to study. There are clear differences between a liberal arts college and a school in which the academic focus is on preparation for a specific profession or career. One difference is in the proportion of courses you will take that either educate you broadly or train you to do a particular job. Another important difference is the attitude of instructors and your fellow students toward specific job training versus using your college years toward becoming broadly educated. People at technically oriented colleges will tend to pressure you to find your niche and to "think career," while those at liberal arts colleges tend to feel strongly that training for a specific job should come *after* a person is more broadly educated and has developed thinking and communication skills to a high level.

Deciding which environment would suit you better is an important factor in selecting a college. Other things being equal, in a career-oriented program you are likely to learn more about a specific field (your major and *possibly* the career it is designed to lead toward), but gain less general knowledge. On the other hand, you will gain a broader base of knowledge and are likely to develop more fully your communication and analytic skills if you choose a liberal arts curriculum, in which more research and writing are generally required of students.

Your Major

Some students emerging from high school know exactly what they want to major in and may even know what career they want to enter after college. Many other college-bound students have absolutely no idea about either. The great majority, however, are simply unsure, one day feeling that a particular major or career sounds great, and the next day thinking either that it would be the bore of a lifetime or that they don't possess whatever it takes to be successful in that field. The fact is that most college students change majors and career directions; some change several times. Students who are certain that they want to major in a particular area may select a college based on the availability of courses in a particular field of study. However, if you are not sure about the major you want, select a school that has some majors you think you might like and let other factors contribute more heavily to your decision about which college to attend.

A variety of paper-and-pencil tests and computer-based instruments are available from school counselors to measure vocational interests and relate them to appropriate college majors. These guidance tools are not designed to make up your mind for you but rather to give you a little more insight into the direction that you might like to take.

Be aware that early commitment to a major based on what a test, a computer, or your parents tell you may exert a subtle (or not so subtle) pressure to continue with that decision even when your feelings tell you otherwise. Selecting a major because it is "hot" could also be a mistake. In the 1960s, education was a popular major because there was a shortage of teachers; in the 1970s, teachers were driving cabs because too many had been attracted to that "hot" major. Business majors in the late 1970s and early 1980s were recruited at high salaries; now only the very best have a choice of jobs, and many have to struggle to find one. The same cyclical swings may be true in engineering, nursing, medicine, and even computer science in the '80s and '90s.

The lesson here is not to select a school based solely on what you think or have been told you should be aiming for in a career unless you feel strongly committed in that direction. If you make an early selection of a major and career direction, you should want it irrespective of what other people say and what the job possibilities look like. Be patient with picking your future, because circumstances in that career area or your interests may change over time. If you feel certain of your career direction no matter what anyone says, move this factor to the top of the list and go for the top-rated college to which you can be admitted that offers this major area. Find out from your guidance counselor and from people who work in your chosen field which are the top schools and which ones have the best record of placing graduates in jobs in that field.

Housing and Social Life

College is a total life experience. It should be far more than classes, studying, team practices, tests, and athletic contests. College should help you to grow into the kind of adult you would like to be. It should help you learn to get along with people, even those who are quite different from you. College should teach you how to open your mind to other people's feelings and opinions, as well as to hold firmly to what you believe is right after examining alternatives. And college should certainly be fun.

Living with other students can help you to enjoy the many opportunities that college offers in addition to classes and sports. The kinds of meaningful social experiences we are talking about tend to happen most readily at residential schools where a large proportion of students live in campus housing or in nearby apartment complexes. They happen least easily at "commuter" campuses, where most students come to school specifically for classes and leave when their classes and library time are finished.

Residential campuses tend to offer a ready-made social environment in which it is easy to make friends. You are all in the same boat, contending with similar concerns (courses, professors, grades, sports, dating, food, transportation) and sharing experiences. The intense, daily contact with your peers will help you to develop your social and communication skills and learn to understand the idiosyncracies of others.

At a residential campus, students have numerous opportunities to share ideas, perceptions, and opinions; there is also more chance to meet and interact with professors outside of class than at a commuter campus. If, however, for financial or other reasons you opt for a commuter college, all is not lost. The student union is often a good gathering place to meet people. Furthermore, at many commuter campuses, clubs and study groups have been formed to serve the social and out-of-class academic needs of students.

ATHLETICS AS A FACTOR IN
SELECTING YOUR SCHOOL

Since you want to be a college athlete, you obviously should study with care all the athletics-related variables at the schools you are considering, before you make your final choice. To an athlete, these will be as important as any of the factors we've already described. Consider the following:

The coach (especially the head coach). If you don't have a good feeling about the coach while you are being recruited or visiting the campus on your own, you probably won't have a good feeling about him or her later. First impressions are not always the best evidence by which to judge people, but in choosing a college you would be foolhardy to go against your first impression of the coach. The most important thing to look for in a coach is whether he or she treats you as a complete human being, one with needs and interests that necessarily will extend beyond those of the team. A coach's record or reputation often may blind prospective athletes to many other factors that will become more important once they are enrolled at and committed to the college.

To test the coach's attitude toward the academic side of college, your conversation might go something like this:

YOU: "I'm really looking forward to going to ZYXWV University and competing on your team. I'm not sure of what I want to major in yet, but I do know that I want to get a solid education."

COACH: "Well, you can certainly get that at good old ZYXWV."

YOU: "I just want you to know right now that I'm not looking to just stay eligible or to slide through school. I'm going to challenge myself with tough courses."

15

At this point, you will want to see how the coach reacts. The coach may say something like:

COACH: "Whatever suits you, but just remember that your first commitment is to the team."

or, alternatively,

"Your first job at ZYXWV U. is to get a good education; we try to fit athletics in along with that."

If the coach says your first commitment is to the team, you know that the cards are stacked against you. If, on the other hand, the coach says that the institution supports your efforts to get a good education, your chances of getting what you are after are promising. Be aware, however, that once you are enrolled and involved in the athletic program, the coach may have to be reminded of your commitment to getting a good education.

Being offered an athletic grant. If you are offered a full-ride athletic grant—one in which tuition, room and board, fees, and books are completely paid for—or even a partial grant, this will surely be an important factor in your college selection decision. Such an offer not only provides financial support but also makes you feel wanted and carries with it some social status. If the college is especially costly, however, consider whether you'll be able to earn your degree in four years while devoting much of your time to the team. Because of the heavy demands made on college athletes, many don't graduate in four years. But seldom does an athletic grant extend beyond the athlete's maximum four years of eligibility for play. Four years of full-ride or even partial scholarship aid at an expensive school may sound tempting, but balance it against the fifth year (or more) that may be needed to complete your degree, at a cost of $10,000 or more per year.

Remember that athletic grants are given on a *one-year, renewable* basis. You may feel that you are committing yourself to a school and its team presumably for the duration of your education, yet any athletic grant you receive is committed to you for only one year at a time. If, for some reason, you don't fit into the coach's plans, you may be left without financial support and have to pay your own way, quit school, or find another college that is less expensive or will give you a grant.

16

If you aren't offered or aren't interested in an athletic grant, you have eliminated a major concern from the college selection process. In terms of your relationship with the coach, paying your own way through college (or having some other nonathletic source of funding) has at least one benefit: It helps to keep the members of the coaching staff from thinking of you as an employee, someone who is dependent on them for an education. While you still may have to practice and train as much as scholarship athletes, at least your mind is free from worrying about the possibility of having to drop out of school if you have a major disagreement with the coach. On the other hand, many coaches feel as if they have an investment in their scholarship athletes and so feel less committed to other athletes. Walk-on athletes usually have to perform especially well before coaches will notice them.

There is little doubt that being offered an athletic grant would play a role in your decision about where to attend college. Maybe you couldn't go to college without it, or maybe the honor is as important to you as the money. But try not to let being offered an athletic grant override all other considerations. If one coach wants you enough to offer a grant, others are likely to want you that much, also. A grant may help you through college, but it also means that you run the risk of being

---

Be Aware of "Rule 48" If You Want
to Enroll at an NCAA Division I School

To be eligible to compete in any sport as a freshman at an NCAA Division I school beginning fall 1986, you must satisfy *both* of the following conditions.

1. You must have earned high school credit and maintained at least a 2.00 average in eleven college-prep courses from the following list (the minimum number of courses from each area is in parentheses).
   English (three courses)
   Mathematics (two courses)
   Social Sciences (two courses)
   Natural or Physical Sciences (two courses, including one laboratory section if one is available at your high school)
2. You must have scored at least 700 total on the SAT (verbal and math sections) or at least 15 on the ACT.

---

treated as "property" by some coaches, to be used as they see fit, with little regard for your own needs. You wouldn't be the first student-athlete that this has happened to. And don't forget that renewal of an athletic grant each year is the *coaches'* choice. After you've committed yourself to their college, they get to decide whether to renew your financial support.

Level of competition. Knowing at which level you will feel most comfortable competing is a factor that is often overlooked when athletes consider which college to attend. This is because the various levels of intercollegiate athletic competition are fairly complicated, at least to the uninitiated.

There are three large-scale national associations that govern college athletics: the National Collegiate Athletic Association (NCAA), the National Association of Intercollegiate Athletics (NAIA), and the National Junior College Athletic Association (NJCAA). The NCAA governs more than 400 colleges, ranging anywhere in size from over 30,000 to under 500 students. The NCAA controls the major television contracts for college football and basketball, and its rules govern most of the major football bowl games and major basketball championships. It also holds regional and national championships in many other men's and women's sports. The NCAA is divided into three competitive levels, the main difference between these levels so far as athletes are concerned being in the area of allowable athletic scholarships. Division I schools in the NCAA are allowed to offer more scholarships (the exact number changes from year to year) than schools in Division II, while Division III schools are not allowed to award any scholarships based on athletic ability or promise. Some Division II NCAA colleges choose not to award athletic-based scholarships. Within a given school, teams in some sports may compete at one divisional level, while those in other sports may compete at another divisional level. When looking into prospective colleges, always ask the coach at which level the school competes in your sport.

For football, the NCAA has separated its top competitive level into Division I-A and I-AA, with the former being considered a kind of super conference in which the very best football teams compete against each other. (These Division I-A football schools presumably produce the future professional players; Chapter 2 discusses just how true that is.) Various differences in recruiting rules exist between Division I schools and Division II and III schools. There is one rule in particular that freshman athletes at Division I schools should be aware of: in order to be eligible to compete as a freshman and receive financial aid during your first year in college, you must have graduated from high school with a minimum 2.00 GPA (on a 4.00 scale). (So-called Rule 48, which was passed by the NCAA in 1983, for implementation in 1986, may make Division I freshman eligibility rules even tougher; however, this new rule is currently being protested and therefore could be subject to change.)

The NAIA governs over 500 colleges, most of which are small or medium-sized. Both men's and women's sports are included in the NAIA. Member schools are located in any of 32 geographical districts. National championships are determined by tournaments held for the top teams in each. Athletic-based scholarships are allowed at NAIA schools, although not all schools choose to offer them. The NAIA has its own set of recruiting regulations and eligibility rules regarding academic progress of student-athletes, as well as rules governing eligibility for competition when an athlete transfers between schools. According to NAIA rules, in order to be eligible to compete as an incoming college freshman, you must have graduated from an accredited high school or be accepted as a regular student in your NAIA-affiliated college.

The NJCAA governs most of the junior college athletic programs in the United States, except for those in California. The NJCAA controls both men's and women's sports, has its own set of recruiting and academic progress rules, and controls the amount and type of allowable financial aid and other awards for athletic ability. (California community colleges do not allow athletic scholarships, one of the reasons that they are not NJCAA members.) As with the other national athletic associations, the NJCAA also is responsible for holding national championships for its member schools. To be eligible for athletic competition as an entering freshman at an NJCAA-affiliated school, you must have graduated or been given an equivalency diploma from high school (or show proof of passing an officially recognized test, such as the General Educational Development test). You also must be enrolled in at least ten units listed in the official school catalog at that junior college.

It is important for you to face that age-old question of whether you want to be a big fish in a small pond or a small fish in a big pond— *before* you jump into the pond. The answer is solely yours and should come from a combination of your goals in competitive sports and your feelings about having ample opportunity to compete. If your main objective as a college athlete is to have the opportunity to compete as much as possible, a lower-level college (Division II or III or a junior college) might suit you better than a college that offers big-time competition in your sport. If you have serious and realistic dreams of becoming a professional athlete, be sure to read Chapter 2 before making your choice of colleges.

19

Graduation rate of athletes. The number of athletes who actually graduate from the college they attend is as important a factor to consider as any in making a good choice among schools. This statistic suggests how serious the athletic department is about the academic progress of its athletes. The College Football Association (CFA), which includes 61 of the top football programs in the country, has taken a step in the right direction by keeping track of the graduation rates of football players at member schools and making this information public.

It would be extremely useful if records of athlete graduation rates were kept at all colleges for all sports, with rankings made public. Recruits from high school and junior college would then be able to make a more intelligent choice of schools based on both academic and athletic factors. At present, however, many colleges do more to hide this information than to make it public. Be especially wary of the recruiters or coaches who say, "Don't worry. We'll get you through school." This sort of comment generally means that they have devised a system to keep athletes eligible—easy courses, easy instructors, easy advisors —but that they are not particularly concerned about when or even whether the athletes graduate. Talk to current and former athletes at each college on your list, particularly any you can find who did not graduate. Find out why they didn't graduate and whether it had anything to do with the way the coaches treated them.

The pleasure of being recruited. We all have a natural tendency to look with favor on those who look favorably on us. It's nice to be liked and wanted. But don't be smitten with gratitude just because a college thinks enough of you to provide a free trip to the campus. Thousands of athletes get those free trips each year, yet thousands of fine athletes will be passed over during recruiting. Restating an important point made earlier, take an active part in the recruiting process. Instead of just going along for a recruiting joyride, ask questions of recruiters and coaches, and ask to speak with professors and students.

STRATEGIES FOR MAKING THE BEST CHOICE

Below are some basic strategies to follow from the point of beginning your search to the final selection of your college. Remember that the best overall approach in school selection is to take the offensive. As coaches so often tell their athetes, you can't just sit around and hope things will work out right. You have to make it happen.

Limit your choices. Having too many choices can make finding your one best choice extremely difficult. A long list of colleges gives you too many comparisons and decisions to make. Before you begin to compare schools based on the factors we've suggested, cut your list to no more than nine or ten likely choices. (If you don't have at least three colleges to choose from, you probably haven't done enough looking.)

Consult with guidance counselors. The counselors at your high school or junior college have reference books and other printed information about colleges and can offer opinions of their own. But don't take their opinions, or anyone else's, as directives that you necessarily should follow. The choice remains yours even though you may seek someone else's views.

Check college catalogs. Once you have limited your list to at least three but no more than ten schools, look carefully through the official college catalog of each. You can learn a great deal about a school from its catalog, including its requirements for admission; procedure and deadlines for application; general course requirements and available majors; housing and eating plans; fraternities, sororities, and social clubs; typical expenses; where to go for advice and assistance in financial, academic, personal, and career concerns; what constitutes a normal course load, graduation requirements, and other academic regulations; and much other information. In short, a college's catalog presents a comprehensive account of what it would be like to be a student at that school.

Your high school or a nearby college library should have catalogs from colleges around the country in printed versions or on microfiche. (The latter are tiny pictures of each page of a school's catalog printed on a small card. You put these cards in a machine that enlarges the picture so you can read it. The librarian will show you how to do this; it takes only a minute or two to learn.)

Some schools also publish helpful books or pamphlets aimed at depicting the more personal sides of college life. *Approaching Stanford* is an example of one such book written especially for new or prospective students to help them see what life as a Stanford student might be like. You can find out if similar publications for incoming students exist at the colleges on your list by contacting their Admisssions Office.

Talk with graduates of the school. People who have gone to a college can provide insights about their school that no one else can. Keep in mind, however, that the information you get from former students reflects their opinions about their own experiences, and every person's experience will be somewhat different. Talk with people who were athletes and those who weren't to get the most complete view of the college. Ask about life in general at the school (e.g., Are professors friendly and helpful, or do they tend to keep their distance from students?), but also ask how athletes are viewed and treated.

You needn't feel shy about taking people's time in asking them to tell you about their college. Most people like to talk about themselves and feel good when someone cares enough to ask their opinion.

Make your campus visits count. On your campus visits, whether they are recruiting trips paid for by the athletic department or are arranged at your own expense, talk to admissions counselors, students, and professors, especially those involved in the major fields you might be considering. Set up appointments with these individuals in advance (maybe ask the recruiter to do this for you), and come prepared to discuss what it would be like to be a student at that school and to be enrolled in a particular major. If you are weak in a basic skill (such as English or math), ask to speak with a professor responsible for freshman courses in the troublesome subject. Find out what the class will require and what you might do to prepare for it; if possible, get a copy of the course syllabus.

Sit in on some classes. Ask the recruiter or admissions counselor to arrange for you to attend some classes so you can experience what being a student at that college might be like. In the few minutes before class starts, ask a student if that class is typical of others he or she has taken or how it might be different. After class, ask a student if that class session was typical of the course. Explain that you are in high school (or junior college) thinking about coming to the college and that you want to know about his or her experience there. The students you talk to will have been in your shoes and will have plenty of insights to pass on.

If you have not been recruited, talk to the coach. As obvious as this piece of advice sounds, many athletes shopping for a college neglect to do this. Maybe they don't think the coach has time for them or they don't want to appear to be "buddying-up" to the coach. There are several very good reasons, however, for meeting with a person who might be your coach. First, as an unrecruited athlete seeking to play on the team, you should know what are your chances of getting an honest tryout. Some coaches recruit heavily and don't leave much time for serious consideration of walk-ons; this even happens at colleges that don't offer athletic grants. It's also important to find out what coaches expect of their athletes in terms of time commitment in-season, living and eating arrangements, and commitment to the team out-of-season. You should certainly obtain a sense of whether or not you like the person who, if you choose his or her school, may mold and control your collegiate athletic experience. In the process of measuring your feelings about the coach, you can gather some important practical information, such as what summer training you might do to prepare for the season, what the schedules for practice, contests, and team travel will be like, and whether or not you would need to have a physical exam in advance, if you decide to enroll at the college.

These are all straightforward questions that any coach should be happy to answer. Write or call ahead of time, both to introduce yourself and to make sure the coach will be available when you visit the campus. Keep in mind that meeting the coach is not a tryout for the team but merely an information-gathering session to aid you in *your* decision about attending that coach's college.

SHOULD YOU GO TO A TWO-YEAR COLLEGE?

Two-year colleges, also called community colleges, serve several functions, one of which is to provide students with a stepping-stone to a four-year college and a bachelor's degree. Students eventually bound for senior college may choose a two-year college because: (1) they cannot afford the cost of four years at a senior college; (2) they want to improve their academic records for future admission to their preferred senior college; or (3) they simply want to ease the transition from high school to senior college. In addition, athletes may want to gain more experience or physical growth before they try senior college competition. College recruiters may suggest that you spend a year or two at a two-year college because they are overloaded with talent in your position or event. You will have to decide whether that advice is really for your benefit (to gain maturity) or for theirs (to keep you available until next year).

Senior college coaches often have their own favorite two-year colleges for placing athletes who are "not quite ready." The college they suggest may or may not be the best choice for you. Remember that even though a coach may promise to have a place for you in a year or two and maybe also a scholarship, the promise does not come with a guarantee. Coaches couldn't give you that guarantee even if they wanted to.

Going to a two-year college is a legitimate and often very beneficial step between high school and senior college. Just be certain that this is a step that you want or need to take, not one that serves someone else's needs. And if you attend a two-year college, be sure to speak with an academic counselor early and let him or her know of your intention to go on for a bachelor's degree. Many courses will not be accepted for credit at senior colleges, so it is important that you take only those courses that will transfer into a bachelor's degree program.

Several states have what are called Articulation Agreements between their public two-year colleges and state-supported senior colleges, which designate exactly which courses can be taken to fulfill bachelor's degree requirements. In the course of two years at a two-year college, you probably can fulfill all or most of the General Education course requirements for the bachelor's degree. At that point, you can then begin a major during your first term at the senior college to which you transfer.

We've listed many factors that you might consider in selecting a college. Each person will feel differently about the relative importance of each of these factors. Unfortunately there is no easy formula for making your final decision. You should be sure, however, to carefully consider each of these factors, so that you can determine for yourself which are more important and which are less important. You should then examine your list of prospective colleges and decide on one or two that stand out above the others. Sit back and think about them. If your list of top choices feels right, stay with it; if not, try to determine why. If you seem to be stuck on a particular variable, either give it more weight or eliminate it from your thinking and, again, see how you feel about revising the list.

Selecting the right college is one of the most important decisions of your life and is certainly worth the trouble of considering all these factors. Transferring from one four-year college to another, of course, is an alternative to a bad decision, but it is costly in terms of money, interrupted friendships, wasted time, lost credits or devalued grades, lost playing eligibility, and having to make your place all over again on a new team. Take the trouble to make a good decision, because you will have to live with the consequences.

2

COLLEGE ATHLETICS:

A LAUNCHING PAD

TO THE PROS?

In This Chapter...

For the Future Pro:
Which Colleges Look Like Your Best Bet?

Professional Football

Professional Basketball

Professional Baseball

Professional Ice Hockey

Professional Soccer

Professional Golf

Professional Tennis

Comparing "Rewards" Among Pro Sports

What If You Are Unsure of Your Pro Potential?

Do you dream of becoming a professional athlete? Have you made a realistic assessment of your athletic ability and do you still believe that you have a reasonable chance at a career in professional athletics? Whether or not your chances are good of making a career in professional sports, would you still like to give it a try for a year or two? If you answered yes to any of these questions, read further in this chapter, since it was written especially for you.

Dreams and reality can be a world apart. Unless, as a high school student, you have already achieved a strong reputation in football, basketball, baseball, ice hockey, soccer, golf, or tennis, your chances of turning pro are slim. In fact, even if you have earned national recognition, your chances of having a career as a professional athlete are not

The three major team sports provide approximately 2,663 jobs for professional athletes, in a nation of 226 million people, roughly half of whom are male. This means that only one American male in about 42,000 is a professional football, basketball, or baseball player.

[Harry Edwards, "Educating Black Athletes,"
The Atlantic Monthly, August 1983.]

good; the competition at the top is that tough. If you have the drive and ability—and enough luck—to become a pro, we don't want to discourage you. You owe it to yourself, however, to approach your goals intelligently, with your eyes open to the realities of professional athletics.

For each pro sport, a few colleges seem to provide an unusually large proportion of successful pro athletes. In this chapter, we will show you which are the most likely "launching pad" colleges in your sport. But please don't assume that we mean for you to consider this as the major factor in selecting one school over others. There are far more important reasons that should go into your choice of a college. However, if your goal is to be a professional athlete, it is something that should enter into your decision.

The Smaller the School, the Longer Your Odds of Turning Pro

We should make one more point about the likelihood of going from college to professional status in team sports. This has to do with the overwhelming tendency for future pro athletes to come from the larger, more high-powered college athletic programs. Why are players from smaller colleges that are little known for their athletic performance relatively rare in professional team sports? There are excellent athletes at all levels of college competition, just as there are excellent coaches at all levels. The difference is in the greater number of excellent athletes at schools that tend to produce top-flight teams. At schools with high-powered athletic reputations, a greater number of highly talented players push and test each other daily in practice. This constant challenge helps them to develop even further, while it eliminates those players lacking an extremely high level of drive and ability. This proving-ground atmosphere on the best college teams is an important reason that professional scouts look primarily to these schools for the bulk of their future talent.

FOR THE FUTURE PRO:
WHICH COLLEGES LOOK LIKE YOUR BEST BET?

What are your chances of making the grade as a pro athlete without a college education or with only a year or two of college? How much does a pro earn in different sports and for how long? How important is it to be drafted by a professional team? Will you be "lost" from the pro scouts if you go to a small school or to one that doesn't play in the top competitive level? The information that we have compiled to answer these and other questions has all been taken from the 1981 sports season (1981–82 for winter sports), the latest year for which full figures are available. Various changes will occur from year to year, of course, and bear in mind that salaries will be subject to inflation. Nevertheless, the body of data that has been assembled from this recent, representative season will enable you to get an overview of the connections between pro sports and particular colleges as well as to make comparisons between the favored schools in each major sport.

Professional Football

The National Football League employs approximately 1,300 players on a regular basis. (This is the number of roster positions available on all 27 teams, including a few on each team's taxi squad.) How important is it to attend and play football in college if you want to be an NFL player? Only three players who began the 1981 season on an NFL team did not play football in college, and all three were foreign-born placekickers. Clearly, if you want to play in the NFL, you must go to college. Why? Because college-level football serves as the training ground for the NFL.

The new United States Football League also looks to colleges for its talent, although as a less established league the USFL also seeks players anywhere they can be found. It remains to be seen whether the USFL will last long enough to be considered a stable marketplace for football talent. (Recall that the World Football League lasted only two years during the early 1970s.)

There are a few minor professional football leagues which exist on shoestring budgets. Each year several of their teams go out of business (some in the middle of a season) or move to new locations. They give former college and high school athletes a marginal opportunity to play football for money. These minor leagues primarily employ players who have no hope of making an NFL team (or even a USFL team) and generally pay less than might be earned in a good part-time job. In fact, most minor league players hold other jobs to make ends meet.

27

The Canadian Football League provides another opportunity to play professional football, but the CFL limits the number of players from the United States allowed on each team. Most of these slots are taken by top-level former college players who have had contract problems with the NFL teams that drafted them.

In order to have any hope of playing in the National Football League, you have to play in college, preferably for the full four years. Which colleges offer the best chance for making the jump from amateur to professional football? As a football player are your chances better at a smaller college where you can be a star or at a big-time "football factory"? To answer these questions let's look at the schools that produced the greatest number of players (15 or more) recently active in the NFL. The top producers of NFL players during the 1981 season were as follows:

School	Number of NFL Players
University of Southern California	43
Ohio State University	26
Pennsylvania State University	26
University of California, Los Angeles	26
University of Oklahoma	26
University of Colorado	25
University of Alabama	24
University of Notre Dame	23
University of Pittsburgh	20
University of California, Berkeley	19
Jackson State University	18
San Diego State University	18
University of Michigan	18
University of Nebraska	18
University of Texas at Austin	17
University of Kansas	16
University of Miami (FL)	16
University of Missouri	16
Louisiana State University	15
Stanford University	15
Texas A & M University	15
University of Washington	15

About one-third of all NFL players in 1981 came from just these twenty-two schools. Knowing which colleges are the top producers of NFL talent is more than merely interesting. If you believe that you possess the talent and desire to have a career playing professional football, your chances appear to be much better at one of these schools with a proven record of producing pro players. NFL teams generally pick their top draft athletes from these schools, and top draft picks sign larger contracts. As a result, coaches often give these top draft picks a greater chance to make the starting squad. This doesn't mean that low draft picks from other colleges aren't considered as well; we often hear about the unknown player from a small school who makes good. It's just that your chances are much harder if you haven't played at a college that has an established reputation as a producer of pro football talent.

For added information, the remaining colleges that, as of the 1981 season, had five or more former students earning a living as NFL players are listed below. This doesn't mean to suggest that these schools consistently send a significant number of players to the NFL each year. If a college has, for example, ten players in the NFL at any one time, it probably means the school is sending, at most, *only one or two players each year to the NFL.* What are the chances it would be you? It is important to have dreams, but this one is extremely unlikely.

School	*Number of NFL Players*
University of Florida, University of Tennessee	14
Clemson University, Michigan State University, Oklahoma State University, San Jose State University	13
Arizona State University, Baylor University, Georgia Institute of Technology, Grambling State University, Purdue University, University of Georgia	12
University of Arkansas	11
Colorado State University, Kansas State University, University of Houston, University of Kentucky, University of Maryland, Washington State University	10
Auburn University, Memphis State University, Syracuse University, University of New Mexico, University of South Carolina, University of Wisconsin	9

Boston College, Brigham Young University, Florida State University, Louisiana Tech University, Mississippi State University, Southern Methodist University, University of Mississippi, University of North Carolina, University of Southern Mississippi, University of Tulsa	8
North Carolina State University, South Carolina State University, Temple University, Tennessee State University, University of Illinois, University of Minnesota, Utah State University	7
Alcorn State University, California Polytechnic State University–San Luis Obispo, Iowa State University, Southern University, University of Louisville, University of Oregon, University of Virginia, University of Wyoming, Virginia Polytechnic Institute and State University	6
Bowling Green State University, Duke University, Eastern Michigan University, Florida A & M University, Montana State University, North Texas State University, Oregon State University, Texas Tech University, West Virginia University	5

The 82 schools listed so far accounted for over 75 percent of NFL players on opening day of 1981. This means that the remaining athletes (less than 300) were drawn from among nearly 1,000 other colleges around the country which field a football team. It's no secret that most NFL players come from NCAA schools competing in Division I-A. But what proportion come from the other levels? The figures for the 1,301 NFL players who were employed in 1981 are as follows:

College Athletic Divisions	Percent of NFL Players	Number of NFL Players
NCAA I-A (139 schools)	79	1,027
NCAA I-AA (46 schools)	8	104
NCAA II (69 schools)	9	110
NCAA III (191 schools)	1	16
NAIA (500 schools)	3	44

Only 60 NFL players came from nearly 700 colleges in NCAA Division III and NAIA schools! Yet, at some time during every televised college game, we are likely to hear an announcer pointing out how well Joe Anybody from tiny West Tech is doing. The announcer then chirps about how wonderful it is that anyone from anywhere can become an NFL player. But making a point of mentioning these players from small schools shows how unusual they are. Don't let this or a coach's sales pitch that "We play a pro-type game" fool you into believing that your chances of playing in the NFL are anything but extremely small if you go to a college other than one of those listed above.

Professional Basketball

The National Basketball Association has space on the rosters of its 23 teams to employ 276 players. As with football, professional basketball does not have a broad and stable minor league training ground for its players. Instead, like the NFL, the NBA uses college-level competition to train its future players (at no cost to the professional teams, we might add). As of the 1981 season, only three basketball players who had bypassed college were regularly employed in the NBA.

A very clear picture emerges as to where NBA players received their collegiate basketball training. The following list shows the 33 colleges that had three or more of their former team members employed as NBA players for the 1981–82 season:

School	Number of NFL Players
Indiana University; University of California, Los Angeles; University of North Carolina	9
University of Notre Dame	7
University of Maryland, University of South Carolina	6
Arizona State University, University of Detroit, University of Michigan, University of Minnesota, University of San Francisco	5
Marquette University, Oregon State University, University of Iowa, University of Kentucky, University of Southern California, University of Utah, University of Washington	4
Central Michigan University; DePaul University; Duke University; Long Beach State University; Michigan State University; North Carolina State University; Ohio State University; Rutgers University;	

31

St. John's University; University of Alabama;
University of Houston; University of Kansas;
University of Nevada, Las Vegas; University of
Tennessee, Knoxville; Villanova University   3

For those who follow basketball, there shouldn't be many surprises in this list, except possibly for the presence of Central Michigan and the absence of a few schools that usually rank high in national polls. Most of the schools on this list are thought of as basketball powers, either nationally or in their own regions.

More than half of the players in the NBA for 1981–82 were drawn from among these 33 schools, while about one-quarter of all NBA players came from only the top 11 schools on the list. Well over 1,000 other colleges fielding basketball teams produced only 132 NBA players. If you dream of making a career of professional basketball and are thinking of enrolling at a small college, be aware that *every one* of the top suppliers of NBA talent was a college in Division I of the NCAA. While we find an occasional Caldwell Jones from Fort Valley State or an Artis Gilmore from Jacksonville, these are unusual cases.

Basketball has been called "the city game" in part because big city playgrounds supposedly produce so much future NBA talent. Eighteen percent of 1981–82's NBA players went to high school in one of 12 urban hotbeds of basketball. New York City produced the greatest number of NBA players that year (16), followed by Chicago (11) and Detroit (10). Out of the many thousands in these cities with no dream for their future other than playing pro hoops, less than 40 players had reached their life goal by playing in the NBA! No other city produced more than 7 NBA players for the '81–'82 season. Major cities may have more basketball players than elsewhere, but extremely few are going on to NBA careers, particularly if they don't get an athletic scholarship to one of those 33 top basketball colleges listed above.

Professional Baseball

College experience is not as crucial for future major league baseball players as it is for NFL and NBA players. Slightly more than half of the players on major league rosters during the 1981 season had bypassed college. There are two apparent reasons for this. First, baseball has its own broad minor league training ground, while colleges serve as the minor leagues for professional football and basketball. Second, about 20 percent of major leaguers come from Latin American countries, where college is limited primarily to the wealthy.

Although fewer professional baseball players attend college compared to football and basketball players, college is no longer seen as a waste of time for baseball players with professional aspirations and talent. The 46 percent of major leaguers in 1981 who had attended college is four or five times as great as the number who played in college a decade earlier. One reason for this change is the decline in opportunity to play in the professional minor leagues. In 1949, 448 minor league teams were in operation, providing on-the-job training for nearly 9,000 minor league players (at roughly 20 players per roster). By 1980 there were only 154 minor league teams, with approximately 3,000 players earning and learning as they prepped for the big leagues. As the minor leagues shrank, colleges filled the void for training future professional baseball players. And since more and more players are now going to college, the quality of college baseball has increased, to the point that it is now considered to be about on a par with the professional Rookie or Class A leagues (depending, of course, on the division in which the college team plays).

Another factor leading to the increased number of talented young baseball players who enter college athletics before going on to a professional career has been "free agency," which began for professional baseball players in 1976. Players who declare themselves to be free agents may leave the team that initially signs them on and sell their services to the highest bidder. The loss of long-term control over players has radically changed the way team owners handle raw young baseball talent. Since major-league players are now in a position to sell themselves to another team after a few years, it is no longer good business to sign contracts with players who are very young, often directly out of high school. Team owners want their players to be older now, with their skills and maturity developed at someone else's expense. Enter the colleges, which provide these benefits at no expense to the professional team owners.

If you are interested in college baseball, you probably know that Arizona State is considered to be a pipeline to the major leagues. For 1981, Arizona State, in fact, could claim 18 major leaguers as former students, more than double the number of alums from the next most-productive college. Here is a list of the top 10 producers of major league baseball talent employed in the 1981 season:

School	Number of Major Leaguers
Arizona State University	18
Southern Illinois University	7
University of Southern California	7

University of Michigan	5
University of Oklahoma	5
California Polytechnic State University-San Luis Obispo	4
Florida State University	4
University of Minnesota-Twin Cities Campus	4
University of South Carolina	4
University of Texas at Austin	4

These 10 schools alone were responsible for more than 20 percent of the major leaguers in 1981 who had attended college. Baseball, however, differs from football and basketball in that many baseball players attend college for only one or two years (often at a junior college), while in the other sports it is usual for athletes to remain in school at least until their four years of playing eligibility expires. Only 25 percent of 1981's college-trained major leaguers spent four years in college. This is probably because, unlike football and basketball, major league baseball still has no agreement with colleges to refrain from recruitment negotiations with professional prospects while they are still in school.

Professional Ice Hockey

For a young male ice hockey player born in the United States, a career in the National Hockey League is even less of a realistic goal than for athletes seeking comparable employment in football, basketball, or baseball. A sample of 17 of the 21 National Hockey League team media guides shows that only about 10 percent of the players during the 1981–82 season had been born in the United States. In fact, European players outnumbered U.S.-born players 49 to 46. Most NHL players (nearly 80 percent), of course, were Canadians.

How important is playing ice hockey in college for those with dreams of professional hockey? More so than used to be the case, but less so than in other sports. According to one report, the NHL fifteen years ago had only five players with collegiate experience. A comparison with 1981–82 rosters indicates a dramatic increase in college training among NHL players. Although fewer than one in ten Canadian-born players had competed in college, almost two-thirds of U.S.-born players had collegiate hockey experience. So, if you are American and want to play professional ice hockey, your best route is probably through college. (Canadian youth have an extensive, highly competitive junior hockey program in which to develop their skills.)

The choice of colleges that serve as launching pads to the NHL, however, is small. Few colleges have ice hockey teams and those that tend to produce NHL players are bunched into two regions, the north-central states and New England. The Western College Hockey Association (including the University of Minnesota-Twin Cities, University of Wisconsin, University of North Dakota, University of Denver, University of Minnesota-Duluth, and Colorado College) produced 41 percent of all college-trained NHL players during the 1981–82 season. A handful of Central Collegiate Hockey Association schools (the University of Michigan, Michigan Tech, Michigan State, and Notre Dame) produced 18 percent of the former college players. Just these ten teams accounted for more than half of NHL players with college experience.

Several East Coast schools, such as the University of New Hampshire, Clarkson, Bowling Green, Boston College, and Boston University, contributed significantly to the 1981–82 roster of NHL players. But, the scale of this contribution can be measured by the University of New Hampshire, which is considered one of New England's leading collegiate feeders to the NHL. New Hampshire has sent only 8 players to the NHL in fourteen years.

Down on the NHL farms (their minor league teams), there is a higher proportion of U.S.-born and college-trained players than on the parent teams. The Montreal Canadiens during the past 10 years drafted 61 players who had played in college (of 166 drafted, overall). While college-trained players may find employment in the minor leagues of professional ice hockey, the minor leagues of any sport can hardly be considered a profitable and attractive career.

Professional Soccer

As in the NHL, the North American Soccer League (NASL) is populated mainly by players born and raised outside the United States. According to information in the 1981 Official NASL Guide, less than 30 percent of the 273 NASL players in 1981 were U.S. citizens. (This includes several foreign-born players who were naturalized only after coming to the United States to play in the NASL.)

Among the U.S.-born NASL players, only 27 competed in collegiate soccer. The leaders in producing future professional soccer players were the University of Connecticut and the University of Akron, each contributing three players, and San Jose State, Seattle Pacific, Indiana University, and Saint Louis University, with two players each. Collegiate soccer players should note, however, that there is a movement afoot within the NASL to look more to U.S.-born players in the future. This effort is in part aimed at attracting more fans to the sport, but also reflects the growing recognition that college-level soccer is improving in quality.

Professional Golf

The men's pro golf tour. The Tournament Players Association listed 295 golfers on the men's professional circuit in the 1982 Official Media Guide of the TPA Tour. This is the number of men throughout the world who were then making a living—more or less—playing professional golf.

We say more or less because the amount of money earned by each golfer ranged (in 1981) from Tom Kite's high of $375,699 to Jaime Gonzalez's meager $320. As in any sport, success can be quicker to leave than to arrive. Kermit Zarley, who won over $66,000 as recently as 1979 (and over $683,000 to that point in his career), earned just $732 in 1981. Although their earnings are typically supplemented by affiliation with a country club and product endorsements, professionals in individual sports don't have contracts providing them a guaranteed wage during the tough times as team sport athletes do. If golfers or tennis players don't perform well in tournaments, they don't make money.

How important does attending college seem to be in the progress of professional male golfers? First, in looking at the 1981 tour, let's discount the 25 (out of 295) tour golfers who were foreign-born. Close to 90 percent of the 270 American players attended college. TPA players appear overwhelmingly to consider college to be a worthwhile investment. Actually, the figures favoring college attendance look even stronger when you consider that of the 32 American players who have not had some college experience, all but five are over 35 years old. Thus, nearly all of the younger generation of male golfers have found good reason to go to college.

Not only do TPA golfers tend to gain playing experience in college, but 48 percent of the college alums on the 1981 circuit had graduated from the colleges they attended. This is a slightly higher percentage than the NFL claims for its players, which is approximately the average for all college students. And considering that professional golf is as much business as sport, it is not surprising to know that about two-thirds of the men pros who attended college listed business or marketing as their major.

Which colleges tend to be chosen by male golfers who have the talent to become professional tour players? Top male golfers flock to just a handful of schools. Not only that, a select group of college campuses seem to sprout future pro golfers like weeds. With 21 of its former students on the 1981 TPA tour, the University of Houston

36

serves as a leading hothouse for men's professional golf. The top ten schools that produced male pros on the tour that year include:

School	Number of TPA Players
University of Houston	21
University of Florida	17
Arizona State University	13
Wake Forest University	11
Brigham Young University	9
Oklahoma State University	9
University of Georgia	8
University of Southern California	7
Ohio State University	6
San Jose State University	6

Nearly half (45 percent) of college-bred players listed in the 1981 TPA guide came from one of these ten colleges. Twice as many golf pros had attended one of the top ten colleges than was the case for the comparable configuration in football, basketball, or baseball. It would seem that if you believe you have the necessary talent and determination to become a pro golfer, one of these ten schools should merit serious consideration.

The women's pro golf tour. The Ladies Professional Golf Association (LPGA) listed records for 135 tour players in the LPGA 1982 Player Guide, less than half the number of men pros. All but 6 of the American women golfers under 30 years of age had gone to college. At least 40 percent of this group had graduated by 1981. Physical education and teacher training were the leading academic majors chosen by women pro golfers.

The top college, as of 1981, for producing future LPGA players was Arizona State, with 8 current tour members. (You may recall that Arizona State also produced the greatest number of current professionals in baseball and was third in men's golf.) The colleges with 3 or more alumnae on the 1981 women's pro golf tour include:

School	Number of LPGA Players
Arizona State University	8
University of Miami (FL)	6
University of Tulsa	6
University of Florida	5

Furman University	4
Rollins College	4
Florida International University	3
San Diego State University	3
Southern Methodist University	3

Professional Tennis

The men's pro tennis tour. More than any other professional sport except soccer and ice hockey, men's tennis is populated by a large proportion of foreign-born players. Only one-third of the 239 players listed by the Association of Tennis Professionals in 1981 were U.S. citizens. Paul Bauman, editor of the 1982 ATP Media Guide, notes that of this group, almost all had gone to college. College tennis provides a showcase for young amateur players and allows the best to test their skills against each other. Playing college tennis also means that participants (or their families) don't have to pay for the extensive travel required to compete against top-level opponents.

Where do top junior-level tennis players choose to develop their games and reputations? We've seen consistently in other sports that future professional athletes tend to gravitate toward a select few schools. This is truer in men's tennis than in any other sport. Almost exclusively, these schools are located either in California or in the Deep South. (The weather requirements of tennis provide an obvious reason.) In 1981, over *half* (31 of 60) of the top-ranked American male tennis professionals played at just three schools: UCLA (12), Stanford (11), and USC (8). Other schools that sent from two to four players to the 1981 ATP Grand Prix tour include UC-Berkeley, Trinity (TX), Miami (FL), University of Texas, San Jose State, SMU, Pepperdine, and Northern Illinois (which snuck into the California-Texas-Florida-dominated "Tennis Belt" through the Gullikson twins, Tim and Tom). A staggering 83 percent of Americans among the top 150 ATP players went to one or another of these 11 schools.

If you have any serious designs on a career in men's professional tennis, you would be wise to consider one of these colleges where the competition is the best. Of course, coaches at these schools already know who are the best junior-level players nearing college age, and they actively seek them out. But rankings can be wrong. If you are both good and hungry for top competition, contact coaches at these schools if they haven't already contacted you. But be aware that the competition within these teams is often more intense than their matches with other schools. Even if you are good enough to star at most other colleges, you may never get to compete intercollegiately at one of these schools in the tennis elite.

The women's pro tennis tour. Women's professional tennis differs in one significant way from all other professional sports. Girls begin playing in the top levels of tennis circuits when they are still so young— 14 or 15 years of age no longer surprises—that by the time they reach college age, collegiate competition would be a step down for many of them. We can only speculate why female tennis players tend to turn professional sooner than males do. Could it be that since so few other avenues in professional sports exist for women, there is a great rush in tennis, where opportunities have long been open to women? Or is it simply that role models like Chris Evert-Lloyd and Tracy Austin established a precedent that became the norm? Despite the number of young teenagers who join the women's pro tour, entry into women's professional tennis for many players comes by way of collegiate competition, since college tennis provides a fine competitive experience.

Of the 216 women players rating a personal profile in the 1982 Women's Tennis Association Media Guide, 102 (47 percent) were Americans. Of these, almost three-quarters went to college. (Some had already turned pro and thus were not competing on their collegiate teams.) The same warm-weather Tennis Belt dominates women's college tennis as it does men's. Also, for the 1981 tour under consideration here, the same three California schools—USC, UCLA, and Stanford—dominated women's tennis, with representation by 43 percent of the top players. The list of launching-pad schools for women's professional tennis includes:

School	Number of WTA Players
University of Southern California	12
University of California, Los Angeles	11
Stanford University	9
Trinity University (TX)	6
Rollins College	4
California State University	3
University of Louisiana	3
Brigham Young University	2
Princeton University	2
Southern Methodist University	2
University of Florida	2

University of Miami (FL)	2
University of North Carolina	2

Three out of four of the college-trained female tennis pros in 1982 attended one of the above schools. Business-related fields were the most popular majors for women tennis players. In 1982, 32 percent of top American female players had graduated from college. This graduation rate may not seem high, but considering that the average age of American WTA players was less than 19 (and thus too young an age for players to have earned a degree), it is impressive. Even though top female tennis players can make a great deal of money while still very young, the statistics suggest that for many of these women, a college degree remains an important personal goal.

COMPARING "REWARDS" AMONG PRO SPORTS

Before leaving the topic of careers in professional sports, let's take a quick look at the average length of careers and the amount of compensation one might expect as a pro athlete. Players' salaries in professional team sports are negotiated by the individual players and their agents. Each sport has a form of union known as a players association, which works to establish a minimum or base salary below which no player on a major league roster can be paid. These agreements for minimum wage and other matters last for a few years and are then renegotiated (sometimes, as with unions in other job fields, at the risk of a workers' strike if no agreement is reached before the old contract ends). The information in the next chart shows how the average length of service and player compensation during our sample year of 1981 compare in various men's professional team sports.

Professional Team Sports:
Average Career Length and Salary (1981)

	Avg. Yrs.	Min. Salary	Avg. Salary
Football	4.3	$22,000	$83,800
Basketball	4.2	$45,000	$215,000
Baseball	6.5	$33,500	$250,000
Ice Hockey	4.8	$25,000	$120,000

Remember that the minimum salary figures for each sport change frequently, as players' union contracts expire and are revised. For example, the contract agreed upon between the NFL Players Association and the league owners in 1982 raised the minimum wage for any full-time player to $40,000. The average salary in each sport tends to vary according to playing position. In football, for example, the average salary for quarterbacks and running backs is considerably higher than for kickers. Centers in basketball tend to earn more than forwards and guards. And in baseball, although the game revolves around pitching, the salaries of pitchers tend to be lower, since pitchers play in rotation and only appear in about one of every four of their team's games.

Golfers and tennis players usually have what are called performance contracts, which link their names to a particular club (e.g., Brian Gottfried "plays for" Bonaventure, FL; Roscoe Tanner "plays for" Hilton Head, SC). But as a form of compensation, all these contracts do is to provide a home base for the players and generally also pay for their travelling expenses. The real earning power of professional golfers and tennis players comes from the money they make by competing successfully in tournaments. The more tournaments they enter, the more chance they have to earn money.

Using 1981 tour earnings as a means of comparison, the chart below shows how men and women golfers and men and women tennis players measure up to each other in earning power.

Professional Golf & Tennis:
Tournament Dollar Earnings By Rank (1981)

Rank:	1st	10th	25th	50th	75th	100th	150th
M Golf	375,000	193,342	127,608	85,624	55,513	36,747	15,018
W Golf	206,978	134,938	48,777	30,181	14,249	8,754	263
M Tennis	972,369	280,697	153,680	73,705	42,708	30,466	N/A
W Tennis	865,437	179,115	68,342	31,987	19,239	12,996	N/A

Since these figures were compiled, both Ivan Lendl in men's tennis and Martina Navratilova in women's tennis have earned well above $1-million during a single season's tournament play. More players are likely to follow, although top professional tennis players and golfers may be nearing the limit in their earning power.

Upon announcing his retirement in 1983, Bjorn Borg was estimated to have earned over *$50-million* directly or indirectly from tennis. More of that amount came from product endorsements and earnings from unofficial tennis competition than from official tour earnings. Of course, professional team sport athletes also often make considerable additional income from product endorsements and personal appearances.

The average yearly salary among all 276 National Basketball Association players exceeded $200,000 in 1981, yet only 14 professional male golfers made over $200,000 in that year. Another 38 earned between $100,000 and $200,000. Still sound pretty good? Eighty-seven male golfers (nearly one-third of the players listed in the TPA Tour Book) made less than $10,000 for their full year's tournament earnings. And there were hundreds more "rabbits" (marginal pros who must play qualifying tournaments each week to get into the main tournaments) struggling to make a living at their sport. Their earnings, like those of the hundreds of tennis players who struggle through early week elimination tournaments for a handful of positions in the real tournaments (the ones reported in newspapers), remain uncharted simply because they make so little money for their efforts.

WHAT IF YOU ARE UNSURE OF YOUR PRO POTENTIAL?

Many college-bound athletes simply don't know whether or not they have a chance to become professional athletes. They may hope to turn pro, but they don't yet know enough about their ability compared to others to make a realistic assessment of their chances. In selecting a college or transferring from one school to another, consider which of the following situations comes closest to your own, and make your decision accordingly. Of course, you must also include academic, economic, family, and other factors in making your choice.

- If you want to be a professional athlete and feel strongly that you have that potential, lean toward enrolling at a school that appears to be a launching pad to the pros. Your risk is in not making the team because of stiff competition, or being only a substitute. Weigh this against the benefits of training and competing in a pre-professional sports atmosphere. If you seriously want to become a pro, challenge yourself with the toughest collegiate competition you can get, which may be within your own team.

- If you feel you may have professional potential, but playing as a starter on a highly competitive team is your first priority, then consider Division I colleges that may have good records yet don't appear on the list of launching-pad schools in your sport.

- If you doubt that you have potential and are not even particularly interested in a professional sports career, consider colleges that play at any level of competition, but especially those whose representatives do *not* try to sell you on the fact that they have one or more former players who became professional athletes. The image of both the team and the athletic program that you receive from the school's representatives during recruiting is a good indicator of the team environment.

- If you feel you simply haven't had enough experience to make judgments about either your ability or your interest in a professional sports career, consider colleges with athletic programs that are less rather than more competitive. By doing so, you'll get more playing experience (and just plain fun) from college athletics, and you will reduce the risk of getting lost among players with better reputations. If you determine after a year or two that you are a much better athlete than you initially thought and that a career in professional sports is what you want, transferring to a launching-pad school is an option you can then consider.

College athletes who strive to become professionals don't play their sport just for the fun in it. Nor do coaches in programs that turn out professionals consider fun as an important goal. Along the way, athletes with professional aspirations certainly may enjoy the experience of college sports, but often they do not.

Some coaches try to sell their program to recruits by claiming that they send players into the pro ranks. Whether or not they actually produce future pros—and whether this occurs regularly or only occasionally—coaches who have this orientation sometimes create an atmosphere of drudgery among their players. To be good at a sport, of course, you have to work at it. And hard work in the right atmosphere can be enjoyable. But some pro-oriented coaches get so serious about their "mission" that the team loses out on the enjoyment of sports, and what was supposed to be fun instead becomes a chore. The coach's attitude toward the sport and how he or she treats athletes are good topics to discuss with other students when you visit a campus.

If college athletics is the highest level of competition you expect to experience, then you should strongly consider programs where you will have a reasonable chance of getting to compete rather than those in which you will spend your energy fighting for a spot on the bench. While there is some pleasure in being around future pros, it wears thin, especially if it comes at the expense of your college playing career.

This again raises the age-old question of whether it's best to be a small fish in a big pond or a big fish in a small pond, a question we all have to answer for ourselves. Just remember that, in sports, you may not get into the water at all, if you don't choose your pond wisely.

43

PROFILE OF AN ATHLETE

Dean Wurzberger

Dean Wurzberger has been one of the few American college-level soccer players to become a professional major league player. But Dean earned a living as a professional soccer player for only two-and-a-half years, first with the Seattle Sounders of the major North American Soccer League, then for a short time with Los Angeles' entry in the minor American Soccer League.

Dean had been a star player at San Diego State. He also had begun college as a good student, but, as his dreams for a pro career grew, his attention to academics declined.

"I paid so much attention to soccer," Dean explains, "that I had to hustle just to get done the 12 units worth of class work that I needed to stay eligible. After a while, I just decided to let my studies slide completely and turn pro.

"Being a professional soccer player was fun while it lasted, but it's hard for Americans to get playing time in the NASL. After seeing the same thing in the ASL, I realized the handwriting was on the wall for me as a pro player."

Dean went back to school, this time at Long Beach State, to finish his degree. Without the distraction of his pro athlete dreams, he became an honor roll student.

"My GPA in college ranged from 2.3 to 3.7, which just shows that I could do the work if I wanted to." Dean feels very lucky to have had even his short pro soccer career, but he wouldn't bank on a pro career if he had it to do again. Dean's love for soccer didn't die, just his unrealistic commitment to becoming a pro player. After successfully completing his bachelor's degree and beginning a master's program, Dean now coaches a junior college team and is producing soccer instructional films.

3

COLLEGE RECRUITERS:

WHO THEY ARE

AND HOW TO COPE

WITH THEM

In This Chapter...

Players in the Recruiting Game

Official Recruiting Rules

Cheating in the Recruiting Game: Rewards and Penalties

What to Look For in a Recruiter's Sales Pitch

Questions to Ask Recruiters

Each year, hundreds of star athletes in high schools and junior colleges throughout the country are hounded by college recruiters at home, at school, and around every bend. For thousands more athletes, the recruiting scene isn't quite so hectic or pressure-filled. Yet it still amounts to a seasonal ritual in which recruiters do whatever is necessary to make their colleges look attractive to young athletes. Promises are made, and sometimes gifts and money are given in exchange for the athlete's commitment to enroll at the recruiter's school.

But more than being simply a ritual, recruiting college athletes is a very serious and competitive game having definite winners and losers. As games go, it is a strange one because those who at first believe they have won may find out later that they really were losers. And those who thought they had lost may turn out in the long run to have won after all. To make it even stranger, in the recruiting game both sides can win or both can lose. Much of this chapter is devoted to explaining how these things can happen.

> *"I never want to go through that again. People who have never done it may think it's great, but it was awful. It got so people that I knew were telling me things, and I didn't know if I could trust them anymore."*
>
> — Kim Oden, volleyball player at Stanford University
> [*The Stanford Observer*, November 1982.]

The recruiting game is like most contests in the way that participants treat the rules. In a sports event, many of the rules set the upper limits of acceptable behavior, the point beyond which we shouldn't go: five fouls in basketball, weight limitations in wrestling, no contact with an opponent in races, etc. We risk penalties or disqualification if we go beyond these limits, but we risk losing if we don't stretch the rules as far as we can. In the recruiting game, the rules describing allowable limits also tend to be seen as really setting the *standard* for behavior, rather than the upper limit.

Among the behaviors that recruiting rules limit are the number of contacts a college recruiter can have with a prospective athlete, the number of free trips to visit the college, allowable gifts, the value of scholarships offered, and other carrots hung out to entice star athletes. For example, current NCAA rules state that a recruiter is allowed to come to your home three times. If a college really wants you, its recruiters will certainly see you those three times, and then they may try to sneak in as many other "accidental" contacts with you or your family as they can. Why? Because many recruiters fear that their competition is sneaking in extra contacts and that you'll forget them when it comes time to make your choice among colleges.

In the recruiting game, those who seem to be on your side at the outset may often turn out to be the enemy, while you may find friends and allies where you least expected them. It's a recruiter's job to seem like your pal and to paint a picture of life at the college and on the team as all sunshine, victories, and rewards. But once you enroll, your pal the recruiter either has become your boss or is off somewhere making the same promises to someone else.

As a participant in the recruiting game, you had better know the rules, many of which were written to protect you. The people who are recruiting you certainly know these rules, although they may do their darnedest to get around them. For recruiters, getting caught and penalized for breaking the rules is a calculated risk. Unfortunately, few athletes who are being recruited fully understand either the rules or the penalties which may come from breaking them. In this chapter, we'll describe who the players are in the recruiting game and their motives, as well as the rules of the game and the penalties for breaking those rules. If you are beyond the point of selecting your college, you may want to skip on to the next chapter. However, if you are still in the process of deciding on a college or if there is any chance that you might transfer to another school, the information in this chapter should prove valuable.

PLAYERS IN THE RECRUITING GAME

The opposing sides in the recruiting game appear to be the various recruiters from different colleges striving to capture athletic talent. But you and the other high school and junior college athletes are more than just the prize catches of recruiters. You are also active participants in the recruiting game. As many athletes have found out, you will benefit by understanding this; and you are more likely to suffer if you don't. Whether you've only been contacted by one college recruiter, or swarms of recruiters are beating down your door, you're in the game, more or less feeling its pressures, but certainly guided by its rules. You're even a player in the recruiting game when the initial contact with a coach is made by you.

Coach-Recruiters

Those recruiters who coach at the college are the official recruiting representatives of the school. In the case of small colleges having small coaching staffs, you are likely to be recruited by the head coach, who also may be in charge of the entire athletic program. Even small schools, though, often may have an assistant coach (more likely in football and

---

"You check out every lead you get on a player (including letters written by athletes, their parents, or coaches). Maybe sometimes you've been stupid and didn't follow up, didn't cover somebody. Maybe you didn't have time. Next year, you look up and there she is out on the court whipping your hindside."

—Sue Gunter, women's basketball coach
at Louisiana State University
[Zoe Ingalls, "The Fine Art of Recruiting Superstars
for Big-Time Women's Basketball,"
Chronicle of Higher Education, March 30, 1983.]

---

basketball; less likely in other sports). The primary job of most assistant coaches is to recruit new talent. Assistant coaches also scout opponents and, in their remaining time, actually do a little coaching.

Assistant coaches are considered to be successful if they catch a large proportion of the athletes they seek, or if they reel in one or two of their top-rated prospects. Assistant coaches who fail to catch enough talent (or the right talent) may lose their jobs. This helps to explain why they often promise recruits the world when they can't even guarantee delivering a spot on the team. Much has been written in recent years about unethical recruiting of athletes, but a couple of examples should be enough to show you how bad it can get. A large college in Texas faces charges that its recruiters—including a head coach—promised full-ride athletic grants to track athletes, then delivered only half-grants once the athletes enrolled. A California school has been taken to court by several athletes who have charged that what had been described to them as scholarships for four years suddenly became loans when their eligibility was used up. And these are not even the worst examples of recruiters allegedly lying to prospective athletes.

A favorite line of recruiters is that you will be the key to the team's next championship. Instead, their real plan for you may be to serve as a backup to someone else. Even if recruiters have great plans for you, they are probably recruiting at least one other athlete for your position or event. Seldom will a coach bank on only one untested young athlete to fill a particular need on the team. While it might make you feel good to believe that you are the exception, it would be foolish.

Recruiters are salespeople. Their job is to get you—and others like you—to commit yourself to their school. An effective salesperson paints a picture that makes his or her product (in this case, the athletic program and college) look irresistible, or at least more attractive than the other choices. After you buy the product, it may turn out to be considerably different from the way the salesperson (recruiter) made it seem. But by then, it's too late. Recruiters' promises don't come with guarantees. One recent college athlete described the situation this way:

> When you're being recruited, it's a whole different world. It's like window shopping, all glamour and bright lights. But once you get in and try to buy the merchandise, it's different. You feel powerless to do anything. The school has locked up all the angles, and there's a no-return policy on the merchandise. It's like the lamb staring the tiger in the face.
>
> [Neil Amdur, *New York Times*, March 21, 1982.]

Hard-sell tactics are an accepted part of the recruiting game. Knowing this, you should take the recruiters' promises with considerably more than a grain of salt. Remember, their job is to get you to enroll at their college, which also keeps you away from their rivals. Recruiters are employed in a tough, competitive job, and keeping their job may depend on hooking you. Some coach-recruiters have even intimated this to prospects in the hope of making them feel guilty if they don't sign with them.

Athletic prospects usually have most of their contact with assistant coaches. In NCAA Division I football, you will meet the head coach before it comes time to commit yourself to the college, but NCAA rules do not permit the head coach to be present at the signing. Your commitment (at NCAA schools) is made official when you sign what is called a National Letter of Intent to attend a particular college. This document binds you to enrolling at that school if you intend to play intercollegiate athletics. It is designed to bring an end to the recruiting process and to keep other colleges from continuing to try to attract you.

Recruiting by Boosters

The following headline appeared in the January 27, 1982, edition of the *Chronicle of Higher Education:* "Excessive Boosterism Plagues Sports Program at Wichita State." The story describes how Wichita State, penalized by the NCAA for a record sixth time, has "a problem with overenthusiastic boosters." (Since that time, Wichita State has received a seventh penalty from the NCAA.) But Wichita State was only one of 18 universities under probation at the same time for breaking the rules of the association. In 12 of the 18 cases, the violations included illegal recruiting. Many of the violations were caused by enthusiastic but illegal recruiting by athletic boosters. The failure of boosters to follow recruiting rules has been such a large problem that the NCAA and other governing groups have developed long lists of rules to stop the practice. If we've learned anything from the history of college athletics, however, we can't expect these new rules to do much more than make booster-recruiting more subtle or sneaky.

Many athletic boosters try to remain within the official recruiting limits and are concerned with doing right by the athletes they try to win over to their college. On the other hand, some athletic boosters are motivated only by dreams of being involved in producing a national championship. They care little for the long-term needs of individual student-athletes and either don't know or don't care about the rules set up to control recruiting. Since boosters are not officially connected with the college, their jobs obviously are not in jeopardy if they break

The NCAA refers to boosters officially as "representatives of an institution's athletic interests." The association has ruled that as of 1983, boosters associated with Division I and Division II schools are not permitted to make in-person, off-campus contacts with athletic recruits. This rule was put into effect because it is difficult for coaches and college athletic directors to control the behavior of boosters. If a booster from a Division I or Division II school visits you at any place other than a campus, you should report this contact to the NCAA. If you don't, it could affect your eligibility to compete on the college team or the eligibility of that team to compete in postseason play.

the rules and exceed the limits of recruiting. They volunteer to spend their own time, energy, and often a considerable amount of money attracting athletic recruits to their schools because they want to be associated with a championship team. The chance of being able to boast that they had a part in producing a winner is worth their time and money.

Recruiters who are alumni or boosters may have your best interests at heart, but don't count on it. If we have convinced you to take the promises of assistant coach recruiters with a measure of salt, be even more cautious when considering the promises of booster recruiters.

Parents and Current or Former Coaches

Besides yourself, the only ones you can count on to have your best interests at heart are members of your immediate family. Even here, you have to take care that they aren't just living out their own athletic fantasies through you. Present or former coaches may care about your welfare, but they also may have ties with particular colleges or, in the worst of cases, may be promised some sort of reward for influencing you to attend a particular school. Weigh whatever is told to you about the benefits or liabilities of a particular college, even when the information comes from someone close. A bad decision by an athlete on choice of college is more costly than a bad decision by a nonathlete. At the very least, it may cost you considerable playing eligibility if you decide to change schools.

OFFICIAL RECRUITING RULES

All recruiters of college athletes should have read, if not memorized, the detailed recruiting rules devised by their conference and national association. If they are breaking the rules, it is probably by choice. Recruiters are rigidly restricted in the number, place, and kind of contacts they can make to get prospects to select their school. Even the transportation, lodging, and meals provided athletes during visits to the campus are restricted. Any benefits either given or promised to athletes are considered illegal if they extend beyond what is officially sanctioned by the athletic association to which the school belongs.

The rules governing recruiting, amateurism, and academic progress exist to ensure that student-athletes are selecting a particular college because of its academic benefits as well as its athletic programs, rather than because one school promises more cash, gifts, or other illegal nonacademic benefits than other schools. These rules also exist to guard against student-athletes being shortchanged in their educations. Among the associations governing college athletics, the NCAA has the most detailed list of rules and guidelines. Exactly what can and cannot be done during recruiting is explained in the following rules, drawn from the NCAA Guide for the College-Bound Student-Athlete (1983–84 version).* While some of the rules may seem picky, they exist because recruiters have tried to gain advantages over each other in any way they can. The rules are written for athletic staff members and boosters, but being aware of them can help to keep you, the student-athlete, out of trouble as well.

In recruiting a prospective student-athlete, IT IS PERMISSIBLE:

1. For a bona fide alumni organization of a member institution (which does not necessarily include all athletic booster groups) to entertain prospects at luncheons, teas, or dinners at which prospective students (athletes and nonathletes) of that immediate locale are guests.

2. For a member institution to request a prospect to undergo a medical examination through the institution's regular team physician at the time of the prospect's visit to the campus to determine the prospect's medical qualifications for athletic competition.

---

*Material reprinted from the NCAA Guide for the College-Bound Student-Athlete by permission of the National Collegiate Athletic Association. Material in the brochure is subject to annual revision by the membership of the association.

3. For a prospect to receive one expense-paid visit to a member institution's campus for a period not to exceed 48 hours. Only actual round-trip transportation by direct route between the student's home or school and the institution's campus may be paid. Such a visit may not occur until after the beginning of classes for the prospect's senior year in high school, and a prospect may not accept expense-paid visits to more than a total of five Division I and Division II member institutions. If commercial air transportation is used, the fare may not exceed tourist (or comparable) class.

4. For a Division III member institution's official athletic representative to transport or pay the transportation expenses for a prospect on one official expense-paid visit, provided the representative accompanies the prospect on the visit at the representative's own expense. (No trips paid by boosters are allowed to Division II and III schools.)

5. For a member institution to reimburse a prospect for actual and necessary transportation expenses incurred in travelling to visit the campus in the automobile of the prospect or the prospect's family even though the prospect is accompanied by relatives or friends on the trip.

6. For a member institution to entertain the parents (or legal guardians) or spouse of a prospect one time only on the institution's campus when they accompany the prospect on the prospect's one paid campus visit.

7. For a member institution to house and entertain a prospect, the prospect's parents (or legal guardians), or spouse during the one paid campus visit in the community in which the institution is located only if on-campus entertainment and facilities are not available and only at a scale comparable to that of normal student life.

8. For a member institution's athletic staff member or athletic representative (only at Division III schools) to make a total of three in-person contacts (at sites other than the prospect's educational institution) with a prospect, the prospect's relatives or legal guardian at any location off the collegiate institution's campus for recruiting purposes; however, they shall not expend any funds for entertainment of the prospect, the prospect's relatives or friends.

Three additional in-person, off-campus contacts per prospect shall be permitted by each member institution on the grounds of the prospect's educational institution and with the approval of that institution's executive officer or authorized representative.

Once a prospective student-athlete has signed a National Letter of Intent with a Division I or II member institution, there shall be no limit (subsequent to the occasion of the signing) on off-campus recruiting contacts with the prospect, the prospect's relatives or legal guardians by the institution with which the prospect has signed.

Any face-to-face encounter that is by prearrangement or that takes place on the grounds of the prospect's educational institution or at the sites of organized competition and practice involving the prospect or the team (i.e., high school, preparatory school, junior college or all-star team) the prospect represents shall be counted toward the limit on permissible in-person, off-campus recruiting contacts, regardless of the conversation which occurs.

In-person, off-campus contacts with prospects shall be permissible in the sport of football only during the period between December 1 (or the date of the completion of the prospect's final high school or junior college contest if it occurs thereafter) and March 1 and in the sport of men's basketball only during the period between September 1 and November 1 and the period between March 1 (or the date of the completion of the prospect's final high school or junior college contest if it occurs thereafter) and May 15, except that no member of a Division I institution's coaching staff shall contact a prospect during the period starting on the Thursday prior to the NCAA Division I Men's Basketball championship game and ending at noon on the Tuesday after the game.

[NOTE: The NCAA has authorized the following change in the recruiting period for men's basketball (Divisions I and II) at NCAA schools beginning in the 1984-85 school year: Coaches may try to recruit athletes from September 1 to October 9 (it used to be until November 1) and from March 1 to May 15.]

9. For a prospect to visit a member institution's campus as many times as it is desirable at the prospect's own expense, it being understood that on such visits the institution may only provide a maximum of three complimentary admissions to a campus athletic event to admit the prospect and those accompanying the prospect on the visit. In addition, during such a visit to a Division II or Division III institution, the institution may provide a meal to the prospect in the institution's on-campus student dining facilities. Any entertainment except the three complimentary admissions and the meal at a Division II or Divi-

THE ATHLETE'S GAME PLAN FOR COLLEGE AND CAREER

sion III institution shall cause the visit to be considered an expense-paid visit, only one of which is permissible to each member institution's campus.

10. For a member institution to pay the actual cost (provided it is necessary and reasonable) of the room and board expenses incurred by a prospect in travelling between the prospect's home and the campus on the prospect's one official expense-paid visit.

11. For an athletic staff member or athletic representative to describe the member institution's grant-in-aid program and recommend a prospect for such aid, it being understood that only an institution's regular financial aid authority can actually award aid; further, this authority must provide the prospect with a written statement setting forth the amount, duration, conditions and terms thereof before the award of aid is official.

12. For a prospect to receive an expense-paid visit to a member institution's campus (in addition to the one athletically related paid visit), provided it is for a purpose having nothing whatsoever to do with the athletic recruitment by that institution (e.g., band trip, senior day, fraternity or sorority weekend) and provided the institution's athletic department or athletic representatives are not involved in any way in the arrangements for the visit.

The twelve rules listed above describe what is allowed during the recruiting process. The following list of illegal recruiting actions is more than twice as long. It is important for you to understand these rules to keep yourself and the school you select from suffering penalties because of illegal recruiting. Of course, you can't control the school if its representatives choose to violate these rules; but you *can* choose not to enroll at a school whose representatives jeopardize your athletic future by breaking the rules.

In recruiting a prospective student-athlete, it is NOT PERMISSIBLE:

1. To give, offer or be involved, directly or indirectly, in making arrangements for a prospect, the prospect's relatives or friends to receive financial aid or equivalent inducements, regardless of whether similar financial aid, benefits or arrangements are available to prospective students in general, their relatives or friends, except as permitted by the NCAA, the institution and the athletic conference of which an institution is a member. Included as improper inducements are such things as cash; the

promise of employment after college graduation; special discounts or payment arrangements on loans, employment of the relatives of a prospect, provision of loans to the relatives or friends of a prospect, involvement in arrangements for professional and personal services, purchases or charges; regular or periodic use of an automobile; transportation to or from a summer job or to any site other than the institution's campus on an official visit; signing or cosigning a note for a loan; the loan or gift of money or other tangible items (e.g., clothes, cars, jewelry, electronic equipment); guarantees of bond; purchase of items or services from a prospect or the prospect's family at inflated prices; transportation to enroll; any financial aid other than that administered by a member institution's regular scholarship awards authority, and the promise of financial aid for a period beyond one year or for a postgraduate education.

2. To make an in-person, off-campus recruiting contact with a prospective student-athlete, the prospect's relatives or legal guardian before the completion of the prospect's junior year in high school.

3. To make in-person recruiting contacts with a prospect, the prospect's relatives or legal guardian other than those specifically permitted as set forth in Item No. 8 above.

[NOTE: The limitations on the number of off-campus recruiting contacts and the dates of the football and basketball recruiting seasons do not apply to Division III member institutions.]

4. For a representative of the athletic interests of a Division I or Division II member institution [i.e., a booster] to make in-person, off-campus recruiting contacts with a prospect or the prospect's relatives or legal guardian.

5. To contact a prospect at the prospect's school (high school, preparatory school or junior college) without permission from the institution's executive officer or an authorized representative.

6. To contact a prospect at the site of the prospect's school's (high school, preparatory school or junior college) athletic competition if the prospect is participating or preparing to participate in a contest or competition. No such contact shall be made with the prospect prior to the competition on the day of competition and then not until the prospect has completed the competition (including all games of a tournament or event extended over several days) and then has been released by the

prospect's school authority, dresses, and departs the dressing room or meeting room facility.

7. To publicize or arrange publicity of the commitment of a prospect to attend an institution, other than to publicize a prospect's acceptance of its tender of financial assistance through the normal media outlets of the institution and the prospect's current and former educational institutions. Press conferences, receptions, dinners, or similar meetings held for the purpose of making such announcements are expressly prohibited.

8. For the head football coach of a Division I-A member institution to be present when an off-campus site is utilized to obtain the prospect's signed acceptance of the institution's written offer of admission or written tender of financial assistance.

9. To publicize or arrange publicity of the visit of a prospect to the institution's campus.

10. For a prospect or the prospect's high school, college preparatory school or junior college coach to appear on a radio or television program conducted by a college coach, a program in which the the college coach is participating, or a program for which a member of the athletic staff of a collegiate institution has been instrumental in arranging the appearance of the prospect or the prospect's coach, or related program material.

11. For any agency, group of individuals or organization outside the NCAA member institution to administer or expend funds for recruiting prospects in any way, including the transportation and entertainment of and the giving of gifts or services to a prospect, the prospect's relatives or friends.

12. For two or more persons to pool resources for recruiting a prospect.

13. For company funds to be used to pay expenses (including the provision of a company airplane) incurred in transporting a prospect to visit a campus or for any other recruiting expenses.

14. For a member institution to conduct or have conducted in its behalf on its campus or elsewhere any athletic practice session, tryout or test in which a prospect reveals, demonstrates or displays athletic ability.

15. For a coach of an NCAA member institution to participate in any coaching school or sports camp which includes as a participant any individual who is eligible for admission to a member institution or has started classes for the senior year of high school.

16. For a high school, preparatory school or junior college athletic award winner to be employed by or receive free or reduced-cost admission to any sports camp operated by an NCAA member institution or member of its athletic staff.

17. For a prospect to receive more than one expense-paid visit to a member institution's campus.

18. For a member institution or athletic representative to pay or arrange the payment of transportation costs incurred by relatives or friends of a prospect to visit the institution's campus or elsewhere.

19. For a member institution's athletic representative to transport the relatives or friends of a prospect to visit the campus or elsewhere in the representative's own vehicle.

20. For a member institution or athletic representative to entertain a prospect, the prospect's parents or spouse anywhere except one time on the institution's campus at a scale comparable to that of normal student life.

21. For a member institution or athletic representative to entertain the friends of a prospect at any site.

22. For a member institution or its athletic representatives to offer, provide or arrange financial assistance for a prospect to pay in whole or in part the costs of the prospect's educational or other expenses for any period prior to the prospect's regular enrollment or to obtain a postgraduate degree.

23. For a prospect to receive cash or the use of an automobile during a campus visit.

24. For a prospect to be excessively entertained during a campus visit or at any other time.

25. For a member institution or its athletic representative to pay any costs incurred by an athletic talent scout or representative of its athletic interests in studying or recruiting a prospect.

26. For a member institution or its athletic representatives to reimburse the coach of a prospect for expenses incurred in transporting a prospect to visit the campus.

27. For a member institution or its athletic representative to entertain high school, preparatory school or junior college coaches at any location except on the institution's campus or in the community in which the institution is located. Such permissible entertainment shall be limited to two tickets to home athletic

contests, but shall not include food and refreshments, room expenses or the cost of transportation to and from the campus.

28. For a member institution or its athletic representatives to provide free admission to its away-from-home athletic contests to prospects, their friends or relatives.

Why are there so many recruiting rules? Why are they so complicated and detailed? Because college recruiters have been known to go overboard in their search for prime athletic talent. Every rule that exists is an attempt to stop some unfair or excessive tactic that recruiters have used in the past.

Competition for high school and junior college athletes is intense, and recruiters are motivated (sometimes, as we mentioned, by fear of losing their jobs) to sign top athletes and produce winners. In many cases, cheating on the recruiting rules is seen as a calculated risk, something which comes with the territory.

Of course, high school and junior college athletes can't be "bought" by recruiters unless they are willing to be bought. But it's fairly easy for someone who is older, presumably wiser, and often richer to sway the mind of a young athlete with cash, cars, clothes, other benefits, and promises of much, much more.

Colleges are supposed to provide a list of recruiting rules to their athletic prospects, although some don't. The list we have provided above covers the specific recruiting practices that the NCAA allows and doesn't allow for both you and college recruiters. But rules are revised each year, and not all colleges are members of the NCAA. So, depending on the appropriate governing body of the schools that you are considering, we suggest that you call or write to any of the following organizations and ask for current recruiting guidelines:

The National Collegiate Athletic Association (NCAA)
P.O. Box 1906
Nall Avenue at 63rd Street
Shawnee Mission, Kansas 66201
(913) 384-3220

The National Association of Intercollegiate Athletics (NAIA)
1221 Baltimore Street
Kansas City, Missouri 64105
(816) 842-5050

The National Junior College Athletic Association (NJCAA)
P.O. Box 1586
Hutchinson, Kansas 67501
(316) 663-5445

CHEATING IN THE RECRUITING GAME: REWARDS AND PENALTIES

The "Rewards" of Cheating

The "rewards" of cheating in the recruiting game are obvious and super-ficially very attractive. By offering unauthorized freebies and other types of inducements to its prospective athletes, a college may attract better athletes, and so increase its chances at a championship, a post-season bowl or tournament, and maybe even sports coverage on TV. To the athletic department and the college, this may mean more in-come and fame, more fans in the arena, and better campus and com-munity relations. For the coach, it may mean the assurance of holding onto a job, or it may even be a stepping-stone to a better position.

What are the rewards of cheating during recruiting to you, the ath-lete? They may range anywhere from cash, a car, clothes, an apart-ment, or use of a credit card, to promises of transportation to and from home, free long-distance calls, or any of the other illegal extras that are sanctioned against in the above rules. Whether you ask for these things or whether they are offered by recruiters, it may not seem like such a bad idea to take advantage of the offer, especially if you know that other athletes are doing the same. The bottom line seems to be that whatever is offered is more than the athlete had before. If the recruiter wants to give it to you, where's the harm in taking what is offered, or even in asking for special treatment? Besides, it's nice to feel wanted and worth something extra. For some athletes, the maximum allowable benefits package (full tuition, fees, room, and board) is the minimum they will consider. Some even bargain between schools to see which will give them more. Digger Phelps, head basket-ball coach at Notre Dame, recently charged that he knows of schools that offer as much as $10,000 to get a star player to enroll. In response, some coaches said that figure was a little high, others said it was too low. Nobody said it doesn't happen.

If some recruiters are "buying" high school and junior college ath-letes, they may wind up with a real powerhouse team. Presumably, the higher the price, the better the athlete. The better the collection of athletes on a team, the better the chance that they will bring home a conference title, or even a national championship. That certainly seems like an attractive reward. Being part of a championship team might be nice, even if you weren't one of those who were offered the extra benefits. Money and other illegal extras might entice some very talented athletes onto the squad, but these athletes are often extremely self-centered and care more for themselves than for the team. It isn't unusual for teams with the best talent to fail to win championships, partly because their players lack a sense of team goals. The purpose of cheating in recruiting, of course, is to gain an advantage over the competition by buying better players. But it often works out that those who play the game straight do much better than those who cheat —and feel better about it.

Keep in mind that rules exist to help people from *being cheated* as well as to stop them from cheating. Say, for example, a coach who recruits you puts a little spending money in your pocket, gets you an extra free trip to the school, or finds some way to do something nice for a member of your family (something beyond the rules, like getting your older brother a job). The coach's purpose was to get you to enroll at his or her college. Let's say you bought the coach's salesmanship and become a student-athlete at his or her school. Now that you are enrolled, many of the rules governing college athletics focus on trying to make sure that you are not cheated out of your education by the coach or anyone else. If your college coach cheats in order to get you, what makes you think he or she won't cheat you out of your education once you are under the coach's control? (We'll deal with how and why a coach may do this in Chapter 6. At this point, just ask yourself why a person who cheats to get you won't also cheat to control you.) Besides, there are very heavy costs for cheating, whether you do it or are just a member of a team where it is done.

The Penalties for Cheating

First and foremost, of course, cheating on the recruiting rules is ethically wrong, beyond any consideration of rewards and penalties. Unfortunately, this doesn't stop a lot of people from becoming involved in rules infractions. If they understood the penalties more fully, however, they might be less inclined to cheat in the recruiting process.

When a college is suspected of violating recruiting rules, it is investigated by its national athletic association, its conference, or both. If the college is found guilty, the team involved or even the entire athletic program might suffer penalties. Individual athletes directly involved are also likely to pay the price. The most common penalties to the team are prohibitions from participation in postseason contests or from appearances on television and cutbacks on its allowable number of athletic grants. These penalties hurt even those athletes who weren't involved in the cheating and didn't benefit from the illegal extras. Worse, the penalties may be suffered by student-athletes who arrive a year or two later than those who were illegally recruited, since the investigation often takes that long to complete.

Since the fall of 1982, athletes at penalized NCAA schools who were not directly involved in the cheating have been allowed to transfer and play immediately for their new school rather than having to sit out the customary year that is required of college-athletes who transfer for other reasons. Not only does this take the unfair burden from the innocent athletes' shoulders, but recruiters and coaches now have to face the possibility of losing many of their athletes if they are penalized for rules violations with a few. This shows real progress in placing the burden of penalties where it belongs, but it was a long time coming.

"Clemson University's football program was placed on a two-year probation [in 1982] by the National Collegiate Athletic Association for more than 150 recruiting and other rule violations committed by coaches and athletic boosters. The NCAA also limited Clemson to 20 football scholarships—instead of the usual 30—in each of the next two years.... In addition, the Atlantic Coast Conference prohibit[ed] the team from appearing in any bowl games in the 1984 season... or to compete for the conference championship in 1983 and 1984. University president William L. Atchley said he would 'reorganize the athletic department as part of a series of reforms to prevent future abuses.'"

[*Chronicle of Higher Education*, December 1, 1982.]

But transferring to another school in order to avoid suffering penalties in the athletic side of your college life will probably cost you plenty academically. Credits are often lost when you transfer, or your GPA might be reduced. Also, transferring is likely to add a term or more to the time you will need to complete your degree.

Ideally, you wouldn't want to find yourself in the position of having to transfer because of something your coach or athletic program did. But if you are being recruited in ways which violate rules, it is highly likely that other athletes are, too. Think carefully before enrolling at a school where recruiters show little respect for the rules and guidelines of recruiting. Whether or not you agree with the rules limiting what recruiters can give (or promise to give) to prospects and the amount and kind of contact they may have with you, these rules must be honored.

WHAT TO LOOK FOR IN A RECRUITER'S SALES PITCH

All high school and junior college prospects face a potential problem when dealing with college sports recruiters. Whether or not you are offered an athletic grant or any "extras" along with it, your problem is to determine which school or schools will be interested in you as a complete person—a student-athlete—rather than merely as a body to serve on the athletic team.

In the recruiting game, recruiters and coaches often assume that your only interest is to play in intercollegiate athletics. This attitude of theirs (and possibly yours also) can become the gravest penalty for you. Far too many recruiters seem bent on selling their school based primarily on the supposed benefits of playing on their team. This happens at all levels in the NCAA, NAIA, and NJCAA, and it happens whether or not the school offers athletic grants. Recruiters may also dangle some choice bait concerning the wonderful social life, and, if they're fortunate enough to work at a campus blessed by nature, they'll provide a glowing description of the glorious climate and geography in which their school basks. (Recruiters who aren't so blessed with climate and geography are not above lying about it if they are recruiting athletes who don't know any better.) Some recruiters are also likely to toss in a comment or two, usually directed toward parents, about how wealthy alumni provide well-paying jobs to ex-athletes from their alma mater. (This is one promise that rarely materializes.) But in their sales pitch recruiters far too seldom point to the college's academic reputation, to the quality of the education that can be gained there, or to the value of a degree from their school.

The recruiters who take an approach that is entirely tuned toward athletics do so because that is what they believe sells a college to young athletes. Unfortunately, they are often right. You will be far better off in both the short and the long run to look for more than athletic opportunities and a social life from college. Base your evaluation of a college on its athletic program but equally on how well recruiters and coaches push the academic side of their school.

QUESTIONS TO ASK RECRUITERS

- Ask *each* college's recruiters for a printed list of the recruiting rules that their association uses. If they won't give you one, or make excuses, take that as a sign to begin doubting their knowledge, and maybe even their honesty.

- Although under present rules they can't promise you an athletic scholarship for more than one year at a time, ask for some names of athletes who were kept on scholarship after their eligibility for competition expired but who still had to take more courses to graduate.
- Ask whether your athletic scholarship will also cover summer courses.
- Ask what proportion of athletes playing on the past three years' teams *in your sport* actually graduated. (The proportion of graduated athletes in the athletic department as a whole may be misleading, since the emphasis that each team's coach places on graduation will differ.)
- Ask whether the college has a counseling or tutoring program for athletes that is conducted by trained personnel other than coaches. (Some coaches may be very bright and really care about your academic progress, but you *still* will want professionals trained in counseling and academic advising available to help you.)
- Ask about housing arrangements. Even though you might want to live in an athletic dormitory, ask whether you are required to live there or to room only with other athletes. (Your interests are likely to broaden during your years in college.)
- Ask what connection each recruiter has to the school. It is better for you to talk with a coach and best to talk with the head coach.
- Ask whether the athletic program has ever been on probation or penalized by its governing association. If the recruiters have something to hide, they might get upset by this question. If their recruiting approach is honest, they'll probably appreciate your concern.

These are some of the questions you should ask recruiters to find out what life as an athlete at their school might be like. Remember, if recruiters are selling you solely on the benefits of playing for their team, they are most likely selling every other athletic recruit the same bill of goods. There are only so many slots on a team roster and usually less than half that number on the starting team. A sharp recruiter will try to sign more athletes than the roster can hold, expecting some to wash out. On the other hand, there is no roster limit on the academic side of college, and there is no starting team. Once you are enrolled, you and every other student will have an equal chance to make it through to a bachelor's degree. So pay special attention to how well athletic recruiters try to sell you on the kind and quality of educational experience their school provides. That is a good indicator of how the coaches at that college will treat the time and effort you devote to schoolwork. Do they consider academic effort as a responsibility worthy of support or merely as something that will interfere with your responsibility to the team?

Once you enroll at a college, you become its athletic property in certain respects. You will do better to enroll at a school where those responsible for the athletic program respect you as a complete person and where they care about your academic needs.

4

FINANCING YOUR

COLLEGE EDUCATION

In This Chapter ...

The Pros and Cons of Athletic Scholarships

Who Gets Scholarship Offers?

How to Generate an Offer

Combining Sources of Financial Aid to Fit Your Needs

Special Rules Governing Financial Aid to Athletes

There are various forms of aid available for financing your college education. Our focus here will be on the types of financial aid that either come directly from the college or are administered by or through the college. Later in the chapter, we will present the special rules that govern the kinds and amounts of financial aid that student-athletes are entitled to receive.

Scholarships (or grants) are financial awards that you don't have to repay. They may be based on need or on merit or achievement, as in the case of athletic scholarships.

Loans are financial aid that you must eventually repay (except in rare cases in which an alternative arrangement is spelled out in the loan agreement). They usually carry an interest rate, which amounts to your fee or cost for having had the use of the money. Most loans to college students have a grace period, usually around six months following graduation, before you have to begin repayment.

Work-study is another form of campus-based financial aid, in which you earn money for jobs provided through the Financial Aid Office.

Most students on financial aid make their way through college by some combination of their own resources (including assistance from their family), scholarship aid, loans, and work-study. But you will have to seek financial aid; in most cases, it won't seek you (unless you are considered a blue-chip athletic recruit).

65

Although scholarships, loans, and work-study are distinct, separate forms of financial aid, people sometimes confuse them. Some unscrupulous coaches describe the aid that they are offering to athletes as scholarships, when the aid really is in the form of a loan. This practice is rare, but it happens enough that you should be sure that whatever scholarship you might be offered is confirmed in writing as a scholarship or grant and is not described as a loan or "indebtedness."

THE PROS AND CONS OF ATHLETIC SCHOLARSHIPS

Athletes who are good enough even to consider competing at the collegiate level frequently dream of being awarded an athletic scholarship. Whether or not their family can afford to pay for their education, potential college athletes think about athletic scholarships because being offered one is a reward, an honor, and a status symbol. An athletic scholarship is a reward for your hard work and success in high school or junior college athletics. It is an honor to be considered good enough to have your athletic services in effect paid for (making you "almost professional"). It is a status symbol because it tells other students that the college wants and needs you at least as much as you want to attend the college.

While many students have to struggle to pay for their years in college, the athlete with a full-ride scholarship cashes in just for being an athlete. This may give you high status in the minds of many students (including nonscholarship athletes), but it also tends to generate resentment and jealousy. The dumb jock myth, which exists more or less on every college campus, is often strongest at schools that give athletic scholarships. Where the athletic program is important enough to have money available to pay for athletes' educations, there is at least a temptation to bring in good athletes who might not meet the same academic standards that other students must meet. Other students sometimes resent the "free ride" that athletes get, while they have to work, save their money, deplete their savings and other assets, go begging to their parents, fill out numerous forms, wait in lines, and hunt sometimes far and wide for enough money to make ends meet in college.*

---

*Some colleges (e.g., the Ivies) have a policy of not granting athletic scholarships at all, believing that all aid should be based on need.

We discussed earlier in the book the tight reins that coaches have over their scholarship athletes. No need to repeat the problems that this causes for athletes who are trying to make the most of their college education. Just remember that as a scholarship athlete, you run the risk of being treated as an employee. In that capacity, much of your life will be governed by your boss-coach. Athletes who have athletic scholarships not only may lose their place on the team if they displease the coach, they also may lose the source of money that is providing their education. If you need that money to afford to go to college, losing it would be devastating. But even if you don't absolutely need it to pay for your education, losing your athletic scholarship could mean a struggle to find new sources of money, often after the financial-aid application season has passed or the money has been awarded to other students.

According to current national athletic association guidelines and practices, athletic scholarships are given on a one-year, renewable basis. So, while your coach may have enticed you to enroll at his or her college with the promise of having your education paid by an athletic scholarship, that scholarship could disappear at the end of any year, leaving you to find some way to pay for the rest of your education. Worse yet, if you then want to transfer to another college, you lose a season of eligibility for athletics. The chances of your getting another athletic scholarship elsewhere are much less if your new coach won't be able to use you until a year passes.

So the question you must decide is whether you both want *and* need an athletic scholarship, or whether you just want one. The status and honor associated with having an athletic scholarship are great; however, are they worth the cost? While some coaches feel more of a commitment to athletes who are their "employees," other coaches will appreciate your getting funds for college some other way, because it frees up a scholarship for them to offer to another athlete.

> *Four basketball players at the University of North Dakota had their athletic scholarships cut in half for the following year (1983–84) and another lost his entire scholarship. Their coach told the athletes he was reducing the level of their financial aid "because they had performed poorly on the court this past season...."*
>
> [N. Scott Vance, *Chronicle of Higher Education*, May 18, 1983.]

In any case, we believe strongly that the availability of an athletic scholarship should not be your primary reason for selecting one college over others. We outlined several better reasons for selecting a school in Chapter 1. There are too many nonathletic sources of financial aid available for you to let the offer of an athletic scholarship determine which school you will attend.

WHO GETS SCHOLARSHIP OFFERS?

Most athletic scholarships at schools with top-level teams are reserved for the best high school and junior college athletes, the ones with established reputations in their sport. Many colleges that can attract such talent now do much of their scouting with the help of computer-based scouting services, which keep running records of the achievements and statistics of the nation's best prospects. Athletes at that level—"blue-chippers"—don't have to search for athletic scholarships; recruiters come knocking at their door (sometimes *knocking down* the door).

Virtually all NCAA Division I schools (except for the Ivy League colleges) offer athletic scholarships, although not all Division I schools are so competitive that they use computerized scouting services. Division II colleges also are allowed to offer athletic scholarships, though not all of them do. The vast majority of Division II schools conduct their own searches for high school and junior college recruits rather than using scouting services. Division III NCAA schools are not allowed to offer athletic scholarships, yet most of them still scout for talent. Remember that NCAA colleges may compete at a particular level in one sport and at another level in other sports. For example, a school with a Division II basketball team (athletic scholarships allowed) may field a Division III soccer team (no athletic scholarships). While this may be confusing, you only need to be concerned about the level at which they field a team in your sport.

Many colleges affiliated with the NAIA also offer scholarships. These schools tend to be smaller and less well known for their sports record, so they generally don't have as much money to put into athletic scholarships. A small number of junior colleges also offer athletic scholarships. Athletic scholarship offers from junior colleges and NAIA or NCAA Division II schools are more likely to be partial (e.g., quarter, half, or tuition-only) scholarships rather than "full rides."

Athletic scholarships for women have increased tremendously in recent years. In part, this is because of Title IX of the Education Amendments of 1972. According to this federal law, colleges must

68

provide equivalent amounts of athletic scholarship aid to female and male athletes. For example, if half of a school's male athletes have athletic scholarships, the school must provide athletics-related financial aid to half of its female athletes. (Title IX also states that all resources, support, and opportunities must be shared equally by males and females.)

Despite these advances, the opportunities women have for obtaining athletic scholarships still tend to lag behind the financial aid offered to male athletes at some colleges. Once you are in college and can see what sorts and amounts of aid are available to female athletes as compared to male athletes, you will be in a better position to determine whether women athletes are being discriminated against at your school. Contact the campus Affirmative Action Office and ask its staff to look into the situation if you think that women athletes are not getting their fair share. You may be considered a troublemaker by some people in the athletic department, but you deserve what the law allows and should be allowed to stand up for your rights.

HOW TO GENERATE AN OFFER

While colleges at all levels of athletic competition scout and recruit athletes, those at levels below Division I in the NCAA are more likely to consider unsolicited information submitted by an individual student who is seeking an athletic scholarship. The amount of scholarship money available each year in any given sport varies greatly, and even if the recruiters have not been knocking down your door, you still may have a chance of getting a scholarship offer if you follow the approach described below:

1. Draw up a preliminary list of colleges that meet the criteria that are important to you as to location, size, overall cost, type of academic environment, availability of particular academic programs or majors, and sports opportunities (including whether the school has a junior varsity team, in case you don't make the varsity your first year).

2. Find out the name of the head coach in your sport at the colleges on your preliminary list by consulting the *Directory of College Athletics* (Ray Franks Publishing, Amarillo, TX 79109; published yearly, with separate editions for men and women). This book should be available at college libraries or in your high school or junior college athletic department or guidance office. Remember that coaches change jobs frequently, so you should use a direc-

tory that is no more than a year old. The directory lists sports offered at each college, coaches' names, school addresses and phone numbers, and the division level for each sport.

3. Starting with the three to six top contenders on your preliminary list, write a letter to the head coach in your sport at each school. In the letter, describe several important reasons why you want to come to his or her college. Explain that you are interested in competing on the team and that you would like to know what sources of financial aid are available for athletes. Don't be shy about telling the coach of your athletic strengths and relating statistics (true ones!) that will generate the coach's interest in you. Include copies of newspaper write-ups and action photos, if you have them. Films of you in competition may also help you to sell yourself to the coach. What you are really doing, after all, *is* selling yourself. There is absolutely no shame in that. In fact, this is good practice for when you graduate and have to sell an employer on your qualifications and accomplishments.

4. If you are short on encouraging replies from the first group of head coaches you write to, work your way down your list of preliminary college choices. Eventually, your efforts are likely to pay off with one or more favorable responses.

5. Ask your present or former coach to write a letter on your behalf to those coaches who show an interest in you. The letter of recommendation should stress how much of an asset you have been to your present squad and would be on a college team. Letters from two coaches are better than one, three coaches better than two, etc.

6. Seldom will a coach offer a scholarship to an athlete sight unseen. Since most coaches operate with a tight recruiting budget, you may have to pay your own travel expenses to see a coach who shows interest. If you are then offered a scholarship—full or partial—your efforts have paid off. (Even if you don't get a scholarship, you've picked up some valuable self-promotion skills.) But beware when a coach promises an athletic scholarship in the future, "if things work out." The offer may come through for you but don't bank on it. Promises such as this one are written on air.

Even if a coach you correspond with does not have an athletic scholarship available, it has probably helped you to let the coach know that you are interested in attending his or her college. You may now be in a better position to get admitted and to be considered for other types of financial aid at the coach's school than someone who is not an athlete. Students who have special talents—and who take the initiative to make these talents known—are often more likely candidates for admission and financial aid than students who spend their time and energy just being students.

COMBINING SOURCES OF FINANCIAL AID
TO FIT YOUR NEEDS

If you are among the majority of college athletes who get only a partial athletic scholarship, or none at all, you may be eligible for financial aid based on need. Determining the extent of your need and the amount and kind of financial aid to which you are entitled is considerably more complicated than simply being told by a coach how much your scholarship is worth. It depends on several factors, including:

- the amount of money your parents can contribute
- the amount *you* can contribute (including such assets as savings or stocks and bonds)
- your summer earnings
- the cost of the college you are attending (tuition along with either room and board or commuting costs)
- the amount of financial aid from other sources (including other scholarships)

As you can see from this list, students seeking financial aid are expected to help pay for their own education. Parents are also expected to help as much as possible. The amount of your parents' income and assets figures heavily into determining how much financial aid you need. But if your parents are retired, disabled, or out of work, they will be able to help you less, and so your "need factor" increases. This means more financial aid is likely to be awarded to you—assuming, of course, that you apply properly and do the other things required to play by the financial aid rules. If your parents have other children in college, or if they have gone into debt because of a brother or sister in college before you, their ability to help is less and your award is likely to be greater.

The actual amount of your financial aid package is likely to change from year to year because of changes in each of these factors as well as possible changes in your family status—marriage or divorce (your own or that of your parents) and births or deaths. In short, there is no way to predict how much need-based financial aid you will receive from one year to the next. You must go through the process of applying each year and let the school's Financial Aid Office make that determination for you.

SPECIAL RULES GOVERNING FINANCIAL AID TO ATHLETES

All students who receive financial aid to attend college are governed by special rules. The basic rule is that the amount of your financial aid *must not exceed* your costs of attending college. Nonathletes who receive financial aid in excess of allowable totals will have to make future adjustments, or, if they were judged to be cheating, they might forfeit any future access to financial aid. Athletes who receive too much aid (i.e., more than their cost of going to school) will suffer in the same way as nonathletes, but they *also* may lose eligibility to compete in their sport. Athletes who receive more aid than the rules allow—whether on purpose or accidentally—may even cause their team to forfeit contests or a chance to compete in championships or on TV.

NCAA Regulations

The NCAA has established the following rules governing financial aid to athletes:*

A Student *MAY:*

1. Receive unearned athletically related financial aid administered by the institution for any regular term the student is in attendance, provided it does not exceed that amount equal to tuition and fees, room and board, and required course-related books, and provided the student is not under contract to or currently receiving compensation from a professional sports organization.

2. Receive unearned athletically related financial aid awarded only by an institution's regular financial aid committee for a maximum period of one year, it being understood that such aid may be renewed for additional, maximum one-year periods by the

---

*Rules reprinted from the NCAA Guide for the College-Bound Student-Athlete, 1983-84, by permission of the National Collegiate Athletic Association. Material in the brochure is subject to annual revision by the membership of the association.

institution while the recipient is an undergraduate or a graduate student with remaining eligibility.

3. Receive income from employment during term time or nonathletic grants for educational purposes in combination with unearned athletically related financial aid, provided the total from all sources does not exceed the actual cost of room and board, tuition and fees, and required course-related books. Income from employment during official institutional vacation periods need not be considered in this limit.

[AUTHORS' NOTE: "unearned athletically related financial aid" means that the athletic scholarship is officially given to you for your athletic ability and potential for success, *not* for any labor you actually perform or on the basis of how well you actually do in competition.]

A Student *SHALL NOT*:

1. Receive athletically related financial aid from an NCAA member institution to attend its summer term prior to the student's initial enrollment as a regular student during the regular academic year at the institution. This prohibition does not apply to a summer orientation program for which participation (by both athletes and nonathletes) is required and financial aid is administered on the same basis for all participants in the program.

2. Receive financial aid other than that administered by the institution if the aid has any relationship whatsoever to athletic ability. This prohibition shall not apply to earnings from a professional organization in a sport other than the student's collegiate sport.

3. Accept financial aid from an organization, individual or agency outside of the student's institution for which selection is based primarily on athletic ability or participation.

4. Receive an extra benefit not available to members of the student body in general.

[NOTE: Division III member insitutions generally may not award financial aid to student-athletes except on a showing of financial need by the recipient.]

NAIA Regulations

The NAIA has rules similar to those of the NCAA governing the limits and kinds of financial aid athletes are allowed. Their general statement about scholarships, grants in aid, and student loans is as follows:

Assignment of scholarships, grants in aid, or student loans shall be controlled by the faculty through the regularly constituted committee on student loans and scholarships. Any financial aid or assistance to a student in money or in kind, except that which comes from members of students' immediate family or from those upon which the student is legally dependent, shall be administered by the college under policies and procedures established by the institution through its regularly constituted committee on student loans and scholarships.

A member institution of NAIA shall award no more financial aid to a student athlete than the actual cost of: 1) tuition, 2) mandatory fees, books and supplies required for courses in which the student athlete is enrolled, 3) board and room for the student athlete only, based on the official board and room allowance listed in the institutional catalog. Further financial assistance to a student athlete, other than listed above, by a member institution shall be prohibited.

[Reprinted from the
NAIA Guide for the College Bound Student,
by permission of the National Association
of Intercollegiate Athletics.]

NJCAA Regulations

The National Junior College Athletic Association (NJCAA) has also established rules governing financial aid to athletes. At NJCAA-affiliated schools, tuitions and fees, room and board, and books and course-related materials can be paid for by athletic scholarship. In addition, athletes at NJCAA schools may receive round-trip transportation costs once a year for travel directly between their home and school. The school must also make sure that for any paid employment (work-study or other), the athlete must work as hard as other students and must not be paid more than other students. All financial aid must be administered through the school's Financial Aid Office. (For additional information regarding NJCAA regulations, see the Official Handbook and Casebook of the National Junior College Athletic Association, from which the preceding information was obtained.)

REMEMBER

Rules for participation in intercollegiate athletics as established by governing national associations (NCAA, NAIA, and NJCAA), as well as by conferences and individual colleges, are subject to change each year. Make sure you keep current with the rules and regulations by obtaining written material from your athletic department at the beginning of each school year, or by writing to the association that governs your school's athletic program.

Great athletes and good ones are sometimes tempted to accept—or even to ask for—money or other financial benefits beyond the amount they are allowed. We made the point earlier that it isn't worth whatever "extra" you might get. Why jeopardize friendships, your teammates' goals, your own ethics, possibly your athletic career, and even your chance at the aid you deserve by taking more than you should? If you have any doubts, see Chapter 8 and our discussion of eligibility and penalties for violating rules.

PROFILE OF AN ATHLETE

Fran Englese

Fran Englese wanted a basketball scholarship, but recruiters weren't exactly beating down her door. Fran decided to take matters into her own hands.

"I wanted to stay either close to home in New York or go out to the San Francisco Bay Area, where I also have family. Women's athletic departments don't have much recruiting money and had even less back in the late 1970s when I was looking for a scholarship, so I couldn't expect coaches to come and look at me play.

"The University of San Francisco was in their first year of giving athletic scholarships to women and, back then, all they could afford were partial scholarships. Since they couldn't afford to send a coach to see me play, I decided to send them a videotape of one of my high school games. This was a big factor in their offering me financial aid. Without the tape the college coach could only take my high school coach's word on my ability."

Actually, both USF and a college in New York State liked what they saw on Fran's videotape. Each offered her a partial athletic scholarship, but Fran chose USF because "the opportunity to attend college and play athletics on the West Coast was too tempting an offer to turn down."

USF began a women's tennis team in Fran's junior year and increased her financial aid to a full-ride scholarship to enable her to play tennis as well as basketball. By being assertive and using some ingenuity in order to get athletic financial aid and then doing well in both her schoolwork and sports, Fran was able to have most of her education paid for.

"Women's sports will never have the budgets that men's sports do," Fran explains, "but if you want it, there are ways to find athletic scholarship aid. After that, it's a matter of making up your mind on other needs, such as educational programs, location, cultural factors, and social life. It seems there are more athletic scholarships available for women every year. You just have to be willing to work to get one."

PART II

GAME PLAN FOR WINNING IN COLLEGE

Winning in college means getting everything that any student-athlete can and should get out of college. Knowing what you want to take with you when you leave college allows you to make strides in the right direction without first having to wander around and wonder what's going to happen next. Success in any environment (athletics, school, or career) is more likely to result from preparation and planning than it is from stumbling into a situation and then having to react.

Game plans work better when you have one specific goal in mind. Your primary goal in college should be graduation. Earning your degree is a tangible goal which can be achieved by following tangible steps.

In sports, every player gains when opponents fall short of their goal. In college, on the other hand, nobody wants to prevent you from getting a good education; no one gains if you fail to receive a degree. But even though nobody *wants* to keep you from your degree, the pressures that some people apply to you may serve the same end. There are far more people who want to see you do well, but you must be alert to the few who would undermine your education for their needs. To be successful as a student-athlete, you must become aware of other people's motives. You must learn to get along with them without being trampled by their needs, so that when you leave college, you take more than memories.

Knowing what your opponents are likely to do is a great advantage in an athletic contest. Likewise, knowing the pitfalls and pressures that await you as a student-athlete, and then developing counter-strategies, will help you reach your primary goal of graduation.

But just having your goal of graduation firmly in mind and knowing what might interfere are not enough to make graduation happen. Successful athletes understand the requirements of their game or contest and develop the necessary performance skills. Successful college students also must know what is required of them and build academic performance skills. Graduation requirements can seem like a jumble and need to be examined well ahead of time.

Athletes, more so than most students, have little time and energy to waste. The most successful students are not satisfied with having skills that simply help them get along. Just as top athletes are always working to improve their skills, so the most successful students work toward raising their level of academic skills. Acquiring these skills and learning to cope with pressure will certainly help you to graduate, but will also provide the basis for you to do well in your career. But that's another game, which we'll get to in Part III.

So, your game plan for success in college should include:

- developing strategies for getting fair return for your effort;
- understanding and learning to get along with others whom you will encounter as a student-athlete;
- knowing who your friends are and how they can help you;
- understanding eligibility rules;
- knowing what requirements you must fulfill to achieve your goal of graduation; and
- developing the skills that will help you to achieve your goals in college and beyond.

5

GIVING AND

GETTING 110%

In This Chapter . . .

Who Is Responsible When Athletes Don't Get Their Fair Share?

Signs of Trouble: How to Tell If You Are Being Exploited

Among the most publicized and troubling examples of student-athletes whose college careers were thrown completely off balance by sports is Kevin Ross. Kevin, like too many other excellent athletes, allowed himself to go lightly on the academics and devote himself almost entirely to his sport. In the process, he not only failed to get a college education, but even failed to realize he needed extra help to do college-level work. Here is Kevin's story, as reported in the *Chicago Sun-Times.*

COLLEGE CAGE STAR
JOINS MARVA'S 7TH GRADE

College basketball player Kevin Ross, who's 23 and 6 feet 9 inches tall, started class this week [in September 1982] with seventh- and eighth-graders.

He has just spent four years at Creighton University in Omaha on an athletic scholarship without getting a degree, and he's intent on learning the basics that he somehow missed in high school and college.

Ross is quite talented at basketball, a captain of the team, but he wasn't wooed by the pros. And he has a clear-eyed determination to be ready academically for whatever life brings.

"I'm here to catch up," Ross said.

"My reading is about 65 percent, my spelling is about 40 percent. And reading comprehension, I can't get a percentage on.

"I just wish people in education would make sure students get an education."

Creighton officials said they agree with Ross on that.

Creighton is paying for his stay at Marva Collins' Westside Preparatory School, and athletic director Dan Offenburger went to Chicago today to help Ross find a place to live.

"We strongly encouraged Kevin" to attend Westside Prep, said Offenburger. "But basically it came down to Kevin accepting the challenge. He is a pioneer student, a 23-year-old man studying with grammar school and junior high kids."

Ross still wants to be a teacher, as he did when he entered Creighton.

Ross said he's considering looking for a job so he can afford to stay here. But Offenburger said that may not be necessary. "We found the (Creighton) stipend is sufficient in Omaha but not sufficient in Chicago. I've just got to get out in the streets with him and find a place for him to live. We're looking to schools or churches or private individuals."

Before Ross enrolled at Westside Prep, Creighton arranged for him and his mother to visit the school. Ross's mother, Opal Ross of Kansas City, Kan., is a postal worker who reared six children. Ross is her youngest. One of his sisters is a college graduate and pharmacist.

"I first heard of Westside Prep on TV," Ross said. The private school has 244 students, was founded by Collins, and is in its eighth year. It is basically for preschoolers through eighth-graders.

Collins, a former Chicago public school teacher, gained a national reputation for teaching youngsters who had been given up for lost educationally.

Ross's education deficit apparently started early. He was an "all-everything" at sports at Wyandotte High School in Kansas City, where he finished 10th, 11th and 12th grades.

He feels he did not get a good education at Wyandotte. "Only once did a teacher lay it on the line and give me 5—that's like an F—in class. And a coach taught me two other classes. I'd get A's and B's in them.

"When I got out of high school, I had a 2.0 grade average, which is what you've got to have to get into Creighton."

When Ross was recruited by Creighton, he said, "they told me 'You're going to be starting (at basketball), you're going to get your degree.

"All those school years, I gave 150 percent in basketball and I got 50 percent of an education."

His first two years at Creighton, Ross said, "I took courses that were not required for my major, a lot of Mickey Mouse courses, Ceramics, Introduction to Football."

But Offenburger said, "I would hate to see us look bad" on that. "With the dean's approval, we arranged, as we do for many students with particular problems, a lighter load in number of hours and types of courses."

When Ross finished his junior year, he said he felt "they were just trying to keep me eligible for basketball. And I was a good jumper and scorer."

Offenburger said, "Midway in his career, we found he had some difficulty with advanced courses in the curriculum. We worked with him through a special testing service in the summertime two years ago at the University of Missouri-Kansas City."

Ross was a forward and center on Creighton's Bluejays, and a captain.

In Ross' junior year, when Tom Apke was coach, the Bluejays won 21 and lost 9. In his senior year, former Knickerbocker star Willis Reed became coach and the team won 7 and lost 20.

Ross felt things changed for him with Reed as coach. "In the next to the last game, everybody played but me." he said. "I was captain but I was getting a backseat. And my worst grade card was in my senior year. My best were as a freshman and sophomore."

Offenburger said Creighton offered to pay for Westside.

"I think we've been working the last two years to best figure out how best to meet our obligations to Kevin," Offenburger said.

Ross said he is determined to stick it out at Westside Prep the full academic year.

Collins called Ross's motives in joining Westside Prep "very admirable" and added that "he hopes to make up in one year what he wasn't able to do in four years."

[Copyright © *Chicago Sun-Times*, 1982.
Column by Bob Herguth.
Reprinted with permission.]

Kevin Ross's educational experience as a college athlete sounds extreme, but it is not all that unusual. More than a few athletes spend four years in college with little to show for it but memories and a few stray credits. Where Kevin's case becomes unusual is in the help that people at Creighton and elsewhere gave him *after* his four years of playing eligibility expired. Although Kevin could no longer play basketball, Creighton, to its credit, extended his scholarship for another year and encouraged him to go back to junior high school to pick up the basic skills that he had somehow missed his first time around. To Kevin's credit, he agreed. Only a person with an uncommonly strong drive to learn and to grow, along with the personal strength to ignore ridicule, could have done this. Needless to say, most athletes who have been cheated out of their education just accept their fate as "the way it is" and fail to recover their lost educational skills—ever.

WHO IS RESPONSIBLE WHEN ATHLETES DON'T GET THEIR FAIR SHARE?

Dan Offenburger, the athletic director at Creighton, is concerned about Kevin Ross and what he represents in college sports. Offenburger wonders where the blame lies:

> The system failed him, Kevin failed the system (presumably by going along with it), maybe his mother failed him, maybe I failed him. But does the school get 60 percent of the blame, the mother 30, the high school 10? I mean, how do you assess who's to blame?
>
> [Edward Menaker, *New York Times*, October 3, 1982.]

Knowing who is responsible for the athlete getting a good education is far more important than assigning blame. Parents of athletes, high school and college coaches, and most important, the athletes themselves must keep alert that they as students are headed in the right direction. Unfortunately, parents are often seen as intruders in the relationship between coaches and athletes. Parents sometimes even see themselves in this light and avoid becoming involved. But it is clearly all parents' right and responsibility to be aware of what is occurring in their children's education, including the athletic part. The trick is for parents to approach their sons and daughters and their coaches in a concerned, inquisitive way rather than in a challenging way. A coach who has nothing to hide is likely to welcome parents who inquire about their son's or daughter's performance in school and request hard data about his or her progress toward a degree.

Many high school and college coaches want to be concerned with the overall welfare, growth, and progress of their student-athletes. But in reality, coaches have to weigh those concerns against the task that keeps them in their job—namely, building and running a competitive and profitable athletic program. When one concern—the long-term welfare of athletes—is weighed against the other—producing a winning team and, in the process, ensuring job security—the latter often tips the scale.

Responsibility for the athlete's welfare is primarily up to the athlete. Knowing that coaches face often intense pressures to produce winning teams should give you incentive to protect yourself. The plight of Kevin Ross illustrates only too well that you can't count on anyone else to look out for your academic interests.

SIGNS OF TROUBLE:
HOW TO TELL IF YOU ARE BEING EXPLOITED

Kevin Ross was passing classes, he just wasn't learning anything. If he had it to do over, only Kevin himself could have made the situation any different. Only he knew how little he was progressing as a student.

Passing only the minimum number of units necessary to stay eligible for sports does not "take care of business." Your business as a student is to get a good education, the kind that will help you thrive in the world after college and athletics. To take care of your educational business, you need:

1. more than 12 units each term so as to graduate in a reasonable amount of time and before your funds dry up (whether that money comes from a scholarship, a loan, or your parents); and

2. the *right* classes (i.e., meaningful and useful ones that make you struggle and stretch your abilities, not just those that provide easy grades).

Whether or not you face the problem of exploitation (having your athletic services used, without receiving fair value in return) largely depends upon the attitude of your college and coach. Some top-level, highly competitive athletic programs are diligent in providing their student-athletes with the best educational and career opportunities available. If you are in this situation, count yourself lucky and make the most of it. At the same time, other top-ranking programs (as well as some very small-time programs) are only concerned with producing winning teams and so drain all that they can from their athletes, with little or no concern for their education and future. In this situation, the only two alternatives you face if you don't want to sacrifice your education are to quit the team or to transfer to another school. A third situation you may find yourself in is one where the coach puts pressure on you to devote so much time and energy to your sport that your academic progress suffers; all the while, however, the coach does not realize that this is happening to you, nor does he intend that this should be so. This is probably the most common circumstance and, fortunately, there are a number of things an athlete can do to correct the situation. But first, how can you tell if you need to do anything?

The following fictitious scenarios represent real situations that many college athletes find themselves in. Each is followed by a likely (and harmful) result.

Profile of a Star Running Back About to Go Down the Tubes
(with a little help from his "friends")

Net yards gained in college career: . . 3,000+

Seasons awarded
  "All-Conference" honor: 2

Semesters spent in college: 7

Semesters of varsity competition: . . . 6 (4 in football, 2 in track)

Semesters on academic probation or
  disqualified and reinstated: 4

Total semester credits earned to date: . 86 (total needed to graduate: 126)

  Credits earned toward
      GE requirements: . . . . 31 (total needed to graduate: 46)

  Credits earned toward
      business major: . . . . 3 (total needed to graduate: 60)

Minimum additional semesters needed
  to graduate (based on a normal
  course load): 5

Overall grade-point average: 2.09

GPA in phys. ed. activities and
  athletics courses: 3.29

GPA in all other courses: 1.42

NOTE: This athlete has been told (by his coaches, among others) that he can expect to be a high draft choice in the NFL. However, the colleges against whom he starred were not big-time caliber and his own school has not placed a single player in the NFL during the past 10 years. Yet, it looks as if this athlete has put all of his efforts into that one dream. What will he do if he doesn't make it in football?

SCENARIO: All Billy Joe ever wanted to do was be an athlete. He doesn't really care about college; instead, he is just happy to be a college athlete. The coaching staff is all too happy to have Billy Joe be nothing more than an athlete and devote all his time to training. They are "taking care of him" and Billy Joe may even graduate, although the few times he goes to class he realizes how much more everyone else knows.

RESULT: Billy Joe may, indeed, be given a diploma, but it won't be worth much. Even if he gets through a job interview and is hired, Billy Joe won't last long, because in the world of work, employers don't tolerate dead weight. Billy Joe may not even be able to get a job as a truck driver because the employer will wonder why someone with a college degree wants to drive a truck for a living.

SCENARIO: Bubba is staying eligible for sports, but he has been avoiding all the tough classes he'll have to take to graduate. He plans to take them after his eligibility expires and he can devote more time to such classes. Coach told him to do this and it sounded pretty reasonable, especially when Coach said he would try to extend Bubba's scholarship or find him a job to help him through that extra year or two of school. "One thing at a time," Coach always says.

RESULT: Bubba couldn't handle all those tough classes at once, especially after having taken easy ones for four years. Bubba hung it up and decided a college degree wasn't worth the effort anyway.

SCENARIO: Barbie competed for four years, used up her eligibility, and then dropped out of school lacking about a year's worth of credits for graduation. She just "got tired of being in school." She thought that, maybe after working for a year or two, she would return and finish her degree. That was five years ago. Besides, she doesn't really mind being a waitress. Rotten hours, and people can be pretty nasty to waitresses, but tips are good and. . . .

RESULT: Barbie probably won't ever return to school. The cost of school is so much more now and the longer she waits, the more she is likely to be intimidated by professors, other students, loss of her study skills, computers, and whatever else is new on the college scene. Waitresses can earn a good living, but work conditions aren't the greatest and there isn't much room for advancement.

SCENARIO: Betty Lou cares about getting an education, but her coach demands so much time that she can't give all she would like to her schoolwork. In fact, her coach has tried to advise her against taking a couple of tough courses that would help Betty Lou get into graduate school. ("Part of the price you pay for being an athlete," the coach said.) Betty Lou took the courses anyway (risking her coach's wrath), but didn't do well since she couldn't devote enough time to them because of team commitments.

RESULT: Betty Lou got into graduate school (although not the one she wanted) but is struggling to keep up with the other students. The stuff that she didn't learn in her undergraduate major they know backwards and forwards. And in graduate school there is no time to go back and learn the basics, especially since she also has to hold down a part-time job to make ends meet. Besides, graduate schools require students to maintain at least a B average. Betty Lou is considering dropping out before they kick her out.

SCENARIO: Bruce's friend Bart did only what was necessary to stay eligible for sports, then dropped out of school, and is now making a lot of money at a pretty good job. Bruce looks at Bart's life and wonders what's so all-fired necessary about making sure he gets a good and complete college education.

RESULT: For every Bart you hear about, there are twenty you don't hear about who are pushing a broom, driving a taxi, or selling used cars.

Graduation Rates of College Basketball Players Following the 1982 Season

Ivy League	*100.0%*
Big East Conference	*77.3%*
Southern Conference	*63.2%*
Big 8 Conference	*50.0%*
Pacific 10 Conference	*40.7%*
Southeastern Conference	*40.0%*
Atlantic Coast Conference	*36.8%*
Big 10 Conference	*30.4%*
Southwestern Conference	*16.7%*

Source: *The Sporting News*, as reported in the *Chronicle of Higher Education*, November 3, 1982. Statistics are for seniors who played as team regulars in 1982.

Other situations that can keep you from getting your fair share from your years in college include:

- majoring in a field that is not of your own choosing.
- taking nothing but gut courses so as to remain eligible for sports; this is called "majoring in eligibility."
- being assigned to courses with other athletes mainly to keep you together.
- avoiding socializing with nonathletes.
- accepting the coach's suggestion (which you construe as a direct order) to take a summer job that will build your body, when you would rather take a job that helps in your major or career plans.

Coaches may exploit athletes in one or all of the following ways:

- by demanding so much time that you cannot perform your best in courses that you want or need for your future.
- by steering you into courses that are easy but less valuable for your future, so that you won't take time and energy away from team commitments.
- by arranging aspects of your life (such as meals, housing, or leisure activities) so that you will interact primarily with other athletes and also be more completely under the control of the coaching staff.

College athletes are all too capable of treating themselves unfairly, engaging in a kind of self-exploitation. They often feel torn in two directions when having to decide between fulfilling their athletic needs and interests and their academic responsibilities and goals. It's very tempting to take the easy way out and put off your academic responsibilities until some later time. Whether you postpone tasks for a given class or avoid your responsibilities for your entire degree and career plans, any delay in taking care of academic responsibilities allows them to pile up and makes it more difficult to take care of them in the future. If you get into this bad habit of taking care of sports now and academics later, you are almost guaranteed to be exploiting yourself. You will end up being the loser. If this happens, you can't blame it on anyone else. You will have done it to yourself.

Grant Darkow majored in biology and played linebacker for the University of Missouri. Honored as an Academic All-America, Darkow believes that the people who run college athletic programs have a responsibility to their student-athletes. Focusing on football, he says:

> So many kids are going to college who have their hearts set on playing pro football but end up just being used. When they get through, what have they got if they didn't study? It's not only the responsibility of the student to study and get a degree, but it's also the responsibility of the administrators and the coaches to see he doesn't waste his time there and gets an education as well as the experience of being an athlete.

[*New York Times,*
December 9, 1981.]

It may seem that at times in this chapter we've painted a bleak picture of college athletics, in which athletes invariably are forced to battle the system if they really want an education. In fact, at many schools that is just how it was for many years (and maybe still is). But you are fortunate in that those who run college athletics, from coaches to administrators to national college athletic associations, are becoming increasingly aware and concerned about athletes getting a fair chance at receiving a solid, well-rounded education and strong career preparation. As a result, the administrators and sports personnel you deal with are more likely to encourage and support you in these pursuits than in the past. Don't expect them to lead you to your academic and career rewards, because many people you will be involved with still may view student-athletes primarily as athletes. However, if you stand up for your rights as a student, your chances of getting all that should be coming your way in terms of a college education are better today than they were for athletes in the past. Being an athlete no longer necessarily means sacrificing important parts of your education. But the responsibility is still yours to make the system work for you, to get your full 110 percent from college in return for the extra effort that coaches expect from you as an athlete.

6

GETTING ALONG WITH COACHES, BOOSTERS, PROFESSORS, AND OTHERS

In This Chapter...

The Athlete and the Coach

The Athlete and Boosters

The Athlete and the College Administration

The Athlete and the Faculty

The Athlete and Other Students

Athletes, Gamblers, and Drugs

Student-athletes often have a different relationship with other members of the campus community than do nonathletes. To the extent that they are identified as athletes, people tend to relate to them as athletes first and students second—or in some cases, as athletes only. Athletes also sometimes attract the attention of fans, boosters, and sports writers, none of whom have an official function on the college campus. Understanding these interpersonal relationships and the expectations people may have of you as an athlete will help you to get along better in college and will keep you from making some serious mistakes.

THE ATHLETE AND THE COACH

It doesn't take a genius to know that in sports, for every winner there is at least one loser. In track and field, gymnastics, swimming, and other sports where more than two teams compete together, there is one winner and several losers. And if a particular team is expected to win a championship, its members can be considered losers, even with a winning record, if they fall short of their championship goal. (The coaching "graveyard" is full of those who earned winning records but not enough championships.)

How much pressure to win each coach feels depends in large part upon the sport and past performance at the college. Obviously there is more pressure to produce a national championship football team at Notre Dame than a winning golf team at Hacker Tech. But to different degrees, most coaches feel some pressure to win, whether the pressure comes from others or is self-imposed. These two factors—that coaches are expected to win, yet everyone cannot win—help to explain why few coaches keep the same job, or even stay in the profession of coaching, for very many years. Those who lose consistently usually are fired or quit; those who win and are ambitious (as coaches tend to be) move on to bigger challenges.

No matter how good a strategist, how well organized, or how deft a psychologist, a coach will not win consistently without good athletes. But many coaches feel that having good athletes (resulting from luck or recruiting effort) is not even enough to help them become and stay winners. They also need *commitment* to the sport from their athletes. Some coaches simply ask their athletes for this commitment, others demand it. What does this commitment mean to you as a student-athlete?

The Time Problem. Commitment to athletics is most apparent in terms of time and energy devoted to training and to the team. As an athlete, you can expect to spend 25 to 50 or more hours each week in your sport. Coaches generally expect the hours required for team-related tasks (practices, travel, games, conditioning, chalk-talks, etc.) to be taken from your leisure time, which they often consider a low priority. This is part of the price athletes are supposed to pay for the privilege of playing for the college. But everybody wants and needs a certain amount of leisure and personal time. Since no one has yet found more than 24 hours in a day, college athletes often have to steal the time required for team-related tasks from somewhere else. Instead of sacrificing their leisure time, that "somewhere else" is often schoolwork or sleep.

Jeff Hembrough, a tackle on the Illinois State University football team who majored in chemistry, was honored in 1981 by the Football

Foundation and Hall of Fame as an All-America Scholar-Athlete. Hembrough describes the time problem facing most college athletes:

> We devoted more than 40 hours a week to football. It's almost like having a full-time job and then having to do schoolwork. For the poor student, this is tough. He needs more time, and when he gets in trouble academically, it is harder for him to find the time as he falls behind.
>
> [*New York Times*, December 9, 1981.]

Time is a problem for student-athletes regardless of whether they are poor students or good ones, starting players or reserves. There is not enough time to do everything that you want to do. To get the most that you possibly can out of your time takes planning and discipline, skills that you should be developing in your sport.

Winning vs. Your Welfare. Coaches feel that the time commitment they demand of athletes is necessary in order to have a winning team. Most coaches are also genuinely concerned about the personal and academic welfare of their athletes. Unfortunately, when the welfare of their athletes conflicts with the chance to win, there are too many coaches who will sacrifice the former for the latter. Try not to get into that situation by carefully selecting your college and coach. But if you find yourself working with a coach for whom your personal welfare is little more than an afterthought, and especially if your academic progress or health are suffering because of the coach's demands, you should seriously consider either transferring to another school or quitting the team. Those are drastic measures, but the consequences of staying in a bad environment and wasting your education are worse. Without question, it is a tough decision to make, but one that you should not avoid.

What Do You Want from Your Coach? Athletes learn early to figure out what their coach wants from them but seldom try to determine, beyond the obvious, what they want and should get from the coach. First, all athletes want the coach to allow them to compete. Next, they want the coach to teach new techniques and strategies and correct their faults. But, in addition, a college coach should be a good counselor and guide, rather than a dictator or guardian figure who takes care of everything. "Taking care of everything" usually means taking most of your choices away from you (even in the selection of classes, who you'll live with, where you'll get a part-time or summer job, and similar decisions). Having someone make decisions for you is *not* what college is supposed to be about; it encourages dependence, which can cripple you when you have to act on your own. Yet, some coaches totally control their athletes in order to better serve the team's needs, at the expense of each athlete's growth. You will gain more from a coach who gives you freedom to make your own decisions.

Dealing with the Coach's Personality. You may like your coach's personality or you may hate it, but you have to deal with it if you want to be allowed to compete. As any athlete knows all too well, the coach holds power over one of the most important concern in your life: your access to competing. If you are not being given a fair chance to compete, an otherwise good relationship is likely to become strained.

Since coaches have ultimate power over who gets to compete, dealing with their personalities generally means adjusting to them rather than having them adjust to you. Some coaches—"Bear" Bryant was the best-known example—are unemotional and distant from their athletes. Others, like Joe Paterno, project a warm and parent-like or even a buddy image to their athletes. Still others present themselves as antagonists, always seeming to dig at their athletes, criticizing and harping on the most minor errors, and keeping everyone on edge. Each has a different coaching style.

Whichever face your coach wears, it is probably one that he or she feels will work most effectively to produce a successful team. The "coaching face"—the way coaches treat and interact with their athletes—is usually a means for motivating and controlling athletes. It may be very different from the way they relate to family and friends. Former athletes often see their coaches in a completely different light after their days of college competition end. They find out that the coach was more of a complete person than he or she dared let on to student-athletes.

Many coaches either can't or won't treat each of their athletes as individuals with different needs. If you don't like the way your coach is treating you, it is your responsibility to do something about it. If you think that your coach has the wrong image of you, your choice is either to suffer along with the old image or to take the initiative to correct that image and establish a new relationship with the coach. Don't expect the coach to take the lead; he or she has a lot of athletes to deal with.

Changing the way we relate to people is not easy. But don't mistakenly believe that the way you've related to coaches or teammates in the past is the way you must continue to act. You always have freedom to change your image; the burden is on you to exercise that freedom, especially if that image is not the way you want it to be. If, for example, you have become the team clown but want to be taken more seriously, it is up to you to change that image. Since the coach often influences what roles people play on their team, let the coach know that you would prefer to be taken more seriously. If you want more responsibility, ask for it and act more responsibly.

Coaches will often respond very well to this kind of direct approach from their athletes. It generates respect as a mature way of dealing with a conflict between two people—such as coach and athlete—who have to work closely together. Some coaches, on the other hand, will react poorly to an athlete who tries to correct the coach's mistaken image and establish a better relationship. Trying to improve the coach's image of you may seem like a gamble, but in the long run it will be worth the risk. You can be sure that it's better than spending a few years not getting along with the coach, hanging onto the futile hope that something will change the situation for you. That something often takes the form of a dream on the athlete's part that a chance will come to win a big contest for the coach. The chance of that happening is not likely when the coach and athlete don't get along.

THE ATHLETE AND BOOSTERS

Who are college athletic boosters? Most people assume that athletic boosters are alumni of the college and, conversely, that all alumni are athletic boosters. In reality, many graduates of a college do not actively support the school's teams. Many do not even like sports. On the other hand, many athletic boosters are simply fans who have affiliated themselves with a particular college, even though they have never taken a class at the school whose teams they support. Their interest in the college lies in having a team to root for.

"People in the business world [sports boosters] are not always interested in the rules and regulations [of college athletics]—they feel they know how to make a sale. We do our best to monitor their activities, but it isn't easy."

—Bob Hitch, athletic director at
Southern Methodist University
[Paul Desruisseaux, "Athletics Deemed
a 'Better Citizen' at SMU,"
Chronicle of Higher Education,
January 5, 1983.]

Boosters invariably appear to athletes as friends, even though they sometimes do more harm to athletes and entire athletic programs than an enemy ever could. The recent probations suffered by the UCLA, Arizona State, and Clemson football teams each resulted from over-zealous booster involvement. Harm to athletes and programs occurs because boosters want so badly for the athletic program to be success-ful. Many boosters feel that athletic success is worth any price. Yet they often seem ignorant of (or unwilling to accept) the fact that tactics which may have led to success in their own businesses and professions are either inappropriate or illegal in college athletics.

QUESTION: Why are athletic boosters interested in you?

ANSWER: Because of your athletic ability and, in particular, what you can do for the team.

QUESTION: What can you do for the team if you suffer a disabling injury or after you use up your playing eligibility?

ANSWER: Nothing!

QUESTION: What interest are boosters likely to have in you if you become injured or after your college athletic career is finished?

ANSWER: Considerably less than when you were an active member of the team. You probably weren't the first athlete they befriended and you won't be the last. There is always someone new coming along on whom boosters can lavish their attention, money, and advice.

Be friendly with athletic boosters, especially if they are friendly to you. But also be wary of them. The history of college sports is filled with incidents where something has gone wrong in the relationship among athletes, athletic teams, and boosters. The problem usually arises when boosters want to help too much, and so offer more to in-dividual athletes than the rules allow. Not long ago, the University of San Francisco decided to drop its entire men's intercollegiate basket-ball program because of excessive booster involvement. The college's administrators stated that they would only reinstate the team when they felt confident that they could control boosters.

What sort of help do boosters frequently attempt to make available to athletes? The following are typical:

Money, from pocket change to thousands of dollars or use of credit cards. (Even the pocket change is illegal.)

Gifts, ranging from "a little something from the store" to cars, trips, and even houses. (All gifts to athletes are illegal, except gifts from family.)

Advice, from game strategy to opinions about majors and careers. (There are better places to get advice than from boosters.)

Contacts with people who can help athletes get started in careers once their college days end. (Career contacts are important, the best legitimate benefit that boosters can offer you.)

Clearly, some athletes don't care about getting an education and willingly sell themselves to the highest bidder. Also, many coaches are only interested in building a winning team any way they can. Even college presidents have been known to look the other way when rules have been broken, and some welcome the involvement and largesse of wealthy boosters. But without the boosters' intense interest in being associated with winning athletic teams, many of the temptations some student-athletes have to face (Should I take the money? Am I a fool if I don't take it?) would not exist.

Many large-scale college athletic programs operate on money donated by boosters. This money pays for scholarships and coaching salaries at a number of large colleges. Donations from athletic boosters to the Stanford University athletic program reached $4-million in the 1980–81 year alone. Clemson's boosters gave $3.1-million, Florida State's $2.1-million, Texas A & M's $1.8-million, University of Missouri's $1.5-million, Purdue's $1-million. These are only a few examples of athletic programs that are among those most heavily funded by boosters' money. The *average* NCAA Division I college counts on over $300,000 each year from boosters to support its athletic programs. And even many small colleges cultivate booster involvement in sports. In fact, budgets tend to be so tight at some small schools that intercollegiate athletics programs might not exist without boosters' donations.

Most boosters mean well for their schools and athletes. The problem lies with those who fail to understand the difficult (and potentially damaging) position in which they are putting athletes by offering them illegal bonuses. Boosters may not want to consider the ethical problems they create for you. Having their team win may be, to them, considerably more important than following the rules. Besides, the rules and penalties apply to you, the athlete, not to them. They have nothing to lose; it's you and your team who will pay the price.

THE ATHLETE AND THE COLLEGE ADMINISTRATION

If athletic programs are so costly and cause so much trouble, why do colleges have them? The answer is that college administrators believe at least one and probably all of the following:

An athletic program earns money for the college.

An athletic program is entertaining and attracts students to the college.

An athletic program provides good public relations for the college.

An athletic program gives students, faculty, and staff a sense of identity with the college.

An athletic program keeps alumni interested in the college and thus ensures a major source of ongoing contributions to the college.

An athletic program provides a kind of learning experience that can't be found in the classroom.

Further, many college administrators believe that if athletics brings these things to their school, then a winning athletic program, particularly in the mass-audience sports of football and basketball, will do even more.

It is not enough just to know that your school's administration supports the athletic program. You should also understand what it expects of your coach, since the expectations that your coach labors under will be felt in one way or another by you, the athlete. The school administration is responsible for setting campus rules for the conduct of athletics and for seeing that coaches and athletes adhere to their conference and national association regulations. Yet it is often the school's administration that demands winning teams and thus inadvertently sets the ball rolling toward cheating on rules and exploitation of athletes. In situations where administrators, boosters, and coaches are all "committed to winning" (a favorite phrase), an even greater commitment is expected of the athletes themselves. As a result, student-athletes may have even great difficulty finding enough time and energy to take care of their own educational and career needs.

The issue boils down to expectations and pressure. The greater the expectations and pressure to win placed upon your coach by the college administration, the greater will be the expectations and pressure placed on you by your coach. Wanting and expecting success is a healthy approach to sports competition and can yield greater success than you might otherwise achieve. But when an expectation becomes a demand for success, people often feel pressured to change their attitudes and behaviors to support that demand, at the expense of other needs. A coach who initially seemed friendly and relaxed may become distant and tense because of the pressure to win. A coach who had always seemed concerned for your welfare may ask you to play when you are injured. Under pressure from the school administration to win, a coach who previously seemed concerned about your future might suggest you take a light or easy class load if difficult courses are diverting your attention from the team. Athletes who find themselves caught in that trap must have the courage to resist pressure from coaches to let their academic efforts and goals slide.

THE ATHLETE AND THE FACULTY

College professors are like coaches in one important way: their job is to help you grow and achieve. A great difference between professors and coaches, however, is that a coach's job often depends on how well his or her team performs; a professor's job, in contrast, seldom depends on the performance of students. A professor can fail over half of a class without being considered "a loser" and jeopardizing his or her job (although the professor's standards and ability as a teacher would likely be questioned). In contrast to professors, coaches who lose more than half of their contests may soon be out of a job. One reason for the difference is that coaches recruit their own athletes; professors, on the other hand, don't have the "luxury" of choosing whom they will teach and so are less directly responsible for students' performance.

On any campus, some professors have a reputation for being pro-athletics, while others are known as anti-jock. You cannot tell if a professor is pro- or anti-athletics by whether or ot they were athletes during their high school and college days. Some former athletes are extremely anti-athletics, particularly regarding the way sports are conducted in colleges. Conversely, many professors who were not athletes themselves are among the strongest backers of athletics.

Whether or not a professor likes sports or approves of college athletics may be completely unrelated to his or her attitude about student-athletes. If a professor has an anti-athletics reputation but treats athletes the same as any other students, you might be missing a good thing by avoiding his or her classes. One of the great benefits of a college education is the opportunity to interact with people who have very different opinions from your own. They may open your eyes to things you hadn't seen, or confirm, after a thorough discussion, your own previous beliefs.

Nearly every college, however, has a few professors who dislike athletics so much that they are unfair to athletes. They group athletes into one or two categories, usually labeled "Dumb" and "Pampered." These professors are biased and their minds are usually closed to any contrary evidence about athletes. Why make college life any harder than it has to be? Avoid taking classes from these anti-athletics professors wherever possible, unless you have a large margin for error in your GPA and feel like being a crusader for athletes' rights. If you can't avoid them, keep a low profile concerning your athletic involvement. Try not to ask for favors (alternative test dates, delayed assignments, etc.) because of team commitments, avoid responding to questions or commenting on assignments in terms of your athletic experience, and certainly don't wear your practice jersey to class.

Some simple techniques can be followed that will help you get along with faculty members no matter what their attitudes toward athletes are. Not surprisingly, these techniques are not just to impress; they will make you a better student. One of the most obvious is to pay attention in class. You'd be surprised how easily professors can identify students who are paying attention. When professors ask a question in class, they usually would like a response from the students rather than having to answer the question themselves. Don't worry about giving the wrong answer. An erroneous yet thoughtful response that indicates you have been paying attention is almost as good as the correct answer. In some cases a thoughtful wrong answer is better than the right answer, because it allows the professor to then explain his or her intention for asking the question in the first place.

Establish your credibility as a student by being on time to classes and meetings and demonstrating the other qualities that professors associate with good students. Specifically,

- Turn in assignments on time or even early.
- Prepare early for tests. Most professors can tell when a student has waited until the last evening to study, and they are not likely to be sympathetic to the excuses of a procrastinator.
- Ask to take tests early when you know there will be a schedule conflict because of your sport. Your best bet is to talk about this the first week of the term by bringing the team schedule to your

professors to discuss the conflicts with them. They will appreciate your foresight and concern. Few things gripe a professor more than to have an athlete (or anyone) come to them after missing a test and ask for a make-up.

- Meet with professors early in the term (or even before the term starts) and ask their advice about what is needed to do well in the course. Professors are used to athletes asking for special favors to get around course requirements, so you will be well received if, instead, you ask *how to do well* in the class.

THE ATHLETE AND OTHER STUDENTS

Getting Along with Nonathletes

Just as with professors, nonathletes come in three varieties: those who are pro-athletics, those who are anti-athletics, and those who couldn't care less about athletics. The main difference you are likely to find among nonathletes in college as compared to high school is that in college, the extremes of either loving or hating athletics are further apart. College students who love athletics are more likely to be in awe of athletes (this tendency is greater in college than in high school possibly because athletic skill is presumably greater at the college level). On the other hand, college students who dislike athletics are likely to be more active and vocal in their feelings. This may affect you in social situations and in classes. An anti-athletic feeling may even hurt your team financially on campuses where athletic funding comes at least in part from student government.

Many nonathletes have their own expectations of what athletes are like and how they are supposed to act. Those who think that athletes are dumb, or aggressive, or not serious about school may cause a problem for you. Sociologists call this problem role conflict, and describe it as stress or tension that results when a person is expected to act two different ways at the same time. For example, student-athletes may feel tension when they are expected to be smart, as a college student, yet dumb, as a jock. Role conflict has burdened many athletes from the early history of college sports. (As noted earlier, the dumb jock image has been well-earned by some athletes; as a result, that stereotype has had to be battled by most other athletes.) Much of the conflict in living the twin roles of student and athlete comes from the perceived need to "live down" to someone else's poor opinion of student-athletes in general. You don't have to match anyone else's opinion of you, especially if it isn't accurate.

Don't fall into the trap of trying hard to make others like and respect you by adopting the attitudes and image you *assume* they expect. Forget about the preconceived notions of others and follow a piece of age-old advice: simply be yourself. And if that isn't enough for some people, it's their loss not to know you.

Getting Along with Other Athletes

Other athletes share an important experience and identity with you, even athletes from other sports. A few of the many things you have in common with all athletes are how to get along with coaches, anxiety over competition and the chance of injuries, balancing sport and school, keeping your scholarship or position on the team, and how to face defeat. Among your own teammates an even closer bond results from your competing against them during practice and with them against other teams. Other athletes probably understand your problems better than anyone else, and they can appreciate both your successes and your failures better than anyone else. You've all been through it, either separately or together.

But don't let the special bond that exists among athletes become a shackle on your social interactions and cause you to associate only with other athletes. To this point in your life, you may have been most comfortable in the company of other athletes, but after you graduate, no longer will there be a distinction between athletes and nonathletes. If you haven't already done so, now is the time to become comfortable with nonathletes and build relationships on other interests.

Some athletes you know, especially those who are unsure of themselves, may try to put you down for associating with nonathletes. Such a response reflects their weakness, not yours. The more you hang around only with other athletes, the more likely you are to think of college (and maybe even life) primarily in athletic terms.

ATHLETES, GAMBLERS, AND DRUGS

A discussion of how an athlete can get along in college is not complete without considering how you can and should handle gamblers and drug usage. It would be nice not to have to concern ourselves with these problems, yet the gambling scandals involving former Ohio State quarterback Art Schlicter in 1983, the point shaving of the 1979 Boston College basketball team, and recent revelations about cocaine use among football and basketball players suggest that these problems are real and very close to college athletes.

100

Handling Your Friendly Neighborhood Bookie

Football and basketball players tend to be more attractive to gamblers than athletes from other sports. Not all gambling, however, is on major contests of national interest. Local gamblers have their own systems and networks for small colleges and even for some minor sports. Gamblers have been known to bet on snail races, so no athlete should assume that he or she is immune from this problem.

Let's say that a gambler, or even a teammate, approaches you to keep the score close—not to lose the contest, but just to shave enough points off the final score so that gamblers can beat the point spread and win their bets. They offer you a few hundred dollars in cash for you simply to take it easy if it looks as if your team is going to beat the point spread. The point spreads for major contests of national interest and even for some local events are listed in the sports section of most newspapers.

The money being offered to you may seem like a lot at the time, especially if you really need it. But in the long run the few hundred or even thousand dollars you might make from gamblers would be meaningless next to what it could cost you, your teammates and coach, and the school. Games, championships, and careers have been lost to involvement with gamblers.

Gamblers will try to make you believe that by shaving points you aren't doing anything too terrible. You might even fool yourself into thinking that all you are hurting are people who are breaking the law by betting with the gamblers. But consider the following:

1. shaving points is illegal and punishable;
2. not trying your hardest in any contest is unethical;
3. not even the best players can control a contest well enough to determine the final score. Many contests have been lost that were just supposed to be kept close.

Being approached by a gambler is a little like getting hit by a truck. You didn't ask for the problem, but you can't ignore it. Don't mistakenly think that you can keep clean by keeping quiet. The rules of collegiate athletics state that you are as guilty by remaining quiet as you are if you participate. Gamblers know that in keeping silent, you have broken a rule, and they will then use that knowledge to draw you further into their web by attempting to involve you in point-shaving or throwing contests. It will probably be hard to report the contact by a gambler to your coach, especially if the contact involves a team-mate. But the consequences of not doing it are worse.*

Drug and Alcohol Use and Abuse

There is considerable disagreement over whether drug and alcohol use and abuse are worse among athletes than among the general American public. What is clear, however, is that athletes at all levels have *no less* of a problem with alcohol and drugs. Athletes actually may take a wider variety of drugs because they believe it will help them compete better. Each drug, however, brings with it more problems than benefits.

"Getting Ready" Drugs. Athletes in many sports must endure considerable pressure in the course of competition. To deal with this pressure, some take uppers, downers, or both in combination. They may look on these drugs as a necessary evil that enables them to be ready for competition. Besides, they often think, taking drugs isn't so terrible since the ones they take are prescription pills that many adults take more or less regularly.

Weight Control Drugs. In some sports, athletes must be concerned with maintaining a particular weight classification in order to be allowed to compete. Some take dietary supplements to gain or diuretics to lose weight. Given the American concern over weight control generally, this practice isn't seen as all that terrible. In fact, the dietary supplements or diuretics may come from or be recommended by coaches or trainers. However, athletes often ruin their competitive edge by trying to "make weight" through chemicals.

"Bulking Up" Drugs. Anabolic steroids have been used by wrestlers, football players, some field-event athletes, weight lifters, and women athletes in many sports in order to gain muscle mass and strength. Steroids, originally devised to reduce inflammation in injured joints, are known to produce several physically harmful side effects. For this reason, and because sports were never intended to be contests between chemicals, steroids may not be used by athletes.

A new system for testing use of steroids by athletes was unveiled at the Pan American Games in 1983, resulting in disqualification of 15 athletes, some of whom were from the United States. Several other athletes left the Games before being tested, for fear that they might

---

*For a horror story involving collegiate basketball and gambling, in which suffering was inflicted on both guilty and innocent parties, read *Scandals of '51*, by Charles Rosen (Holt, Rinehart and Winston, 1978).

be disqualified for the 1984 Olympics. Even apart from considering the problems of being caught as a steroid-using athlete or the effect that use of steroids might have on the fairness of competition, the point that athletes should remember is that steroids are dangerous, especially in the dosages that must be taken to remain or become "chemically competitive." Steroid users have been known to experience significant changes in their reproductive organs and livers. Some who are only in their early 30s are suffering from hardening of the arteries and heart damage.

"Recreational" Drugs. Most people, whether sports fans or not, know of the widespread use of cocaine and other so-called recreational drugs among professional athletes. The point is frequently made that use of recreational drugs, which include alcohol, easily leads to abuse of these drugs. Possibly because of the high price of cocaine, marijuana, and other hallucinogenic drugs, college students who want or need a "rush" often rely on a relatively cheap standby, alcohol. Since alcohol is available, legal (depending on the user's age, of course), and cheap relative to other perception-altering drugs, people may consider alcohol to be less of a problem. But because it is considerably cheaper and easier to obtain than other drugs, too often it is subject to overuse and abuse by college students.

Why is it that so many athletes take illegal drugs or abuse legal ones? Because they believe it will help them improve their performance, deal with the pressures of competition, or fit in better with other athletes. The fact is, however, that drugs are not a solution for any of these problems, and there is a great deal of evidence that considerable damage can result from drug use. Most professional sports leagues, professional players associations, and even the NCAA have programs or are planning to develop alcohol and drug abuse programs for athletes. Some

---

"Drug use is the number one problem in amateur sports. It is of international scope. . . . I remember I was speaking in Philadelphia to a group of heavily recruited young high school athletes. In a way, they were surprised that a person like myself was not into drugs that aid performers. I told them, 'You don't have to be into them (drugs) to be on top.'"

—Edwin Moses, world-record holder in the
400-meter intermediate hurdles
[*Sacramento Bee,* June 16, 1983.]

---

coaches consider athletes who have abused drugs and alcohol to be "damaged merchandise" and remove them from the team.

Our point is not to preach to you about drug and alcohol abuse, however. When people are deciding what to put inside their bodies, few minds have ever been changed by preaching. We only ask that you do two things before indulging: (1) weigh seriously any thought of using alcohol and drugs against the potential physical and legal costs you may face; and (2) consider the respect that any athlete should have for his or her body.

7

YOUR

SUPPORT SYSTEM

In This Chapter...

Is It a Rule, or Do I Have a Choice?

Official Advisors

Special Advising Programs for Athletes

Unofficial Advisors

Special Organizations That Help Athletes

When you need advice about your college education, there are places to get official advice and counseling. "Official" advice comes from people who have been hired by the college specifically to counsel and communicate information to students. "Unofficial" advice comes from anywhere else. Although official sources of advice may take a little effort on your part to contact, the effort is usually worth the trouble. The advice and counseling you get from these official sources tend to be more sound and consistent than any you might come by through unofficial sources, such as alumni, coaches, or the student grapevine. Before describing different sources of official and unofficial advice and counsel, let's make sure you understand the difference between advice and answers.

IS IT A RULE, OR DO I HAVE A CHOICE?

There is a difference between matters of school policy (rules) and matters of choice. Policies and rules are published in the college catalog and other official publications. Although you are responsible for knowing the rules, official school advisors should help you interpret them. Advisors can also give you advice on matters of choice, such as which required courses will best serve your needs. But in these matters of choice, you should not look for *answers* from other people. In

> *"The rewards for collegiate athletic participation are dismal...*
> *for those who are not fortunate enough to have proper guidance*
> *or counseling during their undergraduate career. They could end*
> *up majoring in courses to no-man's land. Too many athletes are*
> *hopeless cases without a chance of a pro sports career or a*
> *degree—after sacrificing four or five years, all at a loss."*
>
> —Oscar Edwards, former UCLA football player
> [Michelle Himmelberg, "Athlete Traded Skills
> for Scholarship at Expense of Grades,"
> *Sacramento Bee,* June 9, 1982.]

general, there is no single right answer in matters of choice. Instead, several viable options usually exist, from which you will have to select the best one for your situation.

Remember: advisors give advice, not answers. The best advisors give you enough information to let you make your own decisions. So weigh advice. Question it. Learn to be a good and intelligent consumer of advice. Take an active part in all matters of choice that affect you.

What sort of advice or counseling do you need? You need or will need advice about how to acquire a solid education and a useful degree, how to make the most of your college athletic career, and how and where to look toward a career. The following sources should help you when you need information, advice about problems, and help with decision making.

OFFICIAL ADVISORS

Professors

Professors often act as advisors to students, explaining academic requirements and other information contained in the official college catalog. You will either be assigned to a professor when you enter the college or be allowed to choose one from the faculty in your major department. As your academic advisor, he or she should help you in developing your academic program, selecting courses each term, and fulfilling your degree requirements in the major.

Just as with coaches, some professors are better advisors than others. Professors are seldom trained as advisors and even less often are paid for it. They are trained, hired, paid, and judged on their teaching and research work. Advising students is a task which comes out of time they might prefer to be doing other things. Some enjoy advising and put a lot of effort into it; others don't. Hold out for one who seems to care about advising and about you. The amount of care and effort put into advising is the best indicator of whether or not a faculty member will advise you well. How can you tell how much care and effort advisors put into advising? Ask yourself the following questions:

- Do they know the rules, regulations, deadlines, etc.?
- If not, are they willing to help you find out this important information?
- Are they willing to spend some time with you exploring your interests, or do you get the feeling that they are rushing you through the advising session?
- Do they simply *tell you* what to take, without exploring your own interests and alternative ways of approaching your degree and career goals?

Professors are very busy with class preparations, research and writing, endless committee work, and other duties. But advising students is one of these duties, and getting good advice and counsel is very important to you. If the professor assigned to you (or chosen by you) for advising isn't doing well for you, either talk to him or her about it (which may be hard for you to do) or look around for someone who might give you better advising service.

Student Services

Academic Advising Center. Some colleges and universities, especially large ones, have special offices for advising students on academic matters. This service is in addition to the departmental advisor to whom you will be assigned in your major. Here, you can expect to find out information about general requirements for graduation, and your state of progress can be monitored and measured. You may also get help with major requirements at the Academic Advising Center; often a member of its staff will serve as your official advisor of record until you select a major.

Besides advice on degree requirements, the academic advising staff can explain the grading system, help you figure out your GPA, and discuss transferring to different majors or even to another school. They also may offer some career counseling, but generally their task is to provide you with help in getting the most out of what college has to offer, in particular a degree.

Realize and remember, however, that no matter what any advisor tells you, even those in the college advising center, the responsibility for your actions—or lack of action—rests on your shoulders alone. If you don't double-check advice and it turns out to be wrong, you are likely to spend extra time and effort making up for the mistake. Be like a bulldog about making sure you have good information; it's your education and future on the line.

Learning Skills Center. This is where you will find tutors, workshops, self-instruction programs, and other help in improving the skills essential to learning. Typical workshops deal with improving reading and writing, test-taking, time management, listening and note-taking, and memory enhancement.

Testing Center. You may take exams here for remedial help or advanced placement (reading, writing, math, etc.) and for identification of your own abilities and interests (such as the Strong Vocational Interest test). Tests for graduate school admission may also be offered, such as the Graduate Record Exam and the Miller Analogies Test. Some schools combine the Testing Center and Learning Skills Center.

Health Center. In addition to seeking medical help at the campus Health Center, you may be able to go there to take any preseason physical exams required in your sport.

Psychological Counseling Center. This is the place to go for help with stress and other personal problems. Many small colleges combine psychological and career counseling in one office; some schools may place psychological counseling in the Health Center.

Career Development and Placement Center. Most colleges have a special office or center for counseling students about their career interests and career alternatives. If your school has a Career Development and Placement Center, check into what it offers. Don't wait until you are about to graduate to seek help from the Career Center. Career advice can be helpful to you as early as your first year in college.

Student Employment Office. This is where you can locate part-time jobs and summer jobs, either on or off campus. Don't confuse the Student Employment Office with the Career Center. (The former deals with your job needs while you are a student; the latter helps you find a career direction and learn the right way to search for a position in your field.)

Educational Opportunity Program (EOP). Students from economically disadvantaged backgrounds can get help through EOP with special admissions (if you don't meet the normal school entrance requirements), counseling to help you adjust to the college environment, special tutors in basic communication and math skills, and small grants (between $200 and $1000) to help you through the school year.

Financial Aid Office. The Financial Aid Office exists to help you determine the amount of aid you need and to help you find appropriate sources of this aid. Your coach may help set up your initial contact with the Financial Aid Office, but don't count on or wait for this to happen. Every coach has his or her personal view of how much initiative student-athletes should take in obtaining financial aid.

The Financial Aid Office may have someone who specializes in helping athletes, but again, don't count on it. Even if the Financial Aid Office has such a specialist, don't expect this person to come to you or to drop everything else when you walk in the door. Financial aid offices are very busy places. At some colleges, more than 80 percent of the students receive some sort of aid. Bear in mind that all aid recipients must apply through the same office. A lesson you should have learned in sports applies also to seeking financial aid: "Persistence pays off!"

Unless you have an athletic scholarship, either full or partial, you will probably be just like any other student to those who work in the Financial Aid Office. Even if they tend to treat athletes in some special way, you will be doing yourself a favor not to expect special treatment. Those who sit around expecting to be fed will probably go hungry.

Large colleges tend to have separate offices for each of the student services mentioned above, while smaller schools may combine the services into one or two offices. A final and very important comment on student services: You must approach them, they won't be likely to find you. If you need any of these services, don't be bashful about seeking them out. They exist to help all students, including athletes.

"Students who want and need financial aid must keep the appointments they make, they must follow through on what they start, and above all, they must be persistent. Don't be shy about coming back time and again to check that your file is in order and to see what's available. We won't get tired of seeing you."

—Kathy Blattner, Financial Aid officer,
California State University, Sacramento

SPECIAL ADVISING PROGRAMS FOR ATHLETES

A growing number of colleges have one or more people whose job it is to work especially with athletes. These specialists provide advice and counsel about any number of concerns in addition to monitoring each athlete's eligibility for competition. About half of the universities in Division I of the NCAA employ at least one advisor or counselor especially for athletes. In Divisions II and III of the NCAA, about one college in nine has a special advisor for athletes. If your school has a special advisor or counselor for athletes, he or she will focus on helping you progress with normal speed toward a degree, select or change majors, find a career direction, and deal with other matters of concern in the life of a college student.

Your college may even have an extensive support program for athletes that gives them a special orientation before their first semester, administers placement or diagnostic tests, operates a tutoring program and/or study tables for athletes, and provides what is normally thought of as academic advising—identifying courses, explaining graduation requirements, helping with choice of the major, and so on. This support program for athletes may also conduct stress counseling, run study skills workshops, bring people onto campus to describe various careers, and even serve as a link to professors on campus. About 200 universities and colleges across the nation currently offer a special support program for athletes, and the number is growing.

In spite of this trend, many colleges don't have enough money to hire a special counselor for athletes, much less an entire support program. Or, they may see their athletes as simply not so different from other students that they need a special advisor. But, other things being equal, consider it a plus if a school has a special advising program for athletes.

UNOFFICIAL ADVISORS

Your Coach

Picture the following scene: The catalog states that Course A is a requirement for graduation. Unfortunately, it conflicts with your team's practice time (a common problem among athletes). You talk with a teammate about the problem, and he or she says the word going around is that you don't really have to take that course in order to graduate. You check with your coach, who says the same thing and adds that a number of students have gotten by without it. You take the coach's advice and don't take the course.

Sometime later, you are about ready to graduate and go through the process (by filing the proper form) of getting your college record officially evaluated. Now, let's really set the scene and say that your family is coming to the graduation ceremony and you even have a job waiting for you once you have the diploma in hand.

In taking the final official look at your academic record, however, the university administration finds that you haven't taken a course that is required for graduation. It happens to be the one that conflicted with the team practice schedule some time ago. You tell the school official that the coach said you didn't have to take it and that a lot of people have graduated without it. The university administrator is likely to say that the advice given you was not only unofficial, but bad. You will probably be stuck with having to take that course before graduating. It may be not only frustrating, but embarrassing to have to change your plans; it may even cost you a job.

The scene just described is one of many potential disasters that can occur when students take hearsay for truth. Even though coaches are hired and paid by the college, their advice on academic matters is unofficial and may serve their own needs more than yours. Many coaches care very much in a personal sense about the welfare of their athletes. At the same time, however, many coaches *primarily* care that their athletes not only stay eligible, but have time and energy free for their sport. When your academic growth and the team's welfare are not in conflict, the advice coming from the coach may be in your best interests. But if there is conflict between athletic and academic interests, you very likely may be hurt in the long run if you follow the coach's advice, even though it may support what you yourself consider most desirable at the time (such as cutting a class to attend special practice sessions).

Because this conflict of interests is a common problem, many schools prohibit coaches from advising athletes on academic matters. If such a rule doesn't exist at your college, you may have trouble knowing if the advice the coach is giving you is in your best interests or will mainly serve the team's interests. Suffice it to say that there are better sources for advice on academic, career, and other matters than your team coach.

The Grapevine

Advice received through the student grapevine may offer some good leads, and often does, but don't make decisions based solely on this kind of information. The grapevine carries much information about good courses and bad courses. It can tell you which professors are better than others (although don't confuse "easier" or "more enter-taining" with "better" in the sense of more knowledgeable and articu-late). The grapevine can help you locate a faculty member who has good contacts in your career area. The grapevine also often carries in-formation about summer jobs or may lead you to a source of financial aid you hadn't known about. The grapevine may even remind you of approaching deadlines and other important information that slipped your mind. The grapevine can provide students with much good and useful information. But you can't bank on it for *reliable* information about requirements, rules, and regulations. You might as well rely on rolling dice for information about important academic and career de-cisions as rely on the grapevine.

SPECIAL ORGANIZATIONS THAT HELP ATHLETES

Two organizations have been formed recently specifically to help student-athletes achieve academic progress. These organizations are geared especially for athletes who feel trapped at a school where the coaches' interests are aimed mainly at keeping their athletes eligible for sports, or where the school's support system has not been helpful. The first of these organizations is the Center for Athletes' Rights and Education. CARE is based in the New York City area but has repre-sentatives in several colleges around the country. CARE's two principal aims are to help college athletes get fair return for their labor and effort and to provide information to high school and college athletes on "the ways that sport can best help them get a college degree." Among the sponsors of CARE are the U.S. Department of Education and the NFL Players Association. Contact CARE at:

Center for Athletes' Rights and Education
391 East 149th Street, Suite 319
Bronx, NY 10455
(212) 665-0602

The second organization, called Athletes for a Better Education, focuses its assistance on basketball players. AFBE is sponsored by the United States Department of Labor and has centers in New York City, Chicago, and Los Angeles. AFBE sponsors free 10-day camps for basketball players that focus on improving their academic skills and attitude. The need for this organization and its work became clear when research by the NBA Players Association showed that four out of every five NBA players had failed to graduate from college, even though most had completed their four years of eligibility. Besides helping students with their college skills and attitude, AFBE workshops provide general counseling and advice on how to get through college successfully. For more information, contact AFBE at:

Athletes for a Better Education Foundation
531 South Plymouth Court, Suite 603
Chicago, IL 60605
(312) 939-6000

PROFILE OF AN ATHLETE

Phil Gayle

Phil Gayle grew up playing basketball in Bayonne, New Jersey. He attracted the attention of the coach at Jersey City State, who got Phil into college through the Educational Opportunity Program (EOP) and found some non-athletic financial aid for him. Phil's EOP counselor enrolled him in basic English and mathematics courses, but after that, according to Phil, "Counseling fell into my own hands. I really had no counseling my freshman year. I took courses here and there and did pretty well, making about a 2.9 GPA but with no direction." But Phil wasn't happy at Jersey City State, so he dropped out.

"I thought I could do better for myself, so I went out to a junior college in California." At junior college, Phil generally took what his coach suggested, usually courses that the coach and the athletic director taught (first aid, sports officiating, etc.).

"I felt that I eventually wanted to go on to a four-year school, but nobody told me how or what to take. "I wanted to go to the University of Hawaii at Hilo, but my JC coach never made the contacts he said he was going to make for me. The coach at Eastern Montana was interested and got me a partial scholarship, but I didn't know I wouldn't be eligible to play because I never graduated from my junior college. Then, somehow my old coach got me an A.A. degree. This kept me eligible, but didn't do much to help me learn to work toward a goal.

"I still didn't know I needed certain classes in different areas to get a B.A. I thought I could just take what I wanted. The coaches seemed happy enough to pick my classes for me anyway."

But after attending three schools over a six-year period, Phil was still two years of course work away from graduation. When his eligibility for basketball expired, so did his scholarship, and Phil left Eastern Montana. Phil returned to California, where he made his living for awhile pushing a mop in a hospital.

"I knew I wanted more from my life than that. I felt I could be a pretty good basketball coach, but knew I couldn't get a job coaching a school team without a degree. I was never dumb; I just didn't have good direction, either from myself or from those who were supposedly taking care of me."

Nine years after graduating from high school, Phil Gayle is about to earn his bachelor's degree in education. What would he have done differently? "From day one, I would seek counseling. I would play basketball again, but I would also keep an eye on my future. I would stress academics more, take courses that would help me progress, not just stay eligible for sports. And I would find someone to advise me right about what all I have to do to earn my degree."

114

8

BECOMING AND
STAYING ELIGIBLE
FOR SPORTS

In This Chapter...

Why Do We Have Eligibility Rules?

Are Eligibility Rules Your Friend or Foe?

NCAA Eligibility Rules

NAIA Eligibility Rules

Penalties for Violating Association Rules

Academic Eligibility Compared to Academic Progress

Before a student can compete in intercollegiate athletics, he or she must be *eligible* to compete. Eligibility for athletics is awarded when you are accepted to a college as a student-athlete in good standing and is maintained as long as you make progress toward a degree and follow the rules of amateur athletic status.

All high school, junior college, and senior college athletes have to deal with matters of eligibility. It is one of the prices you pay for being an athlete in school. Few athletes understand all there is to know about the rules of eligibility; most know only what the coach has chosen to explain to them. Some athletes learn the rules only after they've broken one or two, after it's too late to avoid paying a penalty.

In this chapter, we will present the rules of athletic eligibility that determine which students are allowed to play for college sports teams. The rules focus on two areas: amateur status and academic progress. It's easier to understand and remember rules if we know where they come from and why we have them. So, before listing the rules, we'll take a short side trip to help you better understand why they exist.

115

The NCAA slapped North Carolina State with a one-year probation for football recruiting violations during the 1981–82 school year. North Carolina State was guilty of five violations involving a prospective football player who enrolled at the university, said William L. Matthews, acting chairman of the NCAA Committee on Infractions.

The player, who was not named by the NCAA, will be ineligible to represent the university in a postseason game during the period, although the university may appeal to the NCAA Eligibility Committee for restoration of eligibility.

The violations included providing improper transportation, lodging and meals, providing too many expense-paid visits to the school, and making improper contacts with the athlete.

[*Sacramento Union*, March 21, 1983.]

WHY DO WE HAVE ELIGIBILITY RULES?

Rules of eligibility for playing college athletics have existed almost since the beginning of college sports. The first purpose of eligibility rules was—and continues to be—to ensure that athletes be students and keep on the track toward graduation. The second purpose of eligibility rules is to ensure that student-athletes retain their amateur status, no matter how good they may be or how valuable they are to the college.

These two guiding principles that lie behind eligibility rules for playing college sports complement and support each other. If an athlete is attracted to a college primarily to play a sport, the possibility exists that he or she might have little interest in getting an education. And if athletes could be directly paid to play for colleges, schools might be interested in these athletes only as employees hired to produce athletic victories. College athletes whose main interest is making money from playing their sport interfere with the school's educational purpose and take space in classes that could be filled by students who are interested in getting an education. College athletics exists for students, not for hired hands. If college athletes remain nonprofessional, they are more likely to truly be students. Maintaining what has been called the amateur ideal for student-athletes also saves the school a lot of money. If college athletes were allowed to be paid more than a basic scholarship and living expenses, then colleges would have as hard a time holding salaries in line as professional team owners do.

One problem with this amateur ideal in college sports is that, through the years, the definition of the term *amateur* has changed. In the early era of college sports (roughly the first 40 years, or until the 1920s) no payment to athletes of any kind was legal, not even what we now

116

call athletic scholarships. Amateur athletes, it was believed, should re-. ceive nothing for their skills but the pleasure and privilege of playing for their school. Even organized recruitment of athletes was considered wrong.

But having good teams has always meant a lot to colleges, in both monetary terms and prestige, so athletes were recruited and received scholarships anyway. Although the NCAA had rules against athletes being recruited and paid in any form (whether in free tuition, meals, lodging, cars, clothes, or spending money), the rules had no teeth: The penalties for violating rules were no more severe than a hand slap. The NCAA at that time was a watchdog with a bark but no bite.

Because the practice of recruiting and awarding free tuition, room, and board to college athletes became so common, the officials who oversaw collegiate sports eventually changed their definition of an amateur athlete. For the last 50 or so years, an amateur athlete has been defined as someone who receives *no more than* basic college expenses in exchange for his or her athletic skills. Since other students with special abilities—such as those gifted in particular academic disciplines or the arts—frequently had their way paid through school in the form of a grant or scholarship, it was reasoned that there was little justification for withholding the same sorts of benefits from athletes.

However, there is a difference between top athletes and highly skilled students in other areas. A college cannot earn money or gain popular support based on the talents of its top students and performing artists to the extent that it can from top athletes. As a result, many colleges began to offer athletic prospects a little extra in the way of benefits (sometimes a lot extra) to play for them. The new rules tried to guard against student-athletes being bought, but they fell short of requiring that college athletes really fulfill their role as students—by taking a full range of classes, following a major, maintaining adequate grades, and progressing toward a degree. For many years, college sports were populated by "tramp athletes," professionals who peddled their services to whatever school would pay them the most, sometimes changing names after they had flunked out or in order to play for more than the legal limit of four years. These tramp athletes found many colleges willing to buy their services.

Thus, in spite of the somewhat more relaxed definition of amateur athlete that emerged in the 1930s, it soon became clear that additional eligibility rules were needed, both to guard amateur standing and to monitor the academic progress of athletes. But the imposition of more rules often results in more ingenious ways to get around the rules. As people found loopholes and ways around the rules, even more rules were added, always with the twin purposes of trying to keep college

117

athletes as true students and honest amateurs. It seemed to be a losing battle because the NCAA, whose members included the largest, most competitive colleges, still had no power to punish with meaningful penalties those who broke the rules.

In 1952, after nearly half a century of trying to control college athletics, the NCAA gained the power to penalize schools by banning rule-breakers from bowl games, tournaments, and coverage on television. Avoiding these penalties was important; penalties cost the athletic programs money and prevented them from receiving the national exposure they need to recruit top athletes. The new penalties helped to stop some cheating, but as college sports boomed in the decades that followed, the stakes have continued to increase in college athletics. Star athletes are still being paid more than the rules allow, a practice which, as always, attracts many who aren't particularly serious about being a student and getting an education. To keep star athletes academically eligible for sports, coaches continue to find new ways to sneak them into school and through easy courses.

Not everyone involved in college athletics cheats. Many coaches, school administrators, and alumni remain competitive within the rules. But since the prizes for winning are so great and losing contests can result in lost jobs, there is constant pressure on coaches to cheat as they suspect their opponents are doing. So the rules designed to control amateur competition and the academic progress of college athletes get tougher and more involved. The result is that you and other student-athletes must contend with a long list of detailed rules governing what makes a student eligible to play college sports.

ARE ELIGIBILITY RULES YOUR
FRIEND OR FOE?

The rules governing academic eligibility may seem like obstacles, but they exist for the student-athlete's benefit. They are intended to help ensure that you get an education while you play college sports. Without these eligibility rules, many athletes who don't yet realize the value of a good education would be in college solely to play sports. Worse, without these rules, some coaches would pressure their athletes to forget schoolwork and devote all their time and effort to their sport. Academic eligibility rules are intended to protect athletes from themselves and from others who would exploit them.

Men's basketball coaches Digger Phelps of Notre Dame, John Thompson of Georgetown University, and Bobby Knight of Indiana University, and Penn State football coach Joe Paterno, are examples of big-time coaches who are very concerned about the academic progress of their athletes. They are committed to providing their athletes with a good education. Academic eligibility rules don't exist to control these coaches and others who have good intentions toward their student-athletes. Rather, eligibility rules are made for those coaches who would and do cheat their athletes of an education by demanding too much commitment of time and energy to the team and not enough to school.

Sometimes, the fault is less with the coach than with the student, who would prefer playing to studying. In such cases, the academic eligibility rules protect athletes from themselves. Many athletes keep up with schoolwork simply because eligibility rules force them to.

The remainder of this chapter lists the rules of eligibility for college athletes. Before reading these rules, be aware of three important points: (1) if you've fallen below the minimum academic guidelines and become ineligible, you can always work back into good academic standing; (2) if you've broken the rules of amateur status, on the other hand, you may be *permanently* ineligible for college athletics; (3) if you violate one or more of these eligibility rules—whether on purpose or not—you may cause your team to forfeit some contests or lose the chance for postseason competition or televised coverage and forfeit your own eligibility as well.

Each year before you are allowed to compete, you must sign a statement saying essentially that you have read the rules of eligibility and had a chance to ask questions about them. An athlete's official reading of the rules and signing of a statement, however, is usually done in a large group—either with other members of the team or with all athletes competing during that term. In this environment, it may be difficult for you to read and understand the rules, much less to ask questions about those you don't understand. It's better for you to see these rules in advance so that you can think about them and, if need be, ask a coach, advisor, or athletic director privately about something you are unsure of.

NCAA ELIGIBILITY RULES

Below are the rules governing eligibility as they appear in the NCAA Rules and Regulations Information Sheet (1983–84 version).* (The eligibility rules that directly address the limits and kind of financial

---

*Rules reprinted by permission of the National Collegiate Athletic Association. Material in the information sheet is subject to annual revision by the membership of the association.

aid or gifts a student-athlete may receive are included in Chapter 4. If you have any doubt whether some aid or gift you are being offered would make you ineligible to compete, *by all means* turn to that chapter and read those regulations.) To assist you in your reading, we have added explanations in brackets [...] where we feel the rules might be unclear.

A student-athlete SHALL NOT be eligible in a sport if the student has:

1. Ever taken pay, or accepted the promise of pay, in any form, for participation in that sport.

2. Ever entered into an agreement of any kind to compete in professional athletics in that sport, or to negotiate a professional contract in that sport.

3. Ever directly or indirectly used athletic skill for pay in any form in that sport.

4. Ever signed a contract or commitment of any kind, regardless of its legal enforceability or the consideration (if any) received, to play professional athletics in that sport.

5. Ever received, directly or indirectly, any salary, reimbursement of expenses (except as permitted on one 48-hour visit [to the college] prior to enrollment) or any other form of financial assistance from a professional organization in that sport based upon athletic skill or participation.

6. Subsequent to regular enrollment in a collegiate institution, tried out in that sport with a professional sports organization during any part of the institution's regular academic year.

7. Ever agreed to be or been represented by an individual, agency or organization in the marketing of the student's athletic ability or reputation in a sport or to assist the student for compensation in being placed in a collegiate institution as a recipient of athletically related financial aid.

8. Ever participated in that sport on a team: (a) which was a member of a recognized professional sports organization; (b) which was directly supported or sponsored by a professional team or sports organization; (c) which was a member of a playing league that was directly supported or sponsored by a professional team or sports organization; or (d) on which there was an athlete receiving, directly or indirectly, payment of any kind from a professional team or sports organization for

the athlete's participation. [In other words, you may compete *against* professionals, but not on the same team *with* them.]

9. Ever received compensation, in any form, for a complimentary ticket to an athletic contest involving the student's institution; received money from the institution for or in lieu of such tickets, or purchased tickets from the institution to an athletic event when the tickets were not equally available for purchase by the student body in general.

10. Subsequent to enrollment in a collegiate institution, accepted remuneration for or permitted the use of his or her name or picture to directly advertise, recommend or promote the sale or use of a commercial product or service of any kind, or received remuneration for endorsing a commercial product or service through use of such product or service. [Doing this makes you ineligible in any and all sports, not just the one in which you are known and marketable.]

11. Subsequent to enrollment in a collegiate institution, ever received compensation for employment during which work was not actually performed or [received] compensation at a rate not commensurate with the going rate for the services performed. [You aren't allowed to be paid more than other students receive for doing the same work.]

12. Subsequent to enrollment in a collegiate institution, received compensation in any form from or through the arrangement of the institution for teaching or coaching sports skills or techniques in that sport.

13. Subsequent to enrollment in a collegiate institution, received compensation for officiating games or contests involving teams which are members of or affiliated with a recognized professional sports organization.

14. Ever realized expenses (excluding permissible expenses for athletic competition) from the institution or any representative of its athletic interests to travel for any personal purpose.

15. Subsequent to enrollment in a collegiate institution, received or realized from the institution or any representative of its athletic interests any special arrangements or extra benefits for the student or the student's relatives or friends.

16. Ever received awards or similar mementos prohibited or in excess of those permitted by NCAA Constitution [Bylaw] #3-1-(i) and its subparagraphs. [The list of limits on awards, which

covers two pages in the NCAA Manual, is too lengthy to be provided here. If you have any question about whether or not an award is prohibited, look in section #3-1-(i) of the NCAA Manual. Your coach or the athletic department will have a copy.]

17. Participated in intercollegiate athletics while not in good academic standing or while not maintaining satisfactory progress toward a degree as determined by the regulations of the institution and, for student-athletes at Division I or II institutions, the requirements of Bylaw 5-1-(j)-(6). [This rule is too long to repeat fully here. It refers to the "12/24 Rule," which states, in essence, that those who have been in college for a year may not compete in sports if they are not currently taking 12 units applicable toward graduation and if they have not passed 24 units applicable toward graduation during the previous year.]

18. Practiced in intercollegiate athletics while not enrolled in a minimum full-time program of studies as determined by the regulations of the institution.

19. Ever received financial assistance related to attendance at the student's institution, either for educational expenses or other reasons, which was not administered by the institution's regular financial aid authority or which was not provided by someone upon whom the student was naturally or legally dependent. [Taking gifts or cash from appreciative boosters, coaches, or anyone else, except the people who support you—parents, guardian, etc.—may put an end to your college athletic career. Any scholarship, grant, or loan *must* come to you through the school's Financial Aid Office.]

20. Ever exhibited dishonesty in evading or violating NCAA regulations; knowingly furnished false or misleading information concerning involvement in or knowledge of a violation of an NCAA regulation; refused to furnish information relevant to investigation of a possible violation when requested to do so by the NCAA or the individual's institution; or knowingly been involved in arrangements for fraudulent academic credit or false transcripts.

21. Ever participated following completion of high school eligibility (and, in the case of a high school game, before enrollment in college) in a high school or college all-star game in football or basketball which was not certified in accordance with NCAA legislation or participated in more than two high school all-star

football or two high school all-star basketball games certified in compliance with NCAA legislation. Student-athletes participating on a member institution's women's intercollegiate basketball team shall be exempt from these regulations until August 1, 1985.

22. Subsequent to enrollment in a member institution, ever participated in an extra event in track and field or gymnastics which was not certified by the NCAA Extra Events Committee.

23. Subsequent to being a candidate for an NCAA member institution's intercollegiate basketball team, participated in an organized basketball competition, as defined by NCAA Official Interpretation 10, other than while representing the student's institution or while participating in outside competition or a summer basketball league approved by the NCAA.

24. Subsequent to enrollment in an NCAA member institution and during the student's intercollegiate season in a year in which the student was a member of the intercollegiate squad or team in that sport, competed as a member of any outside team in any noncollegiate, amateur competition in a sport, other than the official Olympic games and the final official tryouts therefor, or competition approved by the NCAA.

25. Participated in intercollegiate athletics at any time after five calendar years have elapsed from the date of the student-athlete's initial registration and attendance at a collegiate institution except as permitted by the provisions of NCAA Bylaw 4-1-(a) for Division I student-athletes or after the first 10 semesters or 15 quarters of full-time enrollment in a collegiate institution for Division II and III student-athletes.

[The following new NCAA regulation, which relates to rule 10 above, is applicable beginning in the 1984-85 school year:

Your name or picture may appear in books, other publications, or films without jeopardizing your amateur standing, but only if all of the following conditions are met:

• Your appearance in such publications or films is for the purpose of demonstrating athletic skill, analysis of a sports event, or instruction in sports.
• There is no indication that you expressly or implicitly endorse a commercial product or service.
• You are not paid.
• You have signed a release statement detailing the conditions under which your name or image may be used, and you have filed a copy of that statement with your school.]

[The following rules concern junior college transfer students. They are drawn from the NCAA Guide for the College-Bound Student-Athlete (1983–84 edition).]

123

If you are moving from junior college to an NCAA college:

1. In order to be eligible for practice, participation in regular-season competition, and athletically related financial aid during the first academic year in residence at a Division I NCAA member institution, a junior college transfer student who graduated from high school with a minimum 2.00 grade-point average (on a 4.00 scale) for all work taken through the accumulative 6, 7, or 8 semesters must satisfy the transfer and eligibility requirements of the institution as well as its athletic conference. For such a student at a Division I NCAA member institution or any junior college transfer student (regardless of the student's high school academic record) at a Division II or III NCAA member institution to be immediately eligible for an NCAA championship event or postseason football game, the student must be a junior college graduate or present a minimum of 24 semester or 36 quarter hours of transferable degree credit from a junior college with an accumulative minimum grade-point average of 2.00 and have spent it at least two semesters or three quarters in residence at the junior college, excluding summer school.

2. In order to be eligible for practice, participation in regular-season competition, participation in an NCAA championship event or a postseason football game, and athletically related aid during the first year in residence at a Division I NCAA member institution, a junior college transfer student who failed to graduate from high school with a minimum 2.00 grade-point average (on a 4.00 scale) for all work taken through the accumulative 6, 7, or 8 semesters must graduate from a junior college.

3. A student who transfers to an NCAA member institution from a junior college after transferring from any four-year college must complete one calendar year of residence at the NCAA member institution in order to be eligible for NCAA championships or postseason football games, unless the student has completed a minimum of 24 semester or 36 quarter hours at the junior college following the student's transfer from the four-year college and also has graduated from the junior college, and one calendar year has elapsed since his or her transfer from the four-year college. Such a student transferring to a Division III member institution need not graduate from the junior college but must meet the other requirements set forth in this paragraph.

4. When a student has been in residence at two or more junior colleges, the terms of residence at all junior colleges may be combined in order to satisfy the residence requirements described in paragraphs 1, 2, and 3 of this section. All grades earned by the student in courses that would be transferable to the NCAA member institution must be included in determining whether the student has earned the required average.

5. A transfer student from a junior college is not subject to the residence requirement for NCAA championships or postseason football games if the NCAA Eligibility Committee concludes that the student changed institutions in order to continue participation in a sport because the student's junior college dropped the sport from its intercollegiate program or never sponsored the sport on the intercollegiate level while the student was in attendance at the institution, provided the student never attended any other collegiate institution that offered intercollegiate competition in that particular sport and provided the student earned at least a minimum 2.00 grade-point average at the junior college.

6. A transfer student from a junior college to a Division III member institution is not subject to the residence requirement for NCAA championships in a particular sport if the student has not competed in that sport at the previous institution or has not competed in that sport for a period of one year immediately prior to the date on which the student begins participation (practice or competition) in that sport at the certifying institution and the student has entered the certifying institution prior to the start of the regular-season competition in that sport and provided the student earned at least a minimum 2.00 grade-point average at the junior college.

NOTE: Divisions II and III member institutions do not apply Bylaw 5-6-(b) [the "2.00 Rule"] to the eligibility of either freshmen or junior college transfer students for practice, regular-season participation or athletically related financial aid and therefore such eligibility is determined on the basis of institutional and conference regulations. In order to be eligible for practice, participation in regular-season competition and athletically related financial aid, an entering freshman as well as a junior college transfer student must also satisfy the transfer and eligibility rules of the member institution in which the individual enrolls and the athletic conference in which the institution holds membership as well as possibly numerous other NCAA individual eligibility rules. Inasmuch as NCAA eligibility rules are oftentimes complex as they might apply to certain students, the NCAA national office should be contacted for proper interpretations in such cases. Inquiries should be addressed to the NCAA enforcement and legislative services department. [Full address and phone number appear on p. 127 of this book.]

For Division I only: For students enrolling in Division I institutions only, any participation by a student as an individual or as a representative of any team in organized competition in a sport during each 12-

month period after the student's 20th birthday and prior to matriculation at a member institution shall count as one year of varsity competition in that sport.

[EXPLANATION: This rule applies to athletes who participate in an organized sport somewhere other than an NCAA school (e.g., an NAIA school or junior college, an armed forces team, a foreign team, an AAU team, etc.). Consider one year of eligibility to be "used up" for each 12-month period following your 20th birthday during which you were involved in *any* organized sports competition.]

The following rules govern academic eligibility for intercollegiate sports for continuing students, i.e., not freshman or transfer students. These rules apply to Division I and II schools only.

i. Eligibility for financial aid and practice during each academic year after the student-athlete's initial year in residence or after the student-athlete has utilized one season of eligibility in a sport shall be based upon the rules of the institution and the conference of which the institution is a member. [This means that if your school or conference has academic progress rules for athletes that are tougher than the ones listed here, you have to follow the tougher rules.]

ii. Eligibility for regular-season competition subsequent to the student-athlete's first academic year in residence or after the student-athlete has utilized one season of eligibility in a sport shall be based upon: (1) satisfactory completion prior to each term in which a season of competition begins of an accumulative total of semester or quarter hours of academic credit acceptable toward a baccalaureate degree in a designated program of studies at the institution which is equivalent to the completion of an average of at least 12 semester or quarter hours during each of the previous academic terms in academic years in which the student-athlete has been enrolled in a term or terms, or (2) satisfactory completion of 24 semester or 36 quarter hours of acceptable degree credit since the beginning of the student-athlete's last season of completion.

[EXPLANATION: For all terms in school since you last competed on a college team, you must have passed an average of at least 12 semester or quarter credits or completed at least 24 semester credits or 36 quarter credits.]

iii. The calculation of credit hours under the provisions of subparagraph (ii) shall be based upon hours earned or accepted for degree credit in a specific baccalaureate degree program for the student-athlete at the certifying institution. Hours earned in the period following the regular academic year at the institution (e.g., hours earned in summer school) may be utilized to satisfy

126

academic credit requirements of this regulation. [Any course won't necessarily apply to your minimum for academic eligibility; the course *must* apply to your degree in some way. (For example, remedial or study skills courses do *not* count.) Before a summer session course can apply to your academic eligibility, it must be approved by an officer of the college. Correspondence, extension, and credit-by-examination courses taken at an institution other than the one in which you are enrolled as a full-time student may not be counted toward this minimum for athletic eligibility.]

iv. A graduate student who is otherwise eligible for regular-season competition shall be exempt from the provisions of this regulation.

The rules governing eligibility to play college sports are indeed complicated. It would be so much simpler to have only two basic rules, one to cover each of the primary concerns for college athletes: that they must be (1) amateurs and (2) progressing toward a degree. Unfortunately, numerous other rules that have been instituted are necessary because the two basic rules have been violated through the years in the attempt by one party to gain a competitive edge over opponents. These opponents, of course, have too often also been looking for their own competitive edge, which serves to escalate the rules violations. New rules are developed to stem the constant flow of new ways found to violate the existing rules—to the point that you, the student-athlete, may feel as if you are buried beneath them.

If you do not understand the academic eligibility rules, or if you are not sure whether one or more rules apply to you, contact the NCAA at the following address:

NCAA Enforcement & Legislative Services Department
P.O. Box 1906
Mission, KS 66201
(913) 384-3220

NAIA ELIGIBILITY RULES

The National Association for Intercollegiate Athletics (NAIA) is an association that oversees athletics programs at over 500 colleges across the country that are not members of the NCAA. If you are going to an NAIA school, you will be expected to adhere to the following rules

which appear in the NAIA Guide for the College Bound Student.*
(Comments appearing within brackets [...] have been added by us
for further explanation.)

To be eligible for any NAIA intercollegiate competition:

1. You must be making normal progress toward a recognized degree and maintain the grade points required to remain in good
   standing, as set forth by the official catalog of the college you
   are attending.

2. You must be enrolled in a minimum of 12 credit hours (or
   equivalent) at the time of participation, or if the participation
   takes place between terms, you must have been enrolled in the
   term immediately preceding the date of participation. You
   become ineligible immediately upon dropping below 12 hours
   of enrollment.

3. You must pass 24 credit hours [or equivalent] between the
   term of competition and the earlier of the two immediate previous terms of attendance.

4. A second term freshman must pass 12 credit hours [or equiva-
   lent] between the beginning of the first term of attendance and
   the start of the second term of attendance.

5. Repeat courses previously passed in any term cannot count
   toward the 24 credit hour rule.

6. You must be eligible in your own conference. [Your conference
   may have tougher eligibility rules than the NAIA.]

7. If you are a transfer student from a four-year school, you must
   have eligibility remaining at the school you are transferring
   from to be eligible for further intercollegiate competition.

8. If you are a transfer student who has ever attended a four-
   year school, you must sit out 16 calendar weeks of residency
   (112 calendar days) not including summer school, before becoming eligible for intercollegiate competition in any sport
   which your previous four-year school sponsored during your
   attendance.

9. You must be within your first 10 semesters (or 12 trimesters
   or 15 quarters) of attendance as a regularly enrolled student.

---

*Material from the NAIA Guide for the College Bound Student and from the NAIA
Handbook reprinted by permission of the National Association of Intercollegiate Athletics.

(A term of attendance is considered to be any semester, tri-mester, or quarter in which you initially enroll for nine or more college credit hours and attend one or more classes. Summer sessions are not included, but night school, extension or cor-respondence classes are applicable to this ruling.)

10. You may not participate for more than four seasons in any one sport. A "season of competition" means participation in one or more intercollegiate contests, whether as a freshman, junior varsity, or varsity participant, or in any other athletic competi-tion in which the college is represented.

11. You shall no longer be eligible for intercollegiate athletics upon completing all requirements for graduation from a four-year college.

12. If you participate for two different colleges in the same sport, in the same season (example—basketball or Fall golf at a junior college and then transfer to an NAIA school and participate in basketball or Spring golf), you shall be charged with a second season of competition in that sport.

13. You must be an amateur, as defined by the NAIA, in the sport(s) in which you participate. [You may be a professional in one sport and still be eligible to compete on an NAIA team in another sport, so long as all the other eligibility rules are met. The exact NAIA definition of an amateur is not listed in their Guide for the College Bound Student but is described in the guidelines below, drawn from the NAIA Handbook, eighth edition (Article VII, Section B).]

The following acts will cause a student-athlete to lose amateur stand-ing for participation in intercollegiate competition recognized by NAIA in the sport where any or all of said acts occur. You may not:

1. Receive money or other forms of remuneration beyond actual expenses for participating in any athletic contest or program.

2. Sign a contract with any professional team in any sport, or re-ceive money, other than actual expenses, or other form of re-muneration.

3. Participate in any athletic contest as a member of a professional team.

4. Coach an organized team or individual for pay beyond actual expenses.

5. Exploit for remuneration athletic ability or fame through exhibition, radio or television appearance, or use athletic fame to write for news media for pay beyond actual expense.

6. Receive remuneration for the use of name or picture to promote any commercial product or enterprise.

7. Enter into an agreement of any kind to compete in professional athletics, either with a professional sports organization or with any individual or group of individuals authorized to represent the athlete with a professional sports organization.

IMPORTANT NOTE: These rules are subject to revision by NAIA. Your Athletic Director or Faculty Athletic Representative should have the complete, updated set of rules. Or, you can contact NAIA as follows:

NAIA
1221 Baltimore
Kansas City, MO 64105
(816) 842-5050

PENALTIES FOR VIOLATING ASSOCIATION RULES

Athletes attending NCAA or NAIA member schools are responsible for knowing and abiding by the rules and regulations of their association. Any violations by you may result in your being ineligible for competition. Of course, you can't control the behavior of coaches, boosters, and others. But what you can do is to know the rules and control your own behavior (i.e., abide by the rules). If you don't follow the eligibility rules, you very well might:

1. Make yourself ineligible, resulting in your immediate withdrawal from intercollegiate competition in your sport for the duration of the season.

2. Find yourself charged with an extra season of competition and a term of attendance for participating. (This will reduce the total number of years you will be allowed to compete.)

3. Cause an investigation by your association's national eligibility committee that could charge against you a second season of participation for playing while ineligible.

4. Cause the disallowance of any honors or consideration of such honors given by your association.

5. Cause your institution to forfeit all contests in which you participated.

The NCAA and NAIA investigate each case of suspected eligibility violations individually, so you cannot tell beforehand what infractions will result in which particular penalties. Your best bet, of course, is not to break any rules and not to cast your lot with coaches and schools that have been in trouble with their association over rules violations.

As a result of recent college sports scandals and increased public alarm over them, the NCAA has recently beefed up its investigation section and is actively looking for rules violations. We don't mean to scare you . . . but the NCAA and NAIA do!

You can avoid bringing these dire circumstances upon yourself by (a) refusing any temptations to illegal behavior and (b) working hard enough in your academics not only to remain within the eligibility guidelines, but to leave yourself a wide margin. The result of doing this, of course, is something called timely progress toward graduation.

ACADEMIC ELIGIBILITY COMPARED TO ACADEMIC PROGRESS

Athletic eligibility rules as laid out by the NCAA, the NAIA, and most schools and conferences do not assure that you will graduate in four years, although four years is the maximum number you can play. Eligibility rules set only the *minimum* number of units you can take and still be eligible to compete. After four years of competing in sports, you may still be a year or more away from graduation if you took only the minimum number of units, as some coaches suggest. So, the minimum academic progress that the NCAA and NAIA talk about in their rules is slow progress that will leave you lagging behind classmates.

Often during the past few years, these national governing bodies have considered upgrading the minimum eligibility requirements to make sure that only truly qualified students are allowed to compete and that they maintain their timely progress toward graduation. Each time, however, rules that would toughen academic eligibility have been defeated, sometimes narrowly. The NCAA and NAIA, however, remain concerned about the academic qualifications and timely progress of their student-athletes toward degrees, and so they may pass tougher rules in the future. Be sure to find out about any changes in current rules as they occur, in order to avoid losing your eligibility for sports.

9

MEETING ACADEMIC

REQUIREMENTS

In This Chapter . . .

The Academic Pie

Finding Out About Academic Requirements

A Checklist for Tracking Your Academic Requirements

Academic Standing: From Dean's List to Disqualification

THE ACADEMIC PIE

Your academic requirements—the number of credits you must earn and the courses you must take in order to graduate—may be thought of as ingredients in a pie that you have at least four years to consume. The pie is divided into three big slices, and all of the courses you take fit into one or another of those slices. You don't have to finish one slice before beginning another. In fact, the pie will probably be more enjoyable if you sample from each slice as you go along. The pie, with its slices labelled, looks like this:

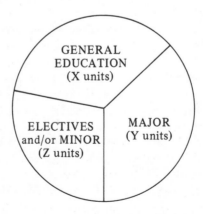

$X + Y + Z$ = THE NUMBER OF UNITS NEEDED TO GRADUATE

General Education

General Education, commonly called GE but also known as Distribution Requirements on some campuses, refers to a group of courses that all students must take, regardless of their majors. At some colleges, all students are required to take exactly the same courses; at other schools students may choose courses from common areas. You will begin taking these GE courses your first term in college, whether you go to a junior college or a four-year school.

The GE slice of the pie is intended to provide you with a well-rounded undergraduate education. It usually includes basic courses in English, history and government, natural sciences and mathematics, social sciences and humanities, possibly a foreign language, and courses designed for lifelong enjoyment, such as art appreciation or physical education. Some colleges may also require you to take courses in computer science as part of GE.

GE is intended to broaden your interests and understanding rather than to address your career goals directly. Students who are particularly career-oriented may resent having to "waste time" in GE courses since they can't see where GE will help them get a job. A well-rounded education *does* have career benefits, although they may not always be immediately apparent.

GE may constitute the largest slice of the academic pie, taking up between one-third and two-thirds of the units required for graduation. The exact pattern and number of units required in GE for graduation varies from one school to another. We will describe each of these GE areas and why they will benefit you.

English and composition requirements. Some athletes feel that their physical skills speak for them. But this is shortsighted and unrealistic. Athletic skills and reputation fade far more quickly than anyone would like or expect. In any field, people who can communicate their ideas well will have an advantage over those who can't.

Communicating well isn't just knowing proper grammar and putting sentences together correctly. Good communication also means knowing how to develop thoughts, how to build an argument, and how to analyze and understand what other people say and write. Whether or not they teach English, professors often reduce students' grades for poor language skills. Take care of your English requirements as soon as possible. You are sure to benefit in your other classes as a result.

Think of your college-level English requirement this way: The more you dread it, the more you probably need it and the better it will be for you in the long run. Rather than seeing the English requirement as a hurdle, consider it an opportunity—maybe your last one—to get some help in developing your ability in the English language.

On the other hand, some students enter college with strong English skills. If your skills are strong enough, you may be exempt from the basic English requirement. One of the more common ways that students gain exemption from the English requirement is to make a high enough grade (4 or 5) on the English Advanced Placement test that is administered by the Educational Testing Service (ETS). The College-Level Examination Program (CLEP) and the American College Testing Program (ACT) exams also may exempt you from English or other core requirements if you earn high enough scores. Even if you are exempt from basic English, we suggest that you take an intermediate or advanced composition course as an elective. Communication is as important as any skill you'll develop in college. It can always stand improvement.

Good citizenship. The history and government courses all students must take are sometimes called the good-citizenship requirements. This suggests that if students know how their society has developed and how it works, they are more likely to support it as good citizens. Whether or not this is the case, all schools recognize that history and government contribute to an understanding of the social system in which we must function and so require a course or two in each. State-supported colleges often insist that students also include a course in state and local government.

Natural science and math. At least one term, and often more, of a natural science is required of all undergraduates. Students can usually take their pick among biology, chemistry, physics, geology, geography, astronomy, and other natural or life sciences. Nonscience majors may be required to take a science course that includes a laboratory component in order to ensure that they have some hands-on experience with the scientific method of investigation and problem solving.

Some schools insist that a formal mathematics subject (e.g., algebra, trigonometry, calculus) be used to fulfill the mathematics requirement. Others consider this requirement to be more in the order of improving your reasoning or computational skills and so allow students to fulfill the math requirement with courses in statistics and computer science. The purpose of this area of GE is to ensure that all students learn skills to help them make decisions through the logical, systematic analyses that these courses teach.

Social science and humanities. Courses in sociology, psychology, anthropology, communication studies, ethnic and women's studies, law, economics, philosophy, and the arts are usually included in this area, as are the disciplines of history and political science. These subjects will help you understand the nature of social and cultural institutions and how people relate to each other as individuals and in small or large groups.

Foreign language. The foreign language requirement is making a comeback after years of disregard. Even beyond the obvious benefits of knowing another language (including increased employment marketability), studying another tongue can help you with your English skills. Many of us paid little attention to grammar when we learned English. But in order to learn another language as an adult, you have to understand its grammar, and in learning grammar you begin to understand your own language better. If you are faced with a foreign language requirement, you may feel like avoiding it for as long as possible (maybe hoping it will go away). We suggest the opposite: take it as early as possible in order to help you with your English skills.

Other GE requirements. This category includes those courses—physical education, dance, drama, art, photography, etc.—designed to enrich the quality of your life through health and cultural activities. Any course credit coming to you from intercollegiate athletics will fall in this category, if it fits into GE at all.

Your Major

Whereas GE is designed to educate broadly in areas you might ordinarily avoid, a major—the second slice of your academic pie—lets you select a particular area of interest and allows you to dig deeply into it. Majors vary widely in the number of units required. Some liberal arts majors (such as psychology, history, or art) may require only about 30 units, while majors in applied or professional areas (such as engineering or nursing) may require more because of prerequisites needed before major courses can be taken. The exact unit requirements vary from school to school.

"Finding yourself" is the best use you could make of your first year or two in college. If you come to college undecided about a major field of study, use your General Education courses and electives (discussed below) to poke around in various subject areas. A course in psychology, one in business, another in computer science, another in history, and one in English would give a student looking around for a major a very nice spread of subject areas from which to choose. During the next term, courses might be taken in social science, art or drama, government, math, and a natural science (geology, biology, etc.).

The simplest and probably the most important piece of advice we can give you on selecting a major is that whatever you choose to major in, you should enjoy it. You should *want* to study it. While taking courses in your major field, you might be thinking about how to apply the knowledge and ideas you are gaining toward your future career, although this isn't necessary. Few college students have an accurate, concrete conception of how their major studies apply to the wide variety of related jobs they might enter. Besides, people tend to change jobs and even career directions several times throughout their working lives.

Most students change majors during college. Is this bad? Does it mean you don't have stick-to-itiveness? Not at all. To change majors simply means your interests have changed, your first choice wasn't carefully considered, or you are finding out more about yourself. Changing majors may set back your timetable for getting your degree, but it is better than continuing in a major that no longer interests you. The NCAA, in its attempt to tighten up eligibility rules governing academic progress of athletes, is considering rules to make sure that enough units apply to the student-athlete's major. But even the NCAA is trying to build into these new rules a formula that won't penalize students who want to change majors.

Electives

The third slice of your academic pie includes the units you will have to take beyond your GE and major courses. This slice is sometimes called your electives, which you may use in a number of different ways. A minor might fit in nicely here, or even a second major, especially if both majors you are considering are "light" (i.e., require relatively few units). Another way to treat this third slice is to use it for those courses that you've always wanted to take but that don't fit into GE or your major. The only requirement for this third slice is that it be used to take enough units to give you at least the minimum number needed to graduate. The examples on page 137 illustrate how to determine the size of this third slice and how all the slices relate to your whole education.

Some majors require a minor, which necessarily will cut into the third slice. For example, a criminal justice major who is specializing in forensic science, might be required to take a chemistry minor. Or, a major in business administration with a specialization in international business might need to minor in a foreign language.

Your major may not actually require you to have an official minor but may still direct you to take several courses in a second area; for

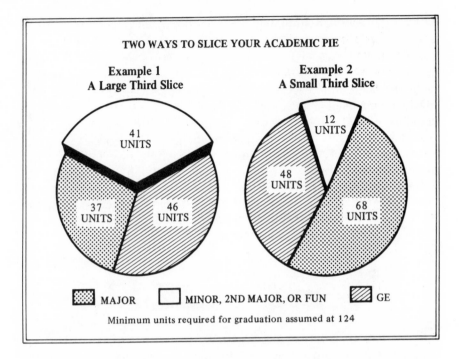

TWO WAYS TO SLICE YOUR ACADEMIC PIE

Example 1
A Large Third Slice

Example 2
A Small Third Slice

41 UNITS

37 UNITS

46 UNITS

12 UNITS

48 UNITS

68 UNITS

▨ MAJOR   ☐ MINOR, 2ND MAJOR, OR FUN   ▨ GE

Minimum units required for graduation assumed at 124

example, computer science majors often must take several courses in mathematics and statistics. In that situation, you might consider taking an additional course or two in this secondary area in order to earn an official minor, which is noted on your transcript. Officially declaring a minor could make you more marketable upon graduation because it attests that you have gained specific knowledge in a second field.

You may dip into many departments to find electives to satisfy your own educational interests or to help in career preparation. For example, if you contemplate a career in business, you may benefit from courses in psychology, political science, math, foreign languages, and even philosophy (an important tool for problem solving). Many students find that taking a broad range of electives is the best strategy for developing career potential, because they can pick the combination of courses from several academic departments that will help most in a given field of work. This is called course clustering.

Don't feel that you have to aim for the minimum number of units required for graduation. Nothing (except, possibly, time and money) prevents you from taking more than that minimum. Taking extra units could turn out to be a wise and profitable decision in the long run, because you are using them to accumulate knowledge and skills that will help you in the future.

Other Graduation Requirements

Graduation requirements involve more than the number of units required in GE, your major, and electives. These other requirements include: *a minimum number of upper-division units*, to ensure that you didn't take the easy way with a light major and a bagful of relatively unchallenging lower-level courses; and *a minimum number of units in residence*, to ensure that your degree bearing the school's name was derived largely from credits earned there. The residence requirement does not refer to where you live (on campus or off campus) but rather to your status of being enrolled and taking courses at that school. The residence requirement usually concerns only those who have transferred and spent less than two years at the school where they intend to graduate, but students who have earned credits through more than one off-campus program may be affected as well.

FINDING OUT ABOUT
ACADEMIC REQUIREMENTS

The College Catalog

The most important source of information about meeting academic requirements is the official college catalog for your school. The catalog (also sometimes called the bulletin) may cost you a few dollars—usually between two and four—but is well worth its modest cost. The catalog is usually available at the campus bookstore.

To avoid possibly taking the wrong path and wasting your time and effort, you should consult the catalog that is in effect the year you first enrolled. Catalogs change every year or two, so borrowing one from someone who graduated or began a year or more before you may cause you trouble. Think of the catalog in effect when you first enter college as a contract between you and the school. The requirements listed for graduation are the requirements you will have to follow, with a few possible exceptions which we will explain shortly.

Much of the catalog is generally devoted to listing the numbers, the titles, and brief descriptions of each course offered by the college. These course listings are separated into academic departments (Mathematics, History, English, etc.). This information will be useful when it comes time to select classes, but the catalog is even more important to you because it also describes the requirements you must follow in order to complete your major and qualify to graduate.

We mentioned above that there may be a few exceptions to the rule holding you to the graduation requirements listed in the catalog for the year you entered college. In some colleges, you may bypass the requirements of your "entry catalog" (the one in effect when you began college), and choose, instead, to follow the requirements listed in the catalog of your graduation year (the "exit catalog"). You might want to choose the exit catalog to follow if the requirements became easier or if your course work just happened to fulfill those later requirements. The problem, of course, is that there is no way you can plan during your first two or three years for requirements listed in a catalog that hasn't been written yet. Blind luck may come your way, but don't count on it.

If you are a transfer student (or plan to transfer) either from a junior college to a four-year school or between four-year schools, be sure to check both your current school's catalog and the catalog of the college you are transferring to so you know what graduation requirements to plan for.

The Class Schedule

Students often confuse the catalog with the class schedule. A new class schedule appears each term and lists the courses currently being offered, along with days, hours, places, and professors for each class. The schedule also is likely to list the courses available for General Education credit. In addition, it provides information about important tests (such as writing or math skills tests, which may be required for graduation), along with the dates, places, and times they are given. The schedule shows important dates, such as deadlines for dropping and adding classes, and information about final examinations. It generally doesn't give descriptions of courses, so when planning your course load, use both the class schedule and the catalog.

The catalog and the class schedule are important resources for you, but they can be very unclear and confusing. If you can't make heads, tails, or elbows of these written explanations of requirements and courses available, don't be bashful about seeking the help of the advisors and counselors mentioned in Chapter 7.

A CHECKLIST FOR
TRACKING YOUR ACADEMIC REQUIREMENTS

A checklist is very helpful for keeping track of the courses you've taken and graduation requirements you've already completed and still have to fulfill. Ask your major advisor or a counselor at the Academic Advising Center if your school has a graduation requirements checklist specifically designed for the programs offered. If not, use the following checklist as a guide, but be sure to alter it to fit your school's particular graduation requirements. Keeping track of your progress on a checklist will save time and worry and can help you avoid unnecessary and unwanted surprises when graduation approaches. One

---

ACADEMIC REQUIREMENTS CHECKLIST

√ WHEN COMPLETED

☐ Total Units Required for Your Degree _____
☐   "In Residence" Units Required _____
☐   Upper Division Units Required _____

                                   Credit Hours or Units
☐ GE REQUIREMENTS: Total Hrs/Units = _____
☐   Communication Skills   _____
☐   Natural Science & Math   _____
☐   Social Sciences   _____
☐   Humanities   _____

☐ MAJOR REQUIREMENTS: Total Units = _____
☐   Lower Division   _____
☐   Upper Division   _____
☐   Concentration or Electives
        in the Major   _____

☐ MINOR REQUIREMENTS: Total Units = _____
☐   Lower Division   _____
☐   Upper Division   _____
☐   Minor Electives   _____

☐ ELECTIVES   Total Units = _____

☐ EXAMS REQUIRED FOR GRADUATION: _____
☐   (writing, math, etc.)   _____
                                        _____

☐ OTHER GRADUATION REQUIREMENTS: _____
☐   (thesis, project, etc.)   _____

---

of the worst experiences would be to discover a forgotten graduation requirement shortly before you thought the degree program would be completed. By monitoring your checklist regularly, you can prevent any oversights that could impede your progress toward the degree.

A Brief Note About Transcripts

In addition to keeping track of your progress on a checklist, obtain (for a few dollars) a copy of your transcript from the Registrar at least every two years. This document will reflect in a single source all the grade reports you automatically receive at the end of each term. Having your own transcript copy handy is useful when meeting with academic advisors. Later, employers may also want to see your academic record and will expect to see a transcript rather than a handful of grade reports.

ACADEMIC STANDING: FROM DEAN'S LIST TO DISQUALIFICATION

Students enter college in good academic standing and most remain there throughout their education. Good academic standing means that a student has been making normal progress toward a degree. For this, a minimum 2.00 GPA is commonly required.

Your academic status can move in either of two directions. It can go up if you qualify for the dean's list, an honor given each term to students who earn outstanding grades. Generally, only full-time students (which includes all intercollegiate athletes) are eligible for dean's list. The minimum GPA required to achieve dean's list varies from school to school, but is usually in the B+ to A– range (3.25 to 3.50 GPA) for the previous term. The standard for making dean's list may be somewhat lower (sometimes a 3.0 GPA) for freshman students.

Obviously, achieving dean's list is something to be proud of. In contrast, falling below good standing spells trouble, possibly including loss of athletic eligibility, and ultimately may bring disqualification from school if your record gets bad enough for long enough. The exact number of steps below good standing differs among schools, but we can show you how a typical system works.

Academic Warning. This is the first level down from good academic standing. It comes when your GPA for the most recent term falls below the minimum standard for passing grades (usually C or 2.00). Even if your overall GPA is extremely high, a bad term in which you make less than 2.00 may put you on warning. The school officials are telling you, "You're still okay, but your bad term means you need to be watched."

Academic Probation. This is a step below academic warning and may cost you athletic eligibility, at least temporarily. Probation comes from letting your overall GPA slip below 2.00 or by making below 2.00 during a term in which you are already on warning. In other words, two consecutive bad terms could put you on academic probation even though your overall GPA may still be well above the minimum for good standing. If you are placed on probation you will probably have to speak with an advisor in an effort to reverse this trend of poor performance and prevent it from becoming a long-term problem.

Continued Probation. This amounts to a last chance before being disqualified from college. Some people need more than one semester to get themselves straightened out, and continued probation gives them that chance.

Disqualification. A third consecutive semester below 2.00 is likely to bring disqualification from school. Disqualified students are not allowed to register for classes the next term. But colleges are not in the business of kicking students out of school, even students who are having trouble meeting the standards. Most colleges will do their best to keep students in school. Some may even reopen the door to students who have been disqualified.

Readmission. Students who are readmitted after being disqualified enroll on a trial basis and are watched closely as they try to work back toward good academic standing. School officials may insist that students who have been readmitted after disqualification sign a special contract in which they agree in writing, and with a counselor, to a course of action aimed at correcting their poor academic performance. This may mean giving up athletics or a job. The contract may also include a statement of how long the student expects to take before reaching the school's minimum standard for good academic standing. A contract may also include strategies to correct the student's problem, such as tutoring, study skills courses, and other measures for improving academic performance.

Beware of ungraded courses (Credit/No Credit, Pass/Fail) as they are handled in a variety of ways in terms of academic status. A No Credit (NC) course may not affect your GPA, but if you have too many, you could be disqualified from school—even if you have a 4.00 GPA! Check with an advisor or in the catalog to determine how NCs are treated at your school.

Competing in Sports While in Academic Hot Water

Athletic conferences and individual colleges vary widely in their rules governing whether athletes on academic probation are allowed to participate in sports. Many conferences and schools require simply that athletes be full-time students in order to compete in intercollegiate sports. Some have no minimum grade-point average nor do they demand that athletes maintain good academic standing for participation in sports.

Some athletic conferences and colleges go further in trying to ensure that their athletes are getting a good education. They do not allow athletes who are on academic probation to compete. In rare cases, a coach will establish a similar rule for participation on his or her team, even when such a rule is not demanded by the school or conference.

Whether or not your conference, school, or coach has a rule preventing athletes on academic probation from participating in sports, you should consider for yourself whether it is wise to compete when you are not doing well in your schoolwork. If you have an athletic scholarship, you may have little choice. Telling most coaches that you want to take time off from the team to build up your GPA is likely to bring a quick end to your athletic financial aid. However, if you are not tied to an athletic scholarship and you are either on probation or are facing it, you should seriously consider taking time away from the team. If that sounds like a rash move, consider what will happen if you don't get off probation and back into good academic standing: You will be disqualified from school and thus removed from the team anyway. Summer school is another possible option for getting back into good academic standing, although it probably would mean you won't be able to earn money you may need for the next school year. The best answer, of course, is working hard to avoid getting into academic hot water in the first place.

Change in NCAA Eligibility Rules
Beginning 1984–85 School Year

Nonfreshman athletes are required to be in good academic standing at their institution to continue playing varsity sports.

["A Summary of the Proposals Approved at the NCAA's Annual Convention," *The Chronicle of Higher Education*, January 18, 1984.]

10

STUDY AND

COPING SKILLS

In This Chapter...

Fighting the Dumb Jock Image

How to Be an Active Student

Time Management: The Critical Skill for Student-Athletes

Improving Learning Skills Needed for College-Level Work

How to Handle Test Anxiety

How Do You Respond to Poor Performance?

The chance at a new beginning comes with every change in environment. Certainly going from high school to college is a new beginning, as is transferring from junior college to a senior college or from one four-year school to another. Each of these new beginnings is an opportunity to improve poor habits (studying, eating, who you hang around with, etc.) and change self-defeating attitudes about your own abilities.

FIGHTING THE DUMB JOCK IMAGE

Unfortunately, athletes aren't always judged on their own merits. The image of athletes as dumb jocks is held by some teachers, some students, and—worst of all—by some athletes. It suggests that if you are an athlete, you are probably less able to do college-level work. Further, the dumb jock image suggests that you probably aren't interested in schoolwork even if you have the ability.

The dumb jock image exists to some degree on most college campuses. Sometimes this reputation is earned; at other times, athletes are stereotyped in this way more as a result of jealousy on the part of those who wish they had some of the attention that athletes enjoy.

The real problem of the dumb jock image lies among athletes themselves, especially when being a good student is considered "uncool."

> *Joke circulating around college campuses—*
>
> *"How many college athletes does it take to change a light bulb?"*
> *"I don't know, but they all get three units of course credit."*

You may find a few teammates, some of whom might even be among the leading players, who seem to take pride in avoiding schoolwork: not studying, failing to meet deadlines, and trying to get around regulations. They don't want to do well in school. Whether this is from lack of ability or lack of interest doesn't really matter. What matters is that these individuals seem to feel better about themselves if they can get their teammates to behave in the same uninterested, negative way about academics as they do. For them, it is a source of pride that they neither know nor care about good study habits. They believe that the coach or someone else will always take care of them.

Athletes who behave this way only help to sustain the dumb jock image. This is why we say that, in some cases, the image is earned. It is a trap that you may fall into, especially if you take the wrong team leaders as your model. Once you've chosen the dumb jock image for yourself, you'll have a hard, though not impossible, time shedding it.

Our best advice here is to be an individual in your schoolwork and be a teammate on your team. This isn't easy. You are both a student and an athlete, but you *may* have to act differently in each situation to feel as if you fit in. You probably would prefer not to have to play these image games, but it may be necessary in order to be considered one of the crew by your teammates and still not sacrifice your education. After all, who but you is supposed to benefit from your education? And who but you will suffer if you squander your years in college?

Even if a dumb jock image is absent at the college you have chosen, you may have doubts about your own ability to do college-level work. Join the crowd! Self-doubt is more common among new college students than homesickness. Again, starting in a new place with a clean slate provides the opportunity to create a new image for yourself and then live up to it. The first thing you may want to change is the way you view yourself, especially if your self-image contains doubts that are keeping you from trying new things and growing. This only takes willpower and the strength *not* to look at small setbacks (such as a low grade on a quiz or assignment) as if they were major failures.

Other people tend to look at us the way we look at ourselves. If we feel and act dumb or shy, others will naturally treat us that way.

If we wear an image of being interested in learning and improving ourselves, others will treat us as if we are bright. Notice that we didn't say you have to act smart to be treated that way. In fact, many people who "act smart" aren't particularly enjoyable to be around. The key to being treated as someone who is bright and interesting is to act interested. After all, college isn't necessarily for people who are already smart; it is for those who are interested in learning and improving.

If you were admitted to college, you are probably as bright as most other students and capable of doing college-level work. Of course, everyone knows that some athletes are admitted to college because of their good athletic skills and in spite of their poor academic skills. Athletes admitted to college on this basis are often called special admissions. First, you must decide whether this is actually your situation or whether you are simply carrying the common but unfounded newcomers' feeling that everyone else is smarter. If you are a "special admit" or if you find from test or writing scores (after giving them a good, honest try) that other students seem to be better than you, you *must* seek extra help. (Refer to Chapter 7 for sources of academic assistance.)

HOW TO BE AN ACTIVE STUDENT

In college you are expected to take an active, interested part in your education to get the most from it. Of course, you may simply sit back, passively taking in what the teacher and readings say and spewing it back on tests; but while you may get away with this approach, you are cheating yourself of an important part of your education and missing the chance to develop habits that will help you thrive in your eventual career. The choice—whether to be an active or a passive student—is yours.

People who say they can't remember what they learned in particular classes are often those who simply memorize information without questioning it or truly thinking about it. They've committed the knowledge they gain to short-term memory, which is lost soon after (if not before) the final exam. In contrast, when you become interested in a topic and question why things are as they are, you not only learn more about it, but retain this knowledge much longer.

Just as important, you'll enjoy your education more by being an active participant. It may seem like the easy way through college to walk into your classrooms, hide in the back, keep your mouth and mind shut, and do the least work that you possibly can to get by with a decent grade. Actually, this is the hard way through college, because going to classes becomes drudgery and you'll tend to either rush through your assignments the night before they are due or forget to do them at all. Students who do this look for excuses to avoid attending classes and gain virtually nothing from their assignments but an intense dislike of their academic responsibilities. This negative behavior pattern too often is carried over into one's work career. This is definitely *not* the easy nor the enjoyable way to get through college.

There are specific things that you can do in order to enjoy and benefit from college classes. But you must choose to do these things; they won't happen on their own.

Set goals. Set long-term general goals for yourself as well as short-term specific goals. Don't just take a course because it is required or because it fits into your schedule. Decide at the beginning what you want to gain from it. Decide before you begin a class project or even an assigned reading what you want to gain from it. (Reading the title and scanning the section and paragraph headings help to provide an idea of what you should get from the article or chapter.) Write your goal on a piece of paper and then after the task is completed, check to see that your goal was accomplished. Setting goals and keeping them in mind helps to keep you alert and alive to what you are doing; it also helps you avoid wasting time. The examples cited here should give you an idea of how simple—yet worthwhile—goal-setting can be:

- *Goal for a GE course on Computers and Society:* To see if I have the interest and ability to take a major in computer science.

- *Goal for a course in conversational Spanish:* Learn to speak Spanish well enough to carry on a one-hour conversation with a Spanish-speaking person who doesn't know English so I can travel in Spain or South America.

- *Goal for a Sociology term paper:* To find out how many college basketball coaches at major universities during the past 10 years have earned a master's degree. (Part of a larger goal: to explore the occupation of college coach.)

Speak up, question. Speak your mind in class whenever class size and instructor's style permit, but certainly speak it out of class as well. College is the perfect time and place to try out new ideas and measure your beliefs (old, comfortable ones as well as new ones) against the beliefs of others. College is meant for trying different ways of thinking and acting on for size. Open your mind to the ideas of others. Student bull sessions can be extremely valuable and enjoyable learning tools.

If you don't involve yourself, you run the risk of making yourself an outsider among other college students.

What you read should also be questioned. The author of a book or article you've read may not often be available to you, but a professor knowledgeable in that area (who likely assigned the reading in the first place) *is* available. One of the best, most valuable parts of a college education is the constant give-and-take among faculty and students on the assigned readings and on reading matter in general.

When you question professors and other students, do so as a genuinely inquisitive person, who may see things a little differently. Don't question other people's beliefs or perceptions in an aggressive, challenging way. We are all more or less emotionally attached to many of the beliefs we hold and probably won't respond well to someone who comes at us as if we were wrong or stupid. On the other hand, we are more likely to give a thoughtful response to someone who approaches us wanting to know more about why we believe what we do, even if he or she disagrees.

Open your mind to learning all the time. Learning habits, like athletic habits, generate their own momentum. A well-trained athlete enjoys training and finds it easy to continue training. A poorly trained athlete, especially one who cuts corners, considers training to be drudgery and finds excuses to avoid it. The same patterns apply to learning.

Does this mean that you have to crack books all the time? NO! It simply means you should also consider the time you spend outside of class and away from assigned readings to be valuable learning time. The content of all classes, from Quantum Physics to Business Law to English 1A, has an application in the real world. Archimedes discovered the Law of Specific Gravity while watching the water being displaced as he sat in his bathtub. This is a classic example of learning in a setting different from the environment where you expect to learn (the classroom, the laboratory, etc.).

Work at making yourself understood. If you don't know what you are saying, no one else will. People who fill their sentences with several "You knows" may be copping extra time to gather their thoughts, but they are also sending a signal to their listener which really says, "I hope you understand what I can't say very well."

No one is expected to know all things. But we all can improve the way we communicate what we do or don't know. Keep a dictionary handy whenever you study, read, or write. It's even a good practice to take a pocket dictionary to class, so you can quickly define words you aren't sure of and thus gain more from the class. College is for learning new things, *not* for hiding what you don't know.

Paraphrase to learn. "What does that mean?" Ask this question of anything you read. Ask it of things that people tell you in and out of class. Ask it of things that come from your own mouth and pen.

Asking "What does that mean?" simply but effectively puts you in the position of stating a thought in different words, that is, *paraphrasing*. If you can put a thought accurately into different words, that thought has been understood. The words are no longer abstractions, or "just words." Instead, they now create a picture in your mind that you can look at, analyze, and understand better.

The best place to begin frequently asking "What does that mean?" is in your reading. Begin by asking it at the end of every paragraph. Read the paragraph and put the heart of the information briefly in your own words (into one sentence, if you can). Then, paraphrase sections of the reading, such as portions that run from one subheading to another. Finally, summarize in your own words whole chapters or articles. With some practice, you should be able to capture the essence of a chapter or article in a few paragraphs, probably no more than five to ten of your own sentences. While it isn't necessary to put detailed information into your summaries, it will be easier to recall the details when you reread these summaries as you study for tests.

By asking "What does that mean?" of your reading and then paraphrasing the answer, you will understand more from reading something *one time* than most others do from reading it several times. So, while it may seem that paraphrasing slows you down, it is actually quicker in the long run and you'll understand and retain more of what you read. A little investment now, a big payoff later.

When a point is made in class, ask yourself, "What does that mean?" If you can't come up with a clear answer, go the next step and ask the professor for clarification. If you find yourself doing this a lot in a particular class or if that professor does not like to be interrupted, write a note to yourself to ask another student or the teaching assistant outside of class. If you still can't get a satisfactory answer, go to the professor during office hours or after a class session and ask for an explanation of the point that isn't clear to you. The professor is likely, then, to paraphrase for you. Hearing the same idea or information expressed two different ways is an excellent strategy to gain an understanding of it, whether you do the paraphrasing or someone else does it.

As a bonus, you may find that talking with the professor outside of class gives you much more useful information than simply clarification of the point that you didn't understand. Professors like students who show interest in their subject matter and often go out of their way to help interested students do well.

Learn to listen. As a child, you may have heard the old saying, "You can learn more by listening than by talking." Listening is a skill that most of us could develop much more fully. Often, we are so busy thinking about what to say next or questioning other people's motives that we fail to hear what they are saying. More arguments probably occur because people misunderstand each other than for any other reason.

Poor listening sometimes comes from drifting attention or plain old disinterest in the topic being discussed. This is a problem both in and outside of class. Resist the temptation to tune out when others are speaking. You will be amazed at how interesting some previously boring topics can become if you just try to listen to what is being said. Actively trying to hear what others say will increase your attention span and will help you understand and remember more. Furthermore, the act of trying to listen is habit-forming.

Improving your listening habits has benefits beyond the classroom. People respond very well to someone who really listens to them. Good listeners are often considered very bright, even without saying anything especially bright. Looking directly at the speaker—without staring—creates a very good impression and also helps you to absorb information and ideas.

In listening to professors and others, you are likely to hear things you don't agree with. Resist the temptation to say so or to discard their message simply because you disagree. Try their thoughts on for size, even though you initially disagree. Try to see where they could be right and you might be wrong. College isn't necessarily for changing your mind, but it *is* for opening your mind. Good listening may be the best tool of all for opening your mind.

Setting goals for yourself, speaking up and making sure you are understood, paraphrasing what you hear and read, opening your mind to the ideas of others, and careful listening are all skills that take effort. They have immediate rewards in school and in your relationships with others, but they also are skills that will help in your future career and relationships. The chance to develop and practice these skills will never be greater than it is in college. You may be able to slide through college without doing these things, but chances are you won't thrive and you'll let some good opportunities slip past unnoticed. It's a matter of choice, and the choice is yours.

TIME MANAGEMENT:
THE CRITICAL SKILL FOR STUDENT-ATHLETES

Managing your time efficiently may be the hardest task you face in college. It is a task that will remain difficult so long as you combine athletic and academic pursuits. All good students have to work at efficient use of their time, but athletes must become even better at this than most students, since athletic and academic responsibilities represent two full-time jobs. You may know of some student-athletes who seem to float through college playing cards, tossing frisbees, telling jokes, and generally playing around. They exist on every campus and are often popular because they are always available to socialize with. But such individuals are not good models to follow for several reasons. First, they are usually in more hot water than they are willing to admit. Wasting time is often their way of saying, "I can't hack it, so I don't really care." Second, beneath the fun-loving image you will probably find a person who is heading down a dead-end street. These people may have a lot of natural talent, but they are wasting it by not working to develop it further. Others who begin with less but are willing to put in the time to develop their talents are likely to pass them by, both in college and in their careers. Third, student-athletes who have a habit of wasting time are looking for others whom they can drag down to their level. If you see three athletes who tend to waste time, you could make a nice profit betting that two of them will flunk out, drop out, or at least lose their eligibility.

Scheduling your time. Making good use of your time requires effort, practice, and vigilance, but it will make college life far more enjoyable and profitable for you. The basic strategy is simple enough: prepare a weekly activities calendar and follow it religiously. Keep your calendar accessible; it does little good inside your desk drawer. Tape it to the inside cover of your notebook. Fill out a new one every Sunday night *before* you begin that evening's study session. (If you wait until after the study session, you may be too tired or forget.)

The first items to fill in on your weekly calendar are class sessions. (As soon as you know your class schedule and fill these into the schedule, make enough photocopies for each week in the term.) Next, fill in team practices, games, and travel. These are the commitments around which everything else in your week will revolve. If it is your sport's off-season, fill in time for conditioning and self-directed practice. If you have a part-time job, your work schedule must also be filled in, of course, although some people are lucky enough to be able to work their job hours around other commitments. Don't forget to include sleep and eating time. Although these may be flexible, they take up significant blocks of time each day, so should appear before you fill in time for studies, fun, and personal chores (laundry, shopping, etc.). Don't forget to schedule time for socializing. To keep efficient at work tasks, you need to relax and socialize, and you'll be able to enjoy this time more without feeling guilty about having fun if you include it as part of your schedule. And finally, take the effort to adjust and refine your schedule so that it is an accurate reflection of your week's activities. Don't be like the dieter who "forgets" the calories in that mid-afternoon candy bar. In order to have a chance at success as both an athlete and a student, you have to be efficient with your time and *know* where you spend it.

Juggling your commitments. We are all created equal in at least one sense: every one of us has no more or less than 168 hours at our disposal each week. The difference is in how we spend our time. Consider the following:

- A normal semester course load is 15 units, which equals 15 hours in class each week.

- The rule of thumb for college courses is that three hours of study should be spent for every hour in class. This equals 45 hours of study each week.

- College athletes often spend 40 to 50 hours each week in such sport-connected activities as practices, games, travel, skull sessions, and conditioning.

- The total of the weekly time commitments listed above is 110 hours, which leaves only about 58 hours (roughly 8 hours per day) for *all* other activities (sleeping, eating, socializing, etc.).

How does a student-athlete fit all of these other activities into only 8 hours per day? Some athletes are unable to fit everything in, and their solution is to let their studies slide. It is the rare coach who will recognize that certain activities may be as important (or even more important) than a player's athletic commitments. Many coaches recommend—or even demand—that their student-athletes take only 12 units during "in-season" terms (this is the least that a student can take and still be eligible for athletics). In addition, some coaches suggest that only easy courses, those that don't require 2 or 3 hours of study time per unit, be taken during the athlete's competitive season.

In the sample week's schedule on the facing page, the student-athlete under consideration is taking five courses, including one lab (16 units

SAMPLE WEEKLY CALENDAR

	MON	TUE	WED	THU	FRI	SAT	SUN
AM 6:00	sleep	GIT/B	sleep	GIT/B	sleep	sleep	sleep
7:00	GIT/B*	ANTHRO	GIT/B	ANTHRO	GIT/B	sleep	sleep
8:00	LAW	lib. read	LAW	lib. read	LAW	GIT/B	GIT/B
9:00	soc./nap	GOV'T	soc./nap	GOV'T	soc./nap	laundry	chapel
10:00	study	study	study	weights	study	study	chapel
11:00	BIOL	soc./nap	BIOL	soc./nap	BIOL	lunch	study
Noon	BIO LAB	lunch	BIO LAB	lunch	lunch	bank, etc.	lunch
PM 1:00	lunch	JOURN	eat/travel	JOURN	study	gme prep	soc.
2:00	practice	practice	team travel	practice	practice	game	soc.
3:00	practice	practice	travel/study	practice	practice	game	soc.
4:00	practice	practice	travel/study	practice	practice	game	weights
5:00	prac/shwr	prac/shwr	travel/eat	prac/shwr	prac/shwr	game/shwr	dinner
6:00	dinner	dinner	gme prep	dinner	dinner	rest	read Law
7:00	Law group	write-J	game	study	study	soc.	read Law
8:00	Law group	write-J	game	study	soc.	soc.	study
9:00	study Govt	read-Bio	game	study	soc.	soc.	study
10:00	study Govt	read-Bio	gme/shwr	study	soc.	soc.	study
11:00	read-Anth	sleep	read-Anth	sleep	soc.	soc.	study
Midn't	sleep	sleep	sleep	sleep	sleep	soc.	study
AM 1:00–6:00	sleep	sleep	sleep	sleep	sleep	sleep	sleep

*GIT/B = Get It Together/Breakfast

> "*I used to go along with the idea that football players on scholarship were 'student-athletes,' which is what the NCAA calls them. Meaning a student first, an athlete second. We were kidding ourselves, trying to make it more palatable to the academicians. We don't have to say that and we shouldn't. At the level we play, the boy is really an athlete first and a student second.*"
>
> —Bear Bryant, legendary football coach
> at the University of Alabama
> [Quoted in *Sports in America,* James Michener
> (NY: Random House, 1976).]

in all), during a semester of intercollegiate competition. This is a heavy academic load for a sports season. In this sample week, the student has scheduled 34 hours for sports commitments (ranging from weight-training sessions to contests); 16 hours for class time and lab work; 33 hours for study outside of class; and 19 hours for socializing. The week is tightly scheduled, and additional hours for sports activities may have to be borrowed from socializing or from sleep time if the coach requires extended practice or that game films be watched, or if team travel time takes longer than anticipated. Taking four courses instead of five (13 units compared to 16) would provide this student with approximately 10 more hours for team and study responsibilities. Some colleges give a unit of academic credit for intercollegiate team participation, which can count toward the 12 units minimum for eligibility and may even apply toward graduation at some schools (although such units rarely can be used for General Education credit or even for credit toward a Physical Education major).

In sports having seasons spanning the entire academic year, there is no latitude to take a heavier course load during off-seasons. A similar problem exists for athletes who must maintain year-round training schedules. Athletes in these circumstances who feel that they can handle only 12 or 13 units per term will probably have to take longer than four years to graduate. If your athletic time commitment is 40 or more hours per week, or if you are in an especially time-consuming major, you might seriously consider either attending summer sessions or stretching your college education over another term or year, rather than shortchanging either academic or athletic responsibilities.

Organizing your study time. When we don't really want to do something or would prefer to do something else, and especially if no one is standing over us to make sure we really do what is scheduled, we often find all sorts of excuses for delay or avoidance. Since the time you have scheduled for studying is probably not the time you most look forward to, you will have to take measures to make sure it is used efficiently. Do the following to help keep from wasting your study time:

- Write down what you will begin the next study session with *before* the session begins. Identify the topic of your study session either in class or before you end the prior study session. This will help to get you out of the starting blocks quickly, the hardest part of studying.

- Just as most coaches lay out schedules detailing what will be covered that day, develop a plan for your study time. Make sure that each course is given adequate study time each week.

- When you use up the allotted time for one subject, leave it even if you aren't finished. Don't borrow from the next subject's study time. This will keep you from shortchanging a course and help you to be more efficient for the next study session.

- Daydreaming belongs to leisure time. Commit yourself to your study time and commit yourself to your play and leisure time. That way you'll enjoy and profit more from each activity.

- Avoid cramming for tests. Study a little at a time, but often. A set schedule helps you do this.

- Study for tests before sleeping. Your subconscious mind tends to repeat the information while you sleep, in essence giving you more hours of study.

- If your mind wanders during a study session and you can't snap it back to the subject, take a 5-minute break (no longer), preferably alone. (Study breaks that involve other people tend to extend well beyond 5 minutes.) Some people need more short breaks than others, but everyone should be able to get through at least half an hour of study without a break.

- If your coach has set up study halls and you must (or want to) attend, sit toward the edge of the group where there is less chance of being bothered by or curious about what others are doing.

- Keep a dictionary by your side as you study and use it whenever you have the slightest doubt about the meaning of a word. When writing a paper, keep a dictionary, a thesaurus (for synonyms), and a manual of style close at hand, and refer to them regularly. Using these resources actually speeds up your studying and writing rather than slowing them down, and you learn more each time rather than continuing to make the same mistakes. (Several writing style manuals are available; ask your advisor or English teacher which they recommend.)

IMPROVING LEARNING SKILLS
NEEDED FOR COLLEGE-LEVEL WORK

You may have gone through high school in a college prep program. Does this mean that you are fully prepared to do college-level work? Possibly. While in high school, some students are not particularly interested in college and so don't consider taking college prep courses—until college athletic recruiters show interest in them. By then it is often too late to shift into a college prep program. Even if these students get admitted to college, they may not be able to compete in the classroom with those who have planned and worked toward college, unless they get special help.

Requirements for college graduation have been getting harder in recent years. Colleges are asking more of their students because many graduates during the past 10 or 15 years simply haven't had the skills that college graduates should have. What are those skills?

The College Board (the people who publish the SAT used for college entrance) have developed a long list of skills they believe students need in order to do college-level work. Following is a shortened list of those skills we consider to be most important in each category.* This will give you an idea of what skills you should have or should be developing during your first years in college:

Reading Competencies

- The ability to use a table of contents, preface, introduction, titles and subtitles, index, glossary, appendix, and bibliography.
- The ability to define unfamiliar words by using contextual clues and a dictionary.

Writing Competencies

- The ability to write standard English sentences with proper spelling, word choice, and grammar, including correct verb forms, punctuation, capitalization, pluralization, and possessive forms.

---

*The complete list can be found in the booklet *Academic Preparation For College: What Students Need to Know and Be Able to Do* (New York, NY: The College Board, 1983).

- The ability to improve one's writing by restructuring, correcting errors, and rewriting.

Speaking and Listening Competencies

- The ability to engage critically and constructively in an exchange of ideas, particularly during class discussions and conferences with instructors.
- The ability to answer and ask questions coherently and concisely, and to follow spoken instructions.

Mathematical Competencies

- The ability to use principles of algebra and geometry, including integers, fractions, and decimals; ratios, proportions, and percentages; and roots and powers.
- The ability to use elementary concepts of probability and statistics.

Reasoning Competencies

- The ability to recognize and use inductive and deductive reasoning, and to recognize fallacies in reasoning.
- The ability to distinguish between fact and opinion.

"Don't Feel Like the Lone Ranger" Department

In a 1982 survey of 188,000 college freshmen, the following percentages of students either had or needed remedial work in the areas listed:

English *16.6%*
Foreign Language *10.8%*
Mathematics *29.7%*
Reading. *9.5%*
Science *13.2%*
Social Science *6.5%*

Source: A. W. Astin, "The American Freshman:
National Norms for Fall, 1982"
(published by the American Council on
Education and UCLA), reported in the
Chronicle of Higher Education, January 26, 1983.

Studying Competencies

- The ability to set study goals and priorities consistent with stated course objectives, to establish surroundings and habits conducive to learning independently or with others, and to follow a schedule that accounts for both short- and long-term projects.

- The ability to locate and use resources external to the classroom (for example, libraries, computers, interviews, and direct observation), and to incorporate knowledge from such sources into the learning process.

Most colleges have a way to help students improve reading, writing, speaking and listening, mathematics, reasoning, and general study skills. At the Learning Skills center, or possibly through the Academic Advising or Counseling centers, you can find assistance to help you improve areas in which you are weak. Colleges often hold workshops or minicourses that provide practical assistance in many of the following areas:

Managing Time and Using It Efficiently

Developing Memory Skills

Efficient Listening and Note-taking

Preparing for and Taking Exams

How to Get More out of Textbooks

Understanding Graphs and Tables

Improving Reading Efficiency and Flexibility

Improving Your Vocabulary

Solving Math Word Problems

Understanding and Using Basic Statistics

Working on Fractions

How to Use a Calculator in Schoolwork

Using Dictionaries and Other Reference Books

Efficient Use of the School Library

If your college offers programs such as these for improving your learning skills, they are well worth the extra effort. They are often available free of charge or for only a modest fee. These workshops and minicourses are usually small (eight to fifteen students), so you will get much individual attention.

Look ahead in your plan for taking classes. If, for example, you don't feel confident about your ability in mathematics and you will be taking a class next semester that requires some math skills, take an appropriate workshop *this* semester. If you know that a future class will require library research and writing, take a related skills workshop the term *before* you will need to use those skills. And if you are having trouble with more general study and coping skills, such as time management, reading, or preparing for tests, by all means, don't wait; take a workshop that will help to improve those skills *immediately,* before you get any deeper into academic trouble.

HOW TO HANDLE TEST ANXIETY

Few people enjoy being tested. Some people have the ability to relax during a test, but most of us feel some nervousness. Feeling anxious or nervous about a test comes from one or a combination of the following factors:

Fear of failure. The habit of feeling anxiety when taking tests often begins with an early failure which grows into an intense fear of failure. From this point, it becomes a self-fulfilling prophecy, with the fear about the possibility of failing causing failure to happen. You may have seen this happen to some athletes in their contests. Athletes who are good in practice, but not in contests, often fail simply because they psych themselves out.

Lack of preparation. Poor preparation for tests is something that is generally under your control. The answer to this source of anxiety, of course, is to prepare better, which is what the previous sections of this chapter have been about.

Not liking to be compared with others. By the time they reach college, athletes generally have grown accustomed to being compared to others. However, some athletes may see comparison of physical skills as very different from comparison of acquired knowledge or intellectual ability. Because they have internalized the dumb jock image, they feel very confident and relaxed about physical comparisons but unsure and anxious about mental comparisons.

Belief that the outcome of the test is crucial to one's future success. Few tests in college are truly crucial to your future. You can usually counteract a poor grade on a particular test with good performance elsewhere in the class.

In sports events, athletes often thrive with mild doses of anxiety. Nervousness gets their adrenalin flowing and they perform better than if they were "flat," that is, without some competitive anxiety. This is most obvious when facing a tough opponent, whom we know we must be up for in order to be competitive. As an athlete, you can take this healthful way of dealing with the anxiety you encounter in your sport's contests and apply it to test-taking in school. Look upon tests as a challenge in which you "show those people what you can do." This attitude will motivate you to prepare well for the test and thus can help you benefit from any anxiety you may experience.

HOW DO YOU RESPOND TO POOR PERFORMANCE?

Does a poor performance in your sport lead you to want to give it up, to slough off in practice and training because you now expect to do poorly? Not likely, or you wouldn't have come this far as an athlete. Instead, a poor performance probably makes you work harder toward the next challenge. There should be no difference between sports and schoolwork; in this respect, at least, your brain works just as your body does. If you did poorly on a test or paper, the answer is probably *not* that you aren't smart enough. You simply need to devote more time to your work or direct your energies better. Instead of giving up, do what is necessary to improve—just as you would in your sport.

Improving poor academic performance boils down to a matter of attitude. Be honest with yourself: Did you do enough in the first place to expect success, or did you almost guarantee failure by hoping to succeed on the test or paper through some miracle? Don't expect enlightened insights to appear while under the pressure of an exam or during an all-night writing session to complete an assignment at the last minute. And don't study only for exam questions that you hope the teacher will ask. With this approach, you are only asking to do poorly, since any test merely samples the material covered in a course and you've gambled your study time on a guessing game.

If, on the other hand, you worked hard and still did poorly, you may need help or direction. Go to the instructor, point out how you prepared, and ask the instructor what you should have done to prepare better. Quite often the problem is in your misunderstanding what the instructor felt was important. Knowing that you are interested in doing better, the instructor is likely to provide hints and direction that will help improve your performance.

Also, check where you characteristically sit in class. It is much easier to stay alert and learn by sitting in the front and center of the class.

160

Good students tend to select seats in a T-formation, with the crossbar formed by the first two rows. Students with poorer performance tend to sit in the back and to the sides. The attitude of those close to you in class is contagious.

Sometimes, poor performance comes from not being active and alert in class. Become more active after a poor test performance rather than retreating into a shell. Make sure that you record in your class notes what the instructor puts on the board. Instructors seldom write on the board things that are not important. Either the specific information is important, or it will help you to recall general ideas and the instructor's organization of the material. Some instructors have a habit of quickly erasing what they've written. If yours does that, don't be embarrassed to ask him or her to leave it on the board a little longer.

Whenever you are unsure of an instructor's meaning in what is said or written, ask for an explanation. Rarely is a question considered stupid, except in the mind of the person who asks it. And even if, in a moment of thoughtlessness, a professor or teaching assistant seems to put you down for your question or idea, everybody (with the possible exception of you) will have forgotten about it in a matter of moments. Unless the professor indicates that he or she does not want questions and comments from the class, you will find your courses to be more stimulating and a better learning experience if you take an active and confident part in them.

Being an active and productive student requires effort, although more effort is needed to begin using these techniques than to maintain them. You will benefit from these good habits throughout your career and personal life.

PART III

GAME PLAN FOR A SUCCESSFUL CAREER

The development of your career begins long before you look for your first job, and even well before you have decided upon a career goal. Careers begin with the competencies and attitudes that you have developed on the field, in the classroom, and through many other experiences, such as extracurricular activities or part-time jobs. Student-athletes often have competencies they do not recognize, as well as hidden talents they fail to take advantage of.

Athletes often believe they are limited in their career potential. "If I can't make a professional team, what good am I?" This narrow viewpoint can be overcome when you recognize that you are excluded from few careers and are a particularly good candidate for many.

In athletics it is understood that a talented, well-conditioned, motivated athlete in one sport can be a good bet in many other sports as well. The same is true of career skills that are nurtured on and off the field. For example, the teamwork that you share as part of a sports organization (such as a football team) translates exceptionally well to all varieties of businesses and other organizations. Likewise, if you are a good talker, have a gift for numbers, write well, or perhaps know a lot about livestock, any of these skills can be marketed in certain

163

fields of work. Anything you have done has career potential, but particularly important are those traits that enable you to manage school, sports, and a social life all at the same time.

Your career game plan begins not with your asking "What can I do as an ex-athlete?" It begins with your saying "I have a lot to offer. Where do I want to use these resources?" Allow yourself to be imaginative; do not limit your thinking to sports-related careers or to those directly tied to your major.

Your game plan will work best if you follow two maxims: ·

1. Investigate and prepare for a career goal during college as fully as you possibly can.

2. Be prepared for change if it occurs (change within yourself or change in the labor market), and be ready to reapply the career exploration process to new situations.

Promising career prospects await any college graduate who is goal-oriented, determined, and disciplined. These qualities define the student-athlete well—the individual who has given fully to a demanding sport while facing the many pressures of completing a college degree.

11

HOW TO USE YOUR COLLEGE EDUCATION IN YOUR CAREER

In This Chapter...

The Career = Major Myth

Playing the Career Game with a Full Deck

Using Your Deck of Cards to Help Find a Career Direction

A Word About Graduate School

This chapter focuses on your life as a student apart from athletics. All those things you do off the field are important for your career development; academic and out-of-class activities enable you to gain skills, knowledge, and experiences that employers want. Since you cannot depend upon athletics alone to lead to a future career, you must examine how nonathletic accomplishments can build your career potential. Some student-athletes waste their time when practice sessions are over, while others are building a wide array of talents. We'll show you how to take maximum advantage of all your classroom obligations and choose out-of-class activities wisely. This chapter is especially useful for freshmen and sophomores in planning how to use their hours off the playing field.

THE CAREER = MAJOR MYTH

Chances are that sometime soon you will find yourself engaged in the following conversation, if you haven't already:

"So, you're a student at ___(fill in the blank)___ College. What are you studying there?"

"Well, my major is _____(fill in the blank)_____ ."

"That sounds like a good field to go into."

This frequent little exchange seems innocent enough, but it points out one of the great misunderstandings about how a college education relates to a career. Many people see a college education simply as vocational training: you choose a major, study it, graduate, and then go into the real world and perform what you've been trained to do. Many students seem to prefer this apparently straightforward relationship between major and eventual career. It seems so clean and simple. It gives students some comfort while they are attending classes, writing papers, and taking exams to feel that at a stipulated time they will be able to get a job and earn a living by using what they're learning. But this comfortable connection between major and career, in most cases, does not match the real world of work.

A major is an artificial and convenient construction of the academic world. The real reason that courses of study are organized by major is to provide a focus for each department in a college; majors provide common ground for the work of faculty members in each department. Majors, however, are not created by colleges in cooperation with the labor market. Sometimes the field you study may correspond to available jobs, but often it is difficult to make the translation between an area of study (e.g., biology or chemistry) and the fields of work you might apply it to (e.g., product development in industry). Or you may study a field that has no apparent relationship at all to the workaday world (e.g., classics, mythology, or comparative literature). Or in another common case, students take a particular major expecting to get a job in an associated field (e.g., teaching or civil engineering), only to find that the job boom that had attracted them to their field has peaked and passed in the four or five years it took them to get the degree.

The major you choose may help you to establish a tentative career direction, and you certainly should work hard in it. But clinging to your major as if it were a guarantee to future success is both short-sighted and self-defeating. Keeping the major = career myth afloat may lead you to believe falsely that the courses you take are sufficient currency to buy you a job. Students who rely on course credits to carry them to a job are like athletes who depend solely on natural talent to succeed. Just as athletic success comes from a combination of natural talent, coaching, training, teamwork, and mental preparation, so does career success result from much more than the courses that appear on your transcript. You can use your major as far as it

166

will take you, but you must be ready and able to draw on other resources when the major does not close the sale. These other resources
are available to you during all of the years you are in college.

PLAYING THE CAREER GAME
WITH A FULL DECK

What are the resources available to you in college, and how can they
help you prepare for a career? Consider the remainder of this chapter
as describing a deck of cards from which you may choose as many as
you like. Each card has potential value for you in a job or career. The
more individual cards you hold in your hand, the better you will be
able to play the career game.

Like a real deck of playing cards, your college-to-career deck has
four suits, each of which contains numerous cards. These four suits are
called Knowledge; Generic Skills; Experience; and Personal Contacts.

The more suits you hold, the stronger your hand. And the more
cards you have in each suit, the better are your chances to win (i.e.,
get the job and career you want). In the Generic Skills suit, for example, the more skills cards you have, the more marketable you will be
when you graduate. As with kings and deuces, some skills are more
valuable to a particular career than others, but all skills have some
value. Many times, people find that a skill they thought was not particularly useful for their work turns out to be valuable; an example is
the microcomputer software programmer who discovers that his or her
artistic skills are immensely useful in constructing visually interesting
yet understandable flow charts for people learning to use computers.

No one expects you to build up the maximum number of cards in
each of these suits while trying to be the best student-athlete that you
can be, but gaining some combination of Knowledge-Skills-Experience-
Contacts during college is highly desirable. After all, if you were hiring
a college graduate, you would prefer the candidate who had some
relevant courses (Knowledge), showed evidence of being able to perform the relevant job functions (Generic Skills), had some direct exposure to the tasks and problems involved in the job (Experience), and
knew people who could vouch for his or her character and future potential (Contacts). Knowledge + Generic Skills + Experience + Contacts
= Career Preparation.

The Knowledge Suit

As noted earlier, many students focus on knowledge in their major
as the key to career advancement. They seek programs where they

can focus on specific courses that relate to particular fields of work. They hope that these courses will provide them with the tools to do specific kinds of jobs. Programs that provide such tools fall into the category of vocational or career training.

Most colleges have some career-oriented programs of study that are keyed to specific areas of the work world. Some of these are in the current high-demand fields, such as engineering, computer science, and accounting. Often, students select these much sought-after majors based on the assumption that the demand for workers in these fields will continue until they graduate and are ready to seek employment. For many, this remains true. However, they forget that thousands of other students—sometimes thousands at the same school—also see these as good fields to enter. Not only is the competition for getting into these programs very high, but competition for jobs also escalates. And eventually, the demand for engineers, computer programmers, accountants, teachers, journalists, or whatever specialty has been in high demand, is equalled by the supply of college graduates. The momentum of this situation is such that colleges continue for awhile pumping out more workers in these fields than the fields can employ.

Vocational or career training in college tends to be concentrated in those fields where the technical knowledge component is high. Many other fields cannot be studied as easily by focusing primarily on specialized knowledge in the form of procedural techniques and job-specific skills. Business administration, journalism, politics, and many other areas of study are concerned less with specific bits of procedural knowledge; instead they are aimed more at transmitting general conceptual knowledge and understanding. For this reason, a specific major is generally *not* a requirement for employment in such fields. People who have not majored in these areas have proven to be just as successful in these jobs as people who have completed the associated majors.

Let's put it another way by returning to our analogy of a deck of cards representing your college preparation for a career. The cards in your Knowledge suit may have high value if you are seeking a career in a technical field, such as engineering or computer science. Your Knowledge cards will always have some value, but just how valuable they will be to your career is more difficult to assess in less technical fields.

Judy chose an education major, with science her subject area focus, because it seemed practical to have a teaching certificate. But she didn't really like teaching. She liked tennis far better and played on the team for four years, yet frequently wondered what she would do with herself after graduation. Judy had taken a wide variety of communication skills courses because she liked them and had worked for a book publisher one summer, where she developed several contacts. Judy also had started a newsletter for her national sorority. She used all of these experiences to find work as an assistant editor for a popular science magazine after graduation. Although Judy did find her major concentration to be instrumental in securing her job, other aspects of her college experience and extracurricular activities far outweighed her major in leading Judy into a satisfying career. What's more, the things she learned in her major courses have served Judy well in her publishing job in very different ways than she had expected while she was a student.

Focusing too much attention on selecting "the right major" (i.e., the one that will guarantee career success) is like asking: "Should I practice fielding grounders so I can be the best second baseman, or should I work on hitting homers so I can bat cleanup, or should I practice stealing bases so I can be the best baserunner?" One-dimensional people are of limited use. To prepare for your sport, you work to become the most complete performer you possibly can. Yes, specialists are needed. But specializing is generally better done after you get your degree. To be a successful career seeker—and to gain more cards in your Knowledge suit—try to get as much from *all* your courses as you can.

The Generic Skills Suit

If jobs could talk, they would say that all this fretting over what is the right major is putting your emphasis on the wrong suit. While some jobs do correlate directly with specific college majors, a far larger portion of them do not. *The most important fact of life in the job market is that most careers are learned and developed on the job, not prepared for in school.* It follows, then, that most college graduates will have to show an employer more than a list of relevant courses on their transcripts, good grades, and a particular major to get a good job.

Generic skills are far more important than particular courses of study, in terms of both the breadth of jobs they prepare you to perform and the long-range growth and advancement potential they give you in whatever field you enter. In spite of the special benefits that come from developing generic skills, many college students ignore or slight this hidden part of the curriculum and depend instead on their major to carry them through. This means that if you don't ignore these skills, you will gain an important advantage in the job market.

Generic skills come in many forms—writing, speaking, research, computer use, problem solving, imagination, detail work, and so on. But, once again, if jobs could talk, they would emphasize strongly

169

> *Samuel H. Armacost, president of BankAmerica Corporation, speaking at UC-Berkeley's 1983 School of Business commencement: "You studied finance and accounting and management science. You learned about economics, organizational behavior, and strategic planning. And you did all of this on the premise that this knowledge, that these tools you now possess, would carry you into your business careers, and give you the base to do the jobs you hoped you'd be hired to do.*
>
> *Well, ladies and gentlemen, I'm here today to tell you that it may not be sufficient. We already have a lot of people in business today who can analyze financial statements. But what we need are more people of integrity and vision. We need people with intuition and good judgment, with sound values and the capacity to truly think."*

that skills are most useful when acquired *in combination*. That is, those who succeed, especially in the leadership positions that college graduates aspire to, do so because of their having many different skills, as many cards in the Generic Skills suit as they can acquire. There are more similarities among the people at the top than there are differences. And these similarities tend to be centered in the area of generic skills.

The individual cards in the Generic Skills suit are as follows:

Technical Skills. Regardless of the career you hope to enter, you should have some technical literacy. This means enough exposure to technical courses that you have an understanding of new developments in science and technology, especially computer technology, the most compelling at this time. Computerese is the newest "native language" in our culture. Courses teaching computer use for non-computer-science majors are now available at most colleges. At an increasing number of campuses (though still mostly among private colleges), students are required either to bring a computer with them or to purchase one from the school. These colleges are making certain that all of their students—including fine arts and philosophy majors—earn the technical card in their Generic Skills suit.

Mathematical Skills. You may be able to avoid math courses. Many colleges allow students to skip or minimize their face-to-face contact with mathematics, but you'll be painting yourself into a corner career-wise if you allow yourself to do this. Business is mathematical, as is public policy and much else, if you look closely enough—even music, for instance. Mathematical thinking is used to solve business problems, to design interiors, to plan research studies, and to work on many social issues. In short, quantitative problems are everywhere, and you should learn to think in these terms.

If you are still cringing from this suggestion because you have a hard time understanding and appreciating the Xs and Ys of math, consider taking a statistics course in the department of sociology, psychology, education, or economics. Statistics is math applied to particular real-world problems. Because of this, many students find statistics easier to understand and appreciate than pure mathematics. Besides, having statistical skills gives you a card in the Generic Skills suit that many other job applicants won't have. Since so many job candidates dislike numbers, those who are not afraid to venture into the quantitative realm will have less competition.

Writing Skills. Writing skills are not learned only in writing courses. Most writing ability is developed in courses that do not have "writing" or "composition" in the title. Any course that requires you to write reports or term projects or even take essay exams can help to develop your writing skills. Ask students and professors which are the best of these courses. Often they are humanities and social science courses, but they can be found in any field where a professor demands that students express their opinions, ideas, and knowledge on paper.

Every challenging job that carries responsibility requires writing skill in some form. Clear, concise writing is the clearest sign of an intelligent, well-educated individual. You can be sure that prospective employers will examine your writing ability in the letters you send, on your application form, and in other situations.

Speaking Skills. Courses to enhance your speaking skills are somewhat harder to find. Beyond public speaking courses (very useful for anyone at any stage in college), the courses that push you to become a better speaker tend to have small classes in which professors are more inclined to ask for oral reports and in-class reactions to lectures or readings, and to have classroom debates. In the best of these, professors take the trouble to give you feedback on your oral presentations. Speaking skills can also be cultivated outside the classroom, in student government positions as well as on the debating team.

People who cannot express ideas orally to others are severely limited in their career development. If you don't like speaking in class or anywhere else in public, now is the time to develop this skill, not later. If you make mistakes while learning to speak in public in college, you might be embarrassed, but it will pass. (You'd be surprised at how many people have fears and self-doubts about speaking to groups.) But if you wait until you've begun your career to make your mistakes, it could cost you advancement—or even your job.

Research Skills. The skill of assembling information relevant to a problem is useful in many careers. This skill can be developed in science courses, history courses, or any course in which you must gather information from primary or secondary sources. The ability to research is actually a set of skills, rather than one skill. It includes imagination in finding information, organizational ability, accuracy in record-keeping, and efficient methods of retrieving information. Computer skills become important especially in this last area. The more that knowledge continues to expand in the modern world, the more that knowing how and where to find it will be a crucial skill in any job.

Analytical/Problem-Solving Skills. Problem solving is the most widely applied and universal skill of all, as it encompasses the ability to think logically. Science courses seem to be the most obvious for nurturing this skill, but many other courses emphasize it as well, including philosophy, critical thinking, and many liberal arts courses. Any course in which students are given a chance to identify and analyze problems and find solutions will provide an opportunity to develop these skills.

The entire hidden curriculum of generic skills should form a very basic part of your college education. Scientists must write and talk to others, managers must comprehend math and science, physical educators and recreation leaders must analyze and communicate, communicators must solve problems, and even social service workers must understand computers. A skill is not powerful by itself but rather in combination with other skills. Focusing your efforts on mastering one or a few skills to the exclusion of others may make your college learning experience "easier," but at the expense of your career potential. You might as well learn to be a superb dribbler on the basketball court and ignore shooting, defense, and moving without the ball. As a "designated dribbler," your use to any organization you join is limited and minor. If someone is to be eliminated from the organization, it will be those with limited skills. And at every opportunity the boss will be looking for someone else who can "do it all."

The worst argument of all for avoiding, skipping over, or mastering only a limited number of skills within the hidden curriculum is, "I'll get all those skills later, as I need them." On the contrary, college is the best and maybe the *only* chance you have to acquire these skills

172

and improve them. College graduates who are deficient in their writing, mathematical, scientific, or speaking skills tend to become worse later on, rather than better, because they have already learned to avoid and fear these skills areas. The longer you wait to enhance a particular skill, the less likely you will ever do it—certainly not once you are on the job.

Generic skills enable you to gain expertise in almost any specific area of knowledge, even if you never encountered the related course work while in college. Graduates with a full complement of generic skills will prosper because they can use their skills to learn new jobs or techniques. In essence, they will have learned how to learn.

The Experience Suit

Employers look for evidence that job seekers know something about the field they hope to enter, over and above the knowledge they have gained through their college studies. If you have done similar work before, they tend to assume that you are motivated to make a living in that area. If you have had some exposure to the line of work, they believe that you will be easier to train.

Together with relevant academic knowledge from course work and a variety of generic skills, the Experience suit can give you a strong hand in the job market. But here is where the age-old lament of recent college graduates hunting for jobs is so often heard: "They're only hiring experienced people, but no one will give me the experience!" How do you build your Experience suit while still in school, *before* you have to lay the cards down to be evaluated by prospective employers? How can you get relevant work experience while you are trying to be both a full-time student and a full-time athlete?

Most colleges offer the following forms of career-relevant experiences:

Internships (sometimes called Field Experiences). An internship gives you an opportunity to relate your academic background to a work situation. (In the medical and teaching professions, internships are requirements for the degree.) You may, for example, work in a child guidance clinic in order to apply your course work in adolescent psychology or social work. Or, as a student interested in earth sciences, you may work with an environmental agency collecting data about water pollution, erosion, and chemical interactions in local streams. In some internships, you can receive pay and/or academic credit. Since internships are gobbled up quickly, look for them early and ask how to build them into your course program. Even if you are not a major in the department offering the field experience you want (maybe *especially* if you are not a major), ask if you may participate. Though regulations occasionally discourage nonmajors, exceptions can be made if you show some real motivation.

Cooperative Education Programs. "Co-op" is usually a paid work experience, arranged by your college with participating employers. "Alternating programs" schedule a semester of study followed by a semester of work; "concurrent or parallel programs" schedule study and work in the same semester.

Independent Study or Research. An academic department often allows its students to do a special project or study that is not connected to a particular course. These studies may be of particular industries, professions, or organizations, or they may focus on a particular topic relevant to the career you may want to enter. A student interested in advertising, for example, might do an independent study of the TV commercials that people in a geographic area recall seeing during the previous night's viewing. The student who conducts the research benefits in several ways. He or she (1) earns academic credit; (2) gains good personal contacts in the project advisor and TV station managers; (3) can show prospective employers that he or she has initiative and experience in advertising-related work; and (4) acquires useful knowledge in an area of primary concern to people who hire young advertising talent. Independent study allows you to observe and gain knowledge of a work area as it exists in the real world at the same time you are studying it for academic purposes. Certainly it's worth the effort when you consider that you may find yourself talking with future employers while gathering information for your project.

Practical Courses. Many courses listed in the catalog offer students an opportunity to gain experience in a work setting or perform functions that are regarded as practical experience by the world of work. These include scientific laboratory courses; studio or applied arts courses; and courses emphasizing field studies, including anthropology, geology, health administration, forestry, and many others. Those who major in a given department may receive preference for enrolling in these courses, but don't assume by this that a specific major is required. Frequently, such courses are open to nonmajors, presuming, of course, that you can satisfy any course prerequisites.

Many things you do in college for which you receive no course credit can also serve as cards in your Experience suit. Among these are jobs, volunteer work and campus activities.

174

Jobs. It's nice to earn as much money from a job as you can, but if you have the chance to work in a field that provides experience for a future profession—even if for less pay—it may be worth more in the long run to do so. Many part-time, summer, or campus jobs offer the chance to work with professionals in a field you hope to enter. If you are a reliable and energetic worker, the supervisor can provide a recommendation that will be very helpful after graduation. In the competition among new graduates for jobs, such recommendations often provide a crucial difference when hiring decisions are made.

Volunteer Work. Often, students are unable to land a paying job that offers relevant career experience, but they can get that experience by working as a volunteer. The understanding between you and the employer should be that you are there for a learning experience: You provide your time and energy in exchange for what you can learn about the field while on the job. Such experience is likely to make a difference when you apply for a full-time job after graduation. Consider it "paying your dues."

Campus Activities. Your involvement in campus activities provides certain skills and experience that can be translated into relevant background for a future job. From treasurer of the Varsity Club to house manager of a fraternity to spokesperson for a dormitory, these experiences enable you to both build generic skills and show evidence of taking responsibility, something employers like to see. Such involvements may seem like "dead time," as they cut into your own time for leisure pursuits, but organizational work in college translates nicely to the organizational teamwork that all employers want in their workers. Participating in campus activities tells employers that you are building "people skills" and are project-oriented. This puts you ahead of the job applicant who has only taken courses and played sports. College students who do not have such experiences are often perceived as loners, overly book-oriented, or perhaps not interested in other people. Much of the business of the world takes place in social groups; thus your experience in groups makes you more attractive as a potential employee.

All of these experiences—paid and nonpaid, credit and noncredit—give you a potential edge for professions that may interest you. Given the variety of experiences we have just outlined, it should be possible for you to assemble cards in your Experience suit that will apply to any field of work you may desire.

The Personal Contacts Suit

Personal contacts are the fourth and last suit in your hand. While contacts have little to do with your ability to do a job well, they have much to do with your being given the chance to do a good job in the first place. Contacts are people whose familiarity with a field of work can help you learn more about it and who can advise you about methods of preparation and entry; they can also "connect" you with a potential job. Contacts are available to any student-athlete who makes the effort to find and talk with them. They can be your neighbors at home, relatives, parents of friends, professors, alumni—in fact, anyone you meet. For you as an athlete, the potential contacts are numerous, because you travel frequently, meet new people, and generally have more exposure to the public than most students.

Keep your career-antenna raised and active. Get in the habit of asking those whom you meet: "What work do you do?" If the answer seems interesting to you, ask, "May I talk with you sometime about it?" Or, "What advice can you give me about preparing for work in __(fill in the blank)__ , and whom should I talk with about getting a job?"

Contacts should be approached as sources of information and potential links to employment. The information contacts provide helps you to sharpen your career choice and may suggest some changes in your course work. Contacts serve as your tour guides to the labor market. You can call or arrange to visit them anytime you are not sure about your career direction. People enjoy helping students find direction and feel good that someone wants to know what they think.

Many of your easiest initial contacts are available right on campus. Faculty, coaches, and friends all may know people who work in fields that interest you. The act of establishing contacts tends to lead you to more contacts, and you can't have too many cards in your Contacts suit. Your first few contacts begin a networking process that looks much like the branching of a tree. The more contacts you make, the more you will know about a field of work. And the more people who know you are interested in a particular field, the more likely it is that some of them may either know of a job or even have a job available when you are ready. A full discussion of making and using contacts is presented in Chapter 14.

USING YOUR DECK OF CARDS
TO HELP FIND A CAREER DIRECTION

Most college students want to be able to say that they are headed in a particular direction after graduation, whether or not they really have a preferred direction yet. This need is clearest whenever somebody asks a college student, "What are you studying to be?" You want to be able to tell them something, just to have an answer. But it would be so much better if the career you mentioned were something that you really might want to pursue. Even better if you feel reasonably confident (not necessarily certain) that you have what it takes to be a success in that field. Choosing a major is one way to head down that path, so long as you realize that it is perfectly acceptable to eventually turn onto another path. Remember, also, that majors do not necessarily equate with careers. The knowledge that you gain from both major and other courses will be important in your career, although in many cases this is so primarily at the beginning. The generic skills that you learn and refine in college will help you throughout any career that you try. Both your prior experiences and your personal contacts are most helpful at the point of getting hired.

The more cards you accumulate in each of the four suits—Knowlege, Generic Skills, Experience, and Personal Contacts—the greater the number of choices and the better career alternatives you will have. The best time to gather these cards is while you are an undergraduate. Paying attention to your cards will give you a sense of direction as well as strategies for further exploration. Even if you are not yet ready to pick a career direction, gather your cards and build strength in your suits. They will pay off regardless of your major or the career choices that you eventually make.

A WORD ABOUT GRADUATE SCHOOL

There is a continuing movement toward professionalization of various fields of work, which often means that a master's or even a doctoral degree may be required for entry into the job market. Often, there is a particular undergraduate program (either a major or a specified combination of courses) required for admission to a graduate degree program, but do not assume that this is the case until you find out firsthand from the graduate school that you'd like to attend. Sciences represent one extreme (a science major or many science courses are usually required for entry to graduate science programs), while law school represents the opposite extreme (in that no particular undergraduate program is required for admission). Although many people assume that a master's degree program in business (an MBA) requires an undergraduate business major, this is seldom the case. Liberal arts majors and others are equally welcome in most

MBA programs, though some schools may insist upon a certain number of math or economics courses.

Admission to graduate school generally depends upon the courses you take as an undergraduate, the grades you earn, and your ability to score well on graduate school admissions tests. Graduate and professional schools vary so widely in terms of how these requirements might be combined (even two schools offering the same graduate program will differ), that you must inquire directly of each school that interests you. Your safest assumption is that each school will have somewhat different entrance requirements than the next.

In certain professional areas—graduate business schools being one of them—applicants who have had some full-time work experience in the field have a better chance of being admitted to graduate programs. Applicants with experience are regarded as more highly motivated, more mature and committed to a career in that area, and more knowledgeable about the field. While this is a growing trend, it is far from universal, and thousands of recent bachelor's degree graduates are admitted directly into professional schools each year.

Graduate school may seem like a long way off, and you may prefer to work for awhile before applying to an advanced degree program. But if you really want to work in a profession in which an advanced degree is required (or in one which gives advanced-degree holders a clear advantage over other job applicants), you should begin preparing for graduate school as early as your junior year. Check with advisors and graduate school catalogs to see what skills are required (statistics? a foreign language? familiarity with computers?) and what particular undergraduate courses are prerequisite to the graduate courses you are interested in.

12

ATHLETICS
AS A BRIDGE
TO CAREER SUCCESS

In This Chapter...

The Role of Athletics in Career Preparation

Special Problems Facing Some Athletes

> What is most revealing about Bradley is [that he] has made himself a great player; it wasn't a gift.... One of his roommates [at Princeton], ...Coleman Hicks, says, "He isn't the smartest guy who ever woke up in the morning." But Bradley wound up winning a Rhodes [Scholarship] and Hicks says of him, "He's very special. He did more with what he had than anybody I know."
>
> [Tony Kornheiser, *Washington Post* article reprinted in the Harrisburg *Sunday Patriot-News*, May 16, 1982.]

Bill Bradley, former Princeton All-American, 1964 Olympics champion, Rhodes scholar, and NBA All-Star for the New York Knicks, is now a highly respected United States Senator, from New Jersey. He grew up in a small town—Crystal City, Missouri. Bradley was intent upon getting the best education possible; he then used his education to transform his abilities into enormous accomplishments.

Sure, you say, an Ivy Leaguer! Anyone can make it big who comes from Princeton (or Harvard, or Yale, or Stanford, or...)! But it ain't necessarily so. There are many Princeton failures, just as there are many successful politicians, executives, doctors, lawyers, scientists, and community leaders who graduated from all varieties of schools—from large state universities to small backwater colleges. Bradley made it as an athlete and a Senator because of his personal qualities, not because of the school he attended. Many of the same qualities that Senator Bradley used to gain career success were ones that he nurtured in sports; they carried over to his pursuit of a career. The message to you? Because of your involvement in sports, you have a good shot at developing those qualities that help lead to career success; fewer nonathletes have that same chance. Why? Because few nonathletes are doing all that you are doing and certainly not under the same kind of public stress.

Are we telling you that sports in college are more than just games and contests, that sports relate to real life? Yes, without a doubt. We are not just talking about an athlete's advantage in which fans do favors for players they once cheered. This may happen, but that kind of assistance is minor in terms of the contribution it can make to lasting career success. We are talking, instead, about how your experiences in athletics can make you more effective in a real job. There is no guarantee that this will happen for you. (Oh, oh. They're hedging now, you might be thinking. I wish they'd make up their minds.) Your sports experience in college *can* help you in many important ways to become a career success, but you must understand *how* this happens and then *make it happen.*

This chapter shows you how to use your athletic experience to cultivate qualities that will help in whatever career you choose. First, a word of caution about your personal athletic successes. Except in the rarified world of pro athletics, your sports record is not going to count in your career. The element that *will* help you in your progress toward your career is the sports *experience,* not your stats and press clippings. All athletes, those who tended to win as well as those who tended to lose, can develop the qualities that spell career success. Because wins and losses are influenced by so many external forces—the level of competition, the fact that at least half of the competitors in sports have to lose in any contest (and all but one lose in the race for championships), the quality of coaching, to name just a few—an athlete's strengths are often buried on a scorecard. A .220 hitter can become an executive as easily as a star player can, maybe even more easily, because the athlete with only average abilities has had to work harder to achieve his or her level of success. What matters most is that as a college athlete you suited up every day, learned to prepare yourself for rigorous competition, took the good and the bad that come from competition, and kept coming back for more.

Athletes are already one step ahead of many other college students in terms of career preparation, since they have worked, risked, succeeded, failed, recovered, and earned the self-respect that comes from doing their job—all while in the public eye. Your college athletic career

ALEX ATHLETE

EDUCATION: Good Ol' State University (or Friendlyville College)

GOAL: A career involving competition and teamwork, in which I can see the results of my efforts, develop new skills, and enjoy the whole experience while I'm doing it.

ALSO: Be around friends, have a few laughs, get some recognition for my work, and learn from smart people.

BUT: Who wants an ex-jock, anyway? All I know much about is sports—how to take orders from coaches, sweat, and keep my eye on the ball.

MEANWHILE: Careers are stocked with college graduates who are goal-directed and can translate their drives into action and performance.

CONCLUSION: What chance do I have to reach my goal?

SKILLS GAINED AS AN ATHLETE:

> Physical and mental alertness
> Endurance – persistence
> Ability to concentrate on goals/objectives
> Ability to work well with others
> Loyalty, supportive of group goals
> Ability to deal well with setbacks or defeats
> Ability to organize time well

WORK SITUATIONS WHERE AN ATHLETE'S SKILLS ARE NEEDED:

> Large corporations
> Small businesses
> Educational organizations
> Public agencies / federal government
> Performing arts / communication organizations
> Nonprofit organizations
> Family businesses
> Self-employment
> et cetera

REVISED CONCLUSION:

> I can work anywhere. An athlete has qualities suitable for every sort of career. I must recognize these qualities in myself before anyone else will.

conditions you to perform under stress, to learn and adjust to variables rapidly, and to become self-disciplined, and it forces you to stretch for your full potential. This is what people must do in preparing for a career, and you've already practiced it in sports. The rigorous demands of sports competition thus form an effective bridge to your future occupational challenges.

THE ROLE OF ATHLETICS IN CAREER PREPARATION

How can college athletics help you to prepare for a career if you are not going to become a pro athlete? Many college athletes, and even many coaches, tend to view sports as a sphere separate from real-world employment. They have cast sports as play—however seriously they take it—and everything else as work. The separation they make is artificial, since diligent striving in any form can be considered work, and a person's work capabilities, skills, and habits are affected by every activity in which he or she participates. Your participation in sports in fact reveals a great many things about you, so you might as well pay attention to the messages you are already sending out to the world.

For the past few years, sports may have been your first priority, the place where you have wanted to devote much of your energy. In doing so, you have made a strong statement about your career potential. Not a statement about the *kind of work* that you expect to go into, but about the *kind of person* you are becoming—highly motivated, hardworking, energetic, and willing and able to take instruction so that in due time you will be capable of leading others. These qualities are highly valued by people who select future employees and organizational leaders, and that is where your athletics involvement enters the career picture. Athletics attracts people who already possess strong personal qualities and provides an environment in which they

> *"In a rapidly developing field such as telecommunications, we need college graduates who have developed skills both in the classroom and on the playing field. Every technical project at AT&T Bell Laboratories involves teamwork as well as technical expertise."*
>
> —Gale Hiering Varma,
> Employment Representative,
> AT&T Bell Laboratories

can cultivate and expand these qualities. The intensity of intercollegiate competition is a particularly good crucible for testing the individual against his or her environment.

Employers look for the job candidate who can be trained, is recep-
tive to learning, strives for perfection, follows organization goals, looks
for new challenges, and supports other people in the organization. All
coaches want these qualities in their players; all employers want these
qualities in their employees. If you are the kind of athlete who pushes
toward your personal limits, you have a four-year head start on the
development of work habits and the highly motivated attitudes that
employers most desire.

All this is great in theory, you might be thinking, but what can you
do right now, while still in college, to help your chances at a successful career? The following guidelines will show you specifically how
to use sports as a bridge to career success:

*Cultivate the abilities, behaviors, and attitudes toward work demanded
in your sport that generalize to competence in any kind of work.*
Improve your interaction with teammates and coaches, your self-
discipline, risk-taking, creative strategies (i.e., developing alternative
plans), and management of time. To people who run organizations, it
is self-evident that success in athletics develops leadership qualities,
primarily because the attributes that contribute to a winning team
(for example, the ability to organize people's efforts) often are needed
to keep members of a company or agency pulling together.

Build the mental side of your sport. A good level of physical fitness
will help somewhat in your future work, but the mental qualities that
you bring to it will be far more crucial. The toughness you need to
endure grueling practices, overcome pain and injuries, and accept losses
in order to bounce back with a better performance in the future, all
breed personal qualities that you can use in your career. The qualities
of emotional endurance and resilience are as necessary in an executive
or a scientist as they are in a trained athlete. The mental side of your
athletic career also cultivates a spirit of reasonable risk-taking, including
awareness of the effects of your risks on others and willingness to accept the consequences of your actions. The emotional steadiness of
an athlete who stands up to crises and enjoys pressure wears well in
the world of work.

Get involved in pregame strategic planning. Get as close as you can to
the thinking that produces results on the field. Involve yourself in the
mental preparation that precedes a game (either by working with the
coaches or by studying the books and manuals in your sport). Take

part in the mental activity that surrounds contests, even if your position or event doesn't involve decision making. Participate in strategy talks when and where you can. Make a habit of asking "Why?" Even individual sports, such as tennis, swimming, gymnastics, and track and field, include strategies such as pacing, psychological combat with opponents, and the judicious placement of individuals in particular events.

No matter what sport you are in, don't just leave the thinking up to coaches and captains. Even if they don't want to hear what you think, you want to hear what they are thinking and why. Use your sport to train your mind to think, to weigh alternatives, to plan and adjust; this is the way a college graduate seeking success in his or her career will be *expected* to think.

Find opportunities for teaching your sport to others. Teach children, sports-minded folks, high school athletes, and others. (Remember, however, that you cannot be paid for this, other than expenses, if you want to remain eligible.) Teaching helps to build communication skills—talking, explaining the way you see things, listening and trying to understand the way others see things—as well as a general sensitivity to other people. Most jobs involve teaching in one form or another, so the earlier you learn to communicate your ideas and perspectives to others, the better. Teaching can also be a form of salesmanship, in that you try to get others hooked on your viewpoint, or persuade them to appreciate different views. "Here's how I see it..." operates in all forms of work.

Mingle with nonathletes as much as you can. There is nothing wrong with having other athletes as friends, of course, but you see enough of them without trying. To get a broader perspective on what life-after-college will be like, get acquainted with people whose interests and abilities differ from yours. Athletics can be a very closed, insulated world. Limiting yourself to jock-talk can lead you to believe there's nothing else going on. Talk with students who don't care about athletics; get into town and meet community people, especially those who don't know that you are an athlete. (Once they find out you're an athlete, many will want to talk about sports. Resist! That's not why you're spending your time doing this.) Talk about what *they* do, not what you do. Especially if your life in college has been wrapped up in sports and classes, take up an activity, no matter how informal, that has nothing to do with athletics, something that forces you to reach people whose interests are entirely different.

You also can broaden your perspective beyond your athletic circle of friends through the elective courses you choose as well as in the places you go and the people you choose to hang around with. We don't mean that you should reject your athlete friends; we simply mean that you should learn to move easily in other groups with various interests. To do this takes practice. You may have to force yourself at first, especially since there is a special in-group magnetism among jocks; but after you beat a few different paths around campus, you'll find it easy to be a citizen of the whole school, instead of just the community of athletes.

Make use of your public recognition. Most athletes are not known publicly by name and reputation, but your school and your sport are known. Take advantage of the relatively public nature of athletics. Tell the people you meet (fans included) that you would like to know more about their field of work. During team trips, try to meet people in work situations that interest you, and get some exposure to their places of work, if possible. Every contact out of town expands your frame of reference for making a career choice.

It is, of course, especially useful to open dialogue with someone who might either have a job available or have inside information in a particular career area. Naturally, you wouldn't go up to this person and just say: "Hi! My name is Joe/Josie and I played basketball at Ole U. How's about a job?" But the following approach, or something like it, could get the ball rolling nicely for you:

> "Pleased to meet you, Mr./Ms. Smith. I've been wanting to talk to someone like you who knows a lot about <u>(fill in the blank)</u>. Playing basketball at Ole U. and keeping up with my schoolwork take up so much time that I haven't had much chance to explore what life is really like in your field."

At this point, Mr./Ms. Smith may pick up your lead and talk about sports or life as an athlete. If so, great! This should completely melt the ice and allow you to slide easily into career talk. But even if Smith doesn't care about or want to talk sports, it gives him or her an image of you as a striving, hardworking, interesting person.

By the way, if you do talk sports with someone who might help you in your career search or in gaining career information, don't speak negatively of your coach or the team, even if you feel that way. Honesty is not always the best policy, especially if the main impression that Mr./Ms. Smith forms of you is that of a bitter or angry person. Even if Smith shares your bad feeling toward, say, the coach, your best response is to say something like, "Well, we all could've done better and we certainly learned by the experience." In this way, you will come across as a person who is capable of profiting by your experiences, both good and bad.

Don't be afraid to promote yourself. As an athlete, you may have had press interviews or at least conversations with friends in which you projected an "Aw, shucks" modesty about your accomplishments. While this modesty is appropriate for athletes, modesty does little good when you are trying to advance your career interests. Tell people that you believe you possess the potential for success in your career goal. Other college graduates have career aspirations similar to yours, and interviewers will pay the most attention to those who show the greatest drive and self-confidence.

Many people interpret modesty as lack of self-confidence. While you may not intend your modesty to be interpreted that way, it is how others see you that is important in career concerns. So, put aside your modesty and say in a straightforward way what you have done and can do. Don't go overboard, obviously; there is a clear line between bragging and an honest accounting of what you believe to be your assets.

SPECIAL PROBLEMS FACING SOME ATHLETES

Although it may be nice to know that athletes have unique advantages that carry beyond their playing field experience, you may be facing a particular problem as a student-athlete, something that is not shared by athletes in general but is a definite source of trouble for you. The athletic experience affects people in different ways. Your own problems will not disappear just because all athletes, including you, have some opportunities for career preparation that are not available to nonathletes. While many athletes benefit from their competitive experience, many others suffer from the ghettoizing effect of athletics. You must face the fact that certain unfavorable characteristics may emerge from your involvement in college athletics. Some athletes have

---

"I felt my whole life had revolved around basketball. I didn't apply my intelligence [while in college] because basketball was all I cared about. I thought I'd be successful at anything, just because I enjoyed success at basketball. But I was wrong, and it took me two or three years to readjust and get into the real world."

—Comments of a former college athlete
[N. Scott Vance, "Life After Sport Found
Difficult for Ex-athletes," *Chronicle of
Higher Education*, November 11, 1982.]

---

a hard time accepting themselves as candidates for the real world. Observe the following brief profiles of athletes, their special problems, and ways that they can overcome them. You may find yourself or a friend somewhere in these four examples, or think of others we have not included. But note that, no matter how troubling the student-athlete experience has been, a successful transition can be made to a postcollege career.

"RITA THE RELUCTANT:" I hung around too many sports nuts who squashed other topics of conversation and read too many comic books. Four years of that stuff and now I think of myself as dumb. I'm afraid to talk with anyone I consider smarter than myself, which seems to be just about everyone. I'm about to graduate and lose even my athlete friends. What's a dummy like me to do?

Answer to Rita: You blew it in college, Rita. But you still have a shot at being one of "the smart ones." Your willingness to admit your fear is the big sign that you want to change. We recommend that you take risks that are manageable, small steps out of the starting block to maintain your balance. (Yes, you are still in the starting block after four years.) After you build some momentum, you can stretch out your stride.

Attend self-help courses, talk with people whom you see as one step above your level. Mix with people, including other athletes, who have interesting things to say. Above all, understand that even though you got off to a late start, it's never too late to catch up. In the career race, many people can win; the race is only over for you when you decide to give up.

Avoid both extremes of people—the muscle-heads who only rehash yesterday's contest or complain about the coach and the high-powered intellectuals who are so impressed with themselves that they talk everyone into a corner. A few months of experience with ordinary folks who cross areas of life away from the sports arena will make you feel like a new person, and will show you that, yes indeed, you can function in the real world.

"FAST BUCKS FREDDIE:" I see so much money being made in sports that it seems stupid to consider doing anything else as a career. Why should I work for a living when I can play? If I don't make it as a player, maybe I can organize sports events—anything to stay close to where the money is.

Answer to Old "Fast Bucks:" There's a little "Fast Bucks" in all of us. This is not so much a personal deficiency, Freddie, as it is your overwhelming desire to get on the gravy train. You simply are unwilling to believe that anything else might compete with what you see as your golden opportunity.

You are right about the riches that await a few people who mine the sports world. But it takes more luck than talent to be one of those rare people who strike pay dirt. You have to allow for the facts of life in sports: franchises die, even whole sports leagues die, players get injured, strikes occur, and darned few people earn an income from sports for more than a small handful of years. Women's professional basketball and softball, professional track and field, team tennis, professional coed volleyball—the professional sports graveyard is littered with "sure things."

If you still want to give it a try after understanding all this, in the immortal words of Rocky Balboa, "Go for it!" Nothing is sacred about working 9-to-5 in a "normal" job. Try your luck and don't second-guess yourself. But be prepared to accept the likelihood that you'll have a hard time making money at all, much less fast bucks. Nobody makes easy money. Scratch someone who has become an overnight success, and you'll probably find a person who worked 100-hour weeks, or slaved for years, or suffered many failures along the way, or all of the above.

"NEVER-MADE-IT NORBERT:" For every name in the newspapers, there are 1,000 of me. Even when I don't get cut from the squad, I never see much action. I have to explain to friends why my uniform never gets dirty and why I'm on campus when the team is travelling. I train hard, try hard, have some ability, and eat the right foods, but never get beyond the sideline. My feeling of failure is causing me to have doubts about my job and career prospects. Are my failures in sports trying to tell me something? Is a loser a loser in everything?

Answer to Norbert: If being a success in college sports were a reliable indicator of future achievement, the top corporations would hire only varsity lineups and most politicians would be ex-jocks. Neither, however, is true. You'll find varsity heroes in the gutter, and third-stringers in the board rooms. The marketable qualities that athletics breeds are available to *all* members of the team, not just those in the starting lineup. The primary effect of collegiate sports is to produce for all who compete—with dedication, willingness to learn, and enthusiasm—qualities that are valued in work. You obviously have dedication and persistence, and these traits will show in your favor when you are involved in a career, where people are not seen as either winners or losers, but rather as good or bad workers and leaders. All members of a working team can win, and unlike sports where only one team or person can be champ, many organizations in the same field can be considered winners.

"FOOTLOOSE FRIEDA:" Competing in sports is such a rollercoaster ride, I don't ever want to get off. Even if I won't ever be a millionaire, I want to live like one—taking trips, being taken care of, seeing important people, and having them care about what I do—just like it's been in college sports. Athletics can provide such a millionaire life-style and pace that anything else seems dull as dishwater by comparison. The idea of a 9-to-5 existence makes me sick. I know I'm jaded about the real world and unrealistic about the sports world, but I love it.

Answer to Frieda: We're as much in favor of an exciting life as anyone. Boredom is the worst curse of the working world. However, realize that your present high life-style has been supported by your college, which believes that your success on the field in some way has something to do with higher learning. Face it: that party is going to end. This doesn't mean the fun ends, only that the game changes. Be ready for the change and roll with it—if you want to continue enjoying life. Before the collegiate party ends, work on developing talents that someone in the work world wants. The more talents you have to offer, the farther you will go in a career, and the more fun and excitement you will have.

In the dual life you lead as a student-athlete, it's not your association with the sport that is marketable as much as it is the obstacles you overcome, in order to keep competing in your sport, while at the same time prospering as a student. Being able to do both things well has set you on the path to your future success. This is your bridge from college to career.

Athletics has as much carryover to other careers as anything else you might have done outside the classroom—probably more. However, if you allow athletics to isolate you from the mainstream of thought and experience in your college, making you feel like an alien in non-athletic areas, you have largely yourself to blame. You've allowed yourself to be defeated by the very thing—your athletic experience—that could have made you special and particularly attractive to employers.

Right now you are surrounded by one of the most intelligent, creative, and socially concerned groups of individuals—a campus community—that you may ever be close to. You have easier access to the members of this community than you ever will have to any similar group of people in the future. Take full advantage of their stimulation, interest, and knowledge. Make yourself more than just an athlete, and let both college and your special athletic experience lead you into success beyond college.

PROFILE OF AN ATHLETE

Mike Cotten

Mike Cotten always looked more like a guard than a quarterback, but in 1961, he got his chance for stardom. The starting quarterback for the University of Texas was hurt at the beginning of that season, and Mike was thrust into the leadership role. He led the team to a winning season, a national ranking, and a victory in the Cotton Bowl over Ole Miss.

In spite of such brilliant successes in his sport, Cotten had his sights set on a nonathletic career from the start. He comments, "I knew early on that I did not have the physical attributes to make it as a professional. So I made sure that I was going to get my degree."

Cotten completed a law degree at the University of Texas Law School and today is a successful attorney with an Austin law firm. He attributes his achievements in both athletics and career more to persistence and thoroughness than to innate talent: "In football, I was short, not especially fast, and others had more talent. However, persistence and thoroughness of preparation for each game paid off for me. It has been the same way in my law work. Others are more intellectual, but I have done well because I take care to attend to everything that needs to be done in preparing for a trial."

Cotten believes strongly that the intensity of competition in collegiate sports gives any athlete an advantage in the career he or she pursues. "If you look for it, you can find competition in just about anything you can do," he asserts. "Any situation in which you are challenged either mentally or physically will bring out the best in you."

13

CAREERS IN AND OUT

OF SPORTS

In This Chapter . . .

Looking Into Athletics-Related Careers

Using Athletics as an Entry Into Other Careers

A Roster of Career Possibilities

The best game plan in choosing a career is to have a Plan A, the plan you will try first, and a Plan B, the one you will turn to if the first plan does not work out. For many college athletes, Plan A is likely to be a career relating to sports, and Plan B will be an alternative to sports. In this chapter, we urge you to consider both plans and recognize that the two may be related to each other. Sports-related jobs you may be thinking of when your college playing days are over generally are part of larger fields of endeavor. Coaching, for example, is part of the larger sphere of education. Sportswriting is part of the larger spheres of journalism and all the communications media. Sports-related businesses suggest private enterprise in general, and so on.

In your personal game plan, you should investigate and weigh many possible Plans A and B before embarking upon any of them. To help you decide upon your Plans A and B, we offer a roster of athletics-related careers that are linked to larger career areas. But first let's review some of the special considerations that athletes who are intent on pursuing a sports-related career should be aware of, along with several self-defeating patterns they should avoid.

LOOKING INTO ATHLETICS-RELATED CAREERS

Taking a Shot at the Olympics or the Pros

Let's say your Plan A is to take a shot at becoming an Olympic athlete or to see if you can earn a living in professional sports. You already

> *"A lot of people leave school, put their eggs in one basket and then don't make it. They have no education, and it's tragic. . . . It's a short life on the circuit. Your body is so vulnerable. It's only a question of time before something breaks down. That's why you always have to be prepared."*
>
> —Ferdi Taygan, professional tennis player
> [Donna Doherty, "Starting Over: Is There
> Life After Pro Tennis?"
> *Tennis Magazine,* December 1981.]

know the odds weigh heavily against you. To give yourself this chance, you may be investing a lot of money in training and travel or borrowing money that you don't have. More likely than not, friends, family, and others are giving you the mixed message of "Go for it!" and "Get serious; prepare for a real career."

You're probably willing to deal with these pressures because you feel no risk is too great if your desire to be an Olympian or pro athlete is strong enough. So what if you fail? You'll try something else when and if that happens.

In earlier chapters, we have discouraged you from expecting a successful professional athletic career, because the odds are so long. (The odds aren't much better in getting to the Olympics, but, of course, you can also actually achieve your Olympic goal while still in college. In fact, achieving Olympic status is easier while you are in college than after, when much of your support for training and travel ends.) Long odds aside, we still like to see people have the experience of shooting for the stars. You can aim for your lofty goal and still keep an eye toward the career you might enter later. Here are several precautions we recommend to those in pursuit of a professional sports-career:

- Minimize your financial risk by encouraging someone to sponsor you. (If you are in a team sport and are drafted immediately, you may not need to take this step.) If you are trying to make it as a golfer or tennis player or as a free agent in a team sport, finding a sponsor may allow you to commit the extra time, energy, and concentration that might make the difference. Ask someone, or several people, to invest in your athletic future; in return, you will have to agree to share a percentage of your earnings with the sponsors, in the event you make it to the pros. However, never make an open-ended deal. Place limits on how much your sponsors will invest and either how much they might eventually make or for how many years the deal will last. In any event, be fully aware of the financial risks you face in your quest for an athletic career. And never put yourself in so great a financial bind that you hurt your chances for developing career alternatives in the future.

- If you haven't already graduated, complete your college degree as soon as possible. It is virtually certain that the kind of employment you will aspire to after a stint as a pro athlete will include jobs that require a degree. The number of jobs in all areas of work for which a college degree is required or preferred is increasing; hence, getting a degree is your best insurance against future career difficulties. In this way, you will avoid going straight to the bottom in earning power after your pro career (or attempt at it) ends.

- If possible, obtain off-season or part-time jobs, preferably in areas providing experience that can be marketed after your professional sports career ends. This means taking a job that holds some prospect for career development rather than any old job to fill time between seasons and earn pocket money.

- Develop an "If I were injured tomorrow" scenario, so that you have a strategy you can use if your athletic career should end suddenly. By having a contingency plan well thought out and firmly in mind, you will not have the added burden of "What will I do...?" while you are still competing. If you deal with this looming question at the proper time—before the crisis occurs—and free from pressure, this kind of "negative thinking" (i.e., what to do in case something bad happens) can help you to survive through rough times.

Are There Special Careers for Ex-athletes?

As a student-athlete, have you imagined or hoped that you would stay in sports in some way, even when your playing days end? Have you considered being a coach, scout, radio announcer, sportswriter, or players' agent? There are three major categories of nonplaying athletics-related careers:

a) Careers in which previous athletic experience as a player is almost always essential, such as coaching and scouting.

b) Careers in which experience and knowledge of a sport may be helpful but in which they are not absolutely necessary. These include positions as sportswriters and announcers, sports publicity directors, athletic trainers, or statisticians. Many people who earn a living in these jobs were never more than casual participants, yet they are hired because they have the necessary academic training or because they have skills—such as writing, public speaking, working with numbers—which make them successful in their line of work.

c) Careers in ancillary industries related to sports, for which previous athletic experience is generally not important. Player representatives (agents), equipment manufacturers, food concessionaires, and employees of fitness centers and organizations that promote sports events fall into this category. Even within the management structure of a professional team, very few employees have had serious playing experience. Just check with the front office of any pro team to find out how few of its staff members have played the sport.

There are numerous athletics-related careers you may want to look into, and there is no reason that you shouldn't investigate them. However, only in coaching and scouting will your playing experience be a specific requirement for the job. For jobs in the two other sports-related categories listed above, you will be competing with nonathletes as well as other athletes. The talents you acquired or refined as an athlete will certainly be of benefit, but they won't mean much unless you possess a variety of other generic job skills and knowledge associated with the position in question.

No matter what kind of sports-related job you may be interested in pursuing, your success will be more a function of those nonathletic skills that relate directly to the job than to any athletics-related skills you might have. If, for example, you want to be an agent for pro athletes, the key hiring consideration would be your talents in sales and public relations, not your previous athletic record. You can be a play-by-play baseball announcer if you had a .210 batting average in college and a truckload of errors, but you won't make it if you have a lousy voice and don't speak proper English. Further, some of the best coaches have been among the worst athletes and vice versa. This may be because top athletes are often "naturals" who don't have to think much about what they are doing on the field to do it right. In contrast, *no* coach will do well without thinking extensively about his or her team.

Give a sports-related occupation a whirl if you really feel the need. But leave room for movement or reexamination of your career goals. Ask yourself if the sports-related occupation meets all of your needs—in terms of income, challenge, life-style, and room for growth and advancement—or if you are primarily taking care of your need to stay close to sports at the expense of other needs.

Self-Defeating Patterns to Avoid

Many college athletes believe that their future work should have a direct relationship to their career as an athlete. Trying to build a connection between the two is sometimes very tempting, and it is quite understandable why individuals might resist letting go of something at which they've been successful and felt comfortable. Unfortunately, a preoccupation with athletics, especially in trying to fit it into the next phase of your life, may lead to nonproductive or even destructive patterns in the careers of former college athletes. Resist the temptation to look at your opportunities in the work world as if they had to pass through the narrow funnel of sports. You've learned from sports, but you aren't limited to work which involves sports. But before discussing how to broaden your view of career options, let's look at the unnecessarily confining patterns that many college athletes set for their futures.

Pattern #1: "I'm going to try to make it as a pro athlete at all costs."
This pattern is fueled by the immense publicity given to highly paid professional athletes. It involves continual workouts to maintain and improve the athlete's physical conditioning and skills, repeated team tryouts or qualifying tournaments in golf and tennis, and frequent contact with and referrals from coaches. These activities become all-consuming and often are done to the exclusion of thought or effort in any other career direction. Dedication is total, with thoughts of failure and what to do next vigorously pushed to the back of the athlete's mind. If you follow this pattern, you may take odd jobs of no consequence or opportunity for advancement while waiting for your big break to happen. Disappointments are accepted as part of the waiting process. You draw hope from the few stories of athletes who eventually made it after long years of obscure struggle. Work harder, you say. You still have eight to ten of your body's best years ahead of you. Why waste these years doing anything else besides following your dream of being a pro athlete?

We do not want to discourage anyone who truly has the potential to be a professional athlete. But we do want you to be aware of the likely consequence of following this pattern. As we showed in Chapter 2, very few athletes ever make even a few dollars as professionals, while only a small percentage of these can claim to earn a regular living

195

at their sport long enough to call it a career. While trying to earn a place in professional sports, you may suffer these consequences:

- Your college education may be curtailed and may end short of a degree. Many student-athletes who believe they have professional potential quit college soon after their eligibility expires.
- You may delay learning about other fields of work because of your preoccupation with your sport. Then, when you eventually give up the dream of being a professional athlete, you'll have to "play catch-up" once you find a career that looks interesting.
- You may find your confidence withering by thinking to yourself, "If I don't make it as a pro, I won't be able to do anything." This pessimism is unnecessary and unfounded, but you may feel it because you have kept yourself from the nonathletic world of work for so long. In short, though it is hard to leave the corps of athletes, you may pay a hard price for hanging on.

Pattern #2: "I'll become a great coach." Coaching is, of course, the first alternative for many athletes whose professional playing aspirations are fading. As noted earlier, it's also a career alternative strongly considered by many other college athletes who have no thoughts of competing as pros. Although your role as a competitive performer ends, coaching keeps you close to the competitive arena, closer to the excitement and the feeling of participation than anything else.

Keeping close to athletics through coaching often entails staying actively involved in some level of the sport, accepting any kind of coaching job no matter what the pay or level of competition, taking other jobs to supplement your income, and waiting for a break. You'll coach Pony League or Bobby Sox, junior high, anything, and push hard for a winning record to show that you're worthy of a coaching job in higher levels of competition. You will probably continue to hope that a top coaching job will open up for you, like magic. But if you think of how many other former athletes are looking for good coaching jobs, you'll begin to understand and appreciate that getting one of these jobs is almost as hard as playing in professional sports. You might waste many years waiting for the big break that never comes.

All former athletes believe they know the sport they played well. Many believe they can transmit this knowledge to others simply because of their experience as players. But if you do not have any appreciation for teaching and the administrative details of coaching, then you probably don't belong there. It's a good profession but a tough one, requiring a great deal of dedication. Having been a player, even a great one, is merely a starting point in the profession of coaching.

The majority of athletes who stay in coaching end up as public school coaches. If this is where your career settles, you had better like teaching children and adolescents and be prepared for very little public recognition and much hard work that has nothing to do with the glamour of collegiate or professional sports. You had better like long hours, paperwork, dealing with parents, and handling troublemakers as well as the "good kids." And all this for relatively little pay. Coaching is a wonderful and stimulating career *if you really want to be a coach and teacher;* coaching is *not* a refuge for frustrated and unfulfilled former athletes who just want to stay close to their sport.

Pattern #3: "Someone will reward me for having been an athlete." A peculiar yet persistent belief espoused by some athletes is that they will do well in their career simply because they have been an athlete. Some athletes are complacent about looking for work and preparing a career strategy because they believe that people *want* athletes to succeed. Whether or not they were star players, athletes generally receive considerable attention while in college and are often admired. It is easy to understand why they feel special and might expect people to want their services later on. Mixed with the inertia that comes from having been taken care of in many ways, an athlete's feeling of special-ness may encourage him or her to wait for opportunities to develop and to avoid taking responsibility for this process. This harmful be-havior pattern is characterized by "biding one's time," coaching here and there, maybe taking a job just because it happens to be there (the extra money is always helpful), and waiting for the good oppor-tunity to come along. "Someone will find me; they won't let me down."

Especially if college athletics has given you success, rewards, and identity, these three patterns may tempt you as your thoughts turn to your future career. No one wants to put down the torch before the flame has expired. But clinging to the past or giving in to any of these three patterns can only delay your immediate task of finding a job that matches your interests and abilities and offers challenge and room for professional growth.

USING ATHLETICS AS AN ENTRY
INTO OTHER CAREERS

Although most college athletes, sooner or later, go on to pursue careers unrelated to athletics, student-athletes fresh out of college often try hard to find sports-related employment. While you may not stay in the first sports-related career you decide to enter, in many cases it will be a sensible way to make the transition between college athletics and the world of employment. If your career ideas are uncertain, look into the work people do that supports the elaborate structure surrounding organized sports—promotion, media communications, physiology, administration, writing, transportation, stadium construction, manufacturing of equipment and clothing, and so on. As you explore these areas, you will notice that each area represents a far broader profession than simply that serving athletes, sports fans, and team managers. Thus, you can use your curiosity about sports-related enterprises to discover many other occupational areas. You may obtain a first job on the basis of your athletic background but later move into the broader profession as your interests widen. As you explore, you will discover that athletics is related to almost every major occupation or profession in some way. Thus, we find sports involved in law, medicine, media, construction, education, finance, retailing, investments, and even politics.

In order to give you a number of different ideas for using athletics-related careers to investigate larger occupational categories, we have presented here a broad sampling of jobs in the sports world and the corresponding larger professions of which they are a part. In each of the sixteen work categories presented here, the sports-related job is defined first, followed by more general employment opportunities, entry requirements, and the job outlook for that occupation in the future. The roster of career possibilities is presented in this way to help you see that your attraction to a sports-related occupation opens up a far broader set of employment possibilities. If, for example, you've thought about being a sports statistician, you should also consider the possibility of being a generalist statistician—one who works in any number of fields. In the long run, your interest in working with quantitative analysis and statistical problem solving may move beyond your interest in working with sports. Similarly, the interest that drew you to the area of sports team management may lead you to personnel and labor relations work. For any sports-related career, there is usually a much larger category of work that might interest you and would offer you a wider array of opportunities.

As you look through the roster of career possibilities that follows, keep in mind that this is but a small sample of your alternatives.* The *Occupational Outlook Handbook,* published by the U.S. Department

---

*In the roster, nonathletic job information comes from the *Occupational Outlook Handbook,* 1982–83 edition, U.S. Department of Labor.

of Labor, lists over 200 broad categories of employment. You should visit your college career center to review the larger numbers of possibilities. Ask for both the *Occupational Outlook Handbook* and the *Occupational Outlook Quarterly*. These government publications will be available along with many other specific career materials.

ADVERTISING

Sports-related Occupation

Sports Promoter: Arranges the financing, facilities, contestants or teams, and schedules for sports events or a series of events. Usually, the event is profit-making and requires publicity beyond that ordinarily provided by commercial press or word-of-mouth. Promoters occasionally organize entire new leagues for a particular sport.

Examples of Other Jobs in This Field

Account Executive: Takes charge of the advertising for each of the agency's clients; determines the nature of the advertising to be produced; coordinates and reviews all the agency's activities involved in producing the advertising package; and maintains good relations between the agency and the client.

Copywriter: Writes the text of ads (called copy) and scripts for radio and TV ads. Good copywriting calls for creativity, imagination, and a sense of salesmanship.

Entry Requirements

There is little agreement on the best preparation for an advertising job. A bachelor's degree with a liberal arts, journalism, art, or business major is a minimum requirement. Those with a master's degree in business are preferred for managerial or research-oriented jobs.

Job Outlook

Employment of advertising workers is expected to increase about as fast as the average for all occupations through the 1980s; however, employment growth is tied closely to the health of the economy. In a recession, some advertisers reduce advertising expenditures, which results in layoffs.

For More Information

American Advertising Federation
1225 Connecticut Avenue, NW
Washington, D.C. 20036

American Association of Advertising Agencies
666 Third Avenue
New York, New York 10017

COLLEGE STUDENT ADMINISTRATION

Sports-related Occupation

Athletic Advisor: Provides individual counseling for all intercollegiate athletes at a particular college or university; assists athletes with course selection, study skills, and personal concerns relevant to sports involvement. Advises athletes regarding eligibility rules for participation in sports.

Examples of Other Jobs in This Field

Director of Student Affairs: Manages the student union; assists student groups in planning and arranging social and cultural activities.

Dean of Students: Heads the entire student personnel program. Evaluates the changing needs of students and helps develop and implement institutional policies.

Entry Requirements

In filling entry-level jobs, colleges often prefer applicants with a bachelor's degree in a social science and a master's degree in student personnel administration. Some student personnel occupations require specialized training. A master's degree is preferred and a doctoral degree may be necessary for advancement to top positions.

Job Outlook

The employment outlook for college student personnel workers is likely to be competitive through the 1980s. Tightening budgets and declining enrollments in four-year colleges and universities are expected to affect employment in those institutions.

For More Information

National Association of Student Personnel Administrators
Central Office
160 Rightmire Hall
1060 Carmack Road
Columbus, Ohio 43210

EDUCATION

Sports-related Occupation

Physical Education Teacher/Athletic Coach: Specializes in teaching physical education courses; depending on training, may also teach other courses. Often coaches one or more athletic teams for the school, which includes direction of practice sessions after school hours. May also direct intraschool athletic activities.

Examples of Other Jobs in This Field

School Counselor: Deals chiefly with the social, behavioral, personal, and career planning concerns of youth. In addition to counseling the students themselves, consults with parents and with other members of the school staff, such as teachers, school psychologists, school nurses, and school social workers.

School Administrator: Occupation includes principals, assistant principals, school district superintendents, and assistant superintendents. School administrators are responsible for improving the quality of instruction. They visit classrooms, review instructional objectives, and examine learning materials. They also confer with teachers and other staff; advise, explain, or answer procedural questions; and talk with parents and members of the community.

Entry Requirements

Prospective teachers need a bachelor's degree from an approved teacher training program with a prescribed number of credits in the subject they plan to teach. They must have completed student teaching and other education courses. Almost half of the states require teachers to have graduate degrees. College students interested in becoming school counselors usually take the regular program of teacher education, with additional courses in psychology and sociology. In states where teaching experience is not a requirement, it is possible to major in a liberal arts program. Experience in education is virtually a must for the individual seeking a job as a school administrator, as is graduate study in educational administration.

Job Outlook

Prospective education workers will face keen competition for jobs throughout the 1980s. Pupil enrollment, the major factor affecting employment, is expected to decline at the secondary level but increase at the elementary level over the next decade.

For More Information

American Personnel and Guidance Association
Two Skyline Place, Suite 400
5203 Leesburg Pike
Falls Church, Virginia 22041

American Alliance for Health, Physical Education, Recreation and Dance
1201 Sixteenth Street, NW
Washington, D.C. 20036

HEALTH AND LEISURE ADMINISTRATION

Sports-related Occupation

Health Club Manager: Supervises and coordinates activities of workers engaged in planning, selling, and structuring fitness plans for clients of health clubs.

Example of Other Jobs in This Field

Hotel Manager: Responsible for operating a hotel profitably and satisfying hotel guests. Determines room rates and credit policy; directs operation of the food service; and manages the housekeeping, accounting, security, and maintenance departments of the hotel.

Entry Requirements

Experience generally is the most important consideration in selecting managers. However, employers are increasingly emphasizing college education. A bachelor's degree in hotel and restaurant administration provides particularly strong preparation for a career in hotel management.

Job Outlook

The employment of hotel managers is expected to grow faster than the average for all occupations of the 1980s as additional hotels are built and chain and franchise operations spread.

For More Information

American Hotel and Motel Association
888 Seventh Avenue
New York, New York 10019

JOURNALISM

Sports-related Occupation

Sports Reporter: Writes stories in magazines or newspapers about the results of sports events. Usually attends these events in person but sometimes obtains the information secondhand. Interviews managers and players and relates current contests to a team's seasonal progress. Often writes subjective pieces analyzing a team's future prospects.

Examples of Other Jobs in This Field

News Reporter: Collects and analyzes information about newsworthy events to write news stories for publication or broadcast. Receives assignments or evaluates leads or news tips to develop story ideas. Gathers and verifies factual information through interview, observation, and research.

Correspondent: Works for newspapers, magazines, and wire services as a station reporter in large cities as well as other countries to prepare stories on major news events occurring in these locations.

Entry Requirements

Most newspapers, magazines, or news wire services prefer to hire college graduates who have a degree in journalism.

Job Outlook

Employment of reporters and correspondents is expected to grow about as fast as the average for all occupations through the 1980s. This growth will come about because of an increase in the number of suburban and small-town daily and weekly newspapers.

For More Information

American Newspaper Publishers Association Foundation
The Newspaper Center
Box 17407
Dulles International Airport
Washington, D.C. 20041

The Newspaper Fund
P.O. Box 300
Princeton, New Jersey 08540

NUTRITION

Sports-related Occupation

Sports Nutritionist: Advises sports teams and individual athletes regarding appropriate foods and training diets that will contribute to maximum athletic performance, prevent injuries, and maintain general health. Usually engages in research to detect the effectiveness of present dietary guidelines and tests proposals for improved training diets. Studies and advises on the effects of nutrition on both short-term (single event) and long-term athletic performance.

Examples of Other Jobs in This Field

Administrative Dietician: Applies the principles of nutrition and sound management to large-scale meal planning and preparation, such as that done in hospitals, prisons, company cafeterias, schools, and other institutions.

Community Dietician: Counsels individuals and groups on sound nutritional practices to prevent disease, maintain health, and rehabilitate persons recovering from illness. May engage in teaching and research with a community health focus.

Entry Requirements

A bachelor's degree, with a major in foods and nutrition or institutional management, is the basic educational requirement for dieticians.

Job Outlook

Employment of dieticians is expected to grow faster than the average for all occupations through the 1980s to meet the rapidly expanding needs of hospitals and long-term health care facilities.

For More Information

The American Dietetic Association
430 North Michigan Avenue
Chicago, Illinois 60611

PERSONNEL AND LABOR RELATIONS

Sports-related Occupation

Sports Team Manager or Coach: Organizes and supervises the preparation, planning, on-field performance and evaluation of an athletic team. Decides who shall represent the team in competition, often recruits the talent, and administers game strategy. Assesses merits of the players and recommends changes in their preparation. Interprets team's performance to the public.

Examples of Other Jobs in This Field

Employment Interviewer: Interviews job applicants to select persons who meet employer qualifications. Reviews completed applications and evaluates applicants' work histories, education and training, job skills, salaries desired, and physical and personal qualifications.

Labor Relations Specialist: Advises management on all aspects of union-management relations. Much of the work of labor relations specialists concerns interpretation and administration of contracts, in particular, grievance procedures.

Training Specialists: Conducts orientation sessions for new employees and arranges on-the-job training. Develops in-house programs as needs are identified; for example, may instruct experienced workers in the impact of new procedures or may teach management skills to new supervisors.

Entry Requirements

A bachelor's degree is required for most beginning positions in this field. Some employers look for individuals who have majored in personnel administration and labor relations, while others prefer graduates with a general business background; still others feel that a well-rounded liberal arts education is best.

205

Job Outlook

The job outlook for personnel specialists is generally expected to be good through the 1980s. Every year, billions of dollars are spent on employee training in the public and private sectors, and the amount is expected to increase in the decade ahead. However, particularly keen competition is expected for the relatively small number of jobs available in labor relations.

For More Information

American Society for Personnel Administration
30 Park Avenue
Berea, Ohio 44017

American Society for Training and Development
600 Maryland Avenue, SW
Washington, D.C. 20024

PHOTOGRAPHY

Sports-related Occupation

Sports Photographer: Takes pictures of game action, usually in conjunction with a sports reporter's story in newspapers or magazines. May also take pre- or post-game photographs of individual athletes to accompany interviews or for use in game stories. Builds file of photos to be used in future articles, yearbooks, promotional literature, or books.

Examples of Other Jobs in This Field

Photojournalist: Photographs newsworthy events, places, people, and things for publications, such as newspapers and magazines, or for television shows. May also prepare educational slides, filmstrips, and movies.

Still Photographer: Usually specializes in a particular type of photography, such as portrait, fashion, or industrial. Portrait photographers take pictures of individuals or groups of persons and often work in their own studios.

Entry Requirements

Photography has no set requirements for formal education or training. Employers usually seek applicants who have a broad technical understanding of photography as well as imagination, creativity, and a good

206

sense of timing. Photographic training is available in colleges, universities, junior colleges, and art schools.

Job Outlook

Employment of photographers is expected to grow about as fast as the average for all occupations during the 1980s. Demand for photographers employed in business and industry is expected to increase as greater emphasis is placed on visual aids in meetings, stockholders' reports, sales campaigns, and public relations work. Employment in photo-journalism is expected to grow more slowly.

For More Information

Professional Photographers of America, Inc.
1090 Executive Way
Des Plaines, Illinois 60018

PHYSICAL THERAPY

Sports-related Occupation

Athletic Trainer: Applies knowledge of human anatomy, the physical demands of athletic performance, and training techniques to treatment and prevention of athletic injuries. Uses this knowledge to prepare athletes for maximum performance and advises them regarding a suitable training regimen. Must be available during practice and games to advise coach or manager about physical condition of players. Must travel with the team and be available on weekends and holidays when there is a heavy load of contests. Acts as link between team members and physician.

Example of Other Job in This Field

Physical Therapist: Plans and administers therapeutic treatment for patients referred by a physician in order to restore bodily functions, relieve pain, or prevent permanent disability following injury or disease.

Entry Requirements

To practice physical therapy, applicants must have a degree or certificate from an accredited physical therapy educational program and must pass a state licensing examination. Athletic trainers must earn a bachelor's degree and become certified through the National Athletic Trainers Association.

Job Outlook

The employment outlook for physical therapists is expected to be excellent through the 1980s, in part the result of increased public support for rehabilitation services. The aging of the American population will also spur increased demand for physical therapists. The number of people completing training programs in this field in the 1980s is expected to fall short of demand.

For More Information

American Physical Therapy Association
1156 Fifteenth Street, NW
Washington, D.C. 20005

PSYCHOLOGY

Sports-related Occupation

Sports Psychologist: Applies the principles of human behavior and motivation to athletic performance. Works with individual athletes and managers to effect the most positive emotional climate for each player. Applies general psychological issues to specific athletic problems, such as aggression, lack of self-control, mental blocks, or emotional conflicts. Also aids players who have no "psychological problems" but seek ways to improve their performance.

Examples of Other Jobs in This Field

Clinical Psychologist: Helps the mentally or emotionally disturbed adjust to life. Interviews patients, gives diagnostic tests, provides individual, family, and group psychotherapy. Generally works in hospitals or clinics or maintains a private practice.

Counseling Psychologist: Uses several techniques, including interviewing and testing, to advise people on how to deal with personal, social, educational, or vocational problems of everyday living.

Industrial/Organizational Psychologist: Applies psychological techniques to personnel administration, management, and marketing problems. Is involved in policy planning, training and development, counseling, and organizational development and analysis.

Entry Requirements

Bachelor's degree holders are qualified to assist psychologists in community mental health centers or other organizations. Applicants with a master's degree may teach in two-year colleges or work as school psychologists or counselors. A doctoral degree, required for self-employment as a psychologist, is increasingly important for advancement and tenure in the academic world.

Job Outlook

The employment outlook for psychologists is generally expected to be favorable through the 1980s, although those seeking academic positions are likely to encounter stiff competition.

For More Information

American Psychological Association
1200 Seventeenth Street, NW
Washington, D.C. 20036

PUBLIC RELATIONS

Sports-related Occupation

Sports Information Director (or Sports Promotion Director): Informs the general public about sports events related to a particular team, sports organization, or educational institution. Writes articles, arranges interviews for the commercial press, and produces in-house materials for public consumption, to enhance ticket sales and promote the general reputation of the athletic organization. Acts as a salesman of his or her employer's athletic program to the press and to the public.

Example of Other Jobs in This Field

Public Relations Representative (or Public Information Officer): Plans and conducts public relations programs designed to create and maintain a favorable public image for an employer or client. Plans and directs development and communication of information designed to keep the public informed of the employer's programs, accomplishments, or point of view.

Entry Requirements

Although most beginners in public relations have a college degree in journalism or communications, some employers prefer to hire those with a background in a field related to the firm's business. Some firms seek college graduates who have worked for the news media.

Job Outlook

Demand for public relations workers may slacken as employers delay expansion or cut their staff during business slowdowns, but over the long run, corporations, associations, health facilities, and other large organizations are expected to maintain or expand their public relations staffs through the 1980s. Competition for entry-level jobs is keen.

For More Information

Public Relations Society of America
845 Third Avenue
New York, New York 10022

RADIO AND TV

Sport-related Occupation

Sports Announcer: Provides play-by-play and pregame or postgame coverage of a particular sports event. Does research on teams and players prior to the game, interviews individuals from teams or management, and reviews history of previous encounters. Interprets and analyzes action during the game. Also conducts sports talk shows.

Examples of Other Jobs in This Field

Announcer: Presents radio or television programs to a listening or viewing audience. Memorizes script, reads or ad-libs to identify the station, introduces and closes shows, and announces station breaks, commercials, or public service information.

News Analyst (or News Commentator): Discusses and interprets current events or news stories for a radio or television broadcast audience.

Entry Requirements

A bachelor's degree in liberal arts provides an excellent background for an announcer. College graduates hired by television stations usually start out as production assistants, researchers, or reporters, and are given a chance to move into announcing if they show aptitude for broadcasting.

Job Outlook

The broadcasting field will continue to attract many more job seekers than there are jobs. It will be easier to get an entry-level job in radio than in television because more radio stations hire beginners. These jobs generally will be located in small stations.

For More Information

Broadcast Education Association
1771 N Street, NW
Washington, D.C. 20036

RECREATION

Sports-related Occupation

Sports Recreation Leader: Organizes and supervises group recreation which focuses on athletic activity but may also include dance, arts and crafts, and other leisure-time activity. Arranges events, obtains equipment, and often provides instruction in sports techniques. Sees that all interested parties have an opportunity to participate, regardless of their abilities.

Examples of Other Jobs in This Field

Recreation Leader: Provides face-to-face leadership and is responsible for a recreation program's daily operation. Keeps records and maintains recreational facilities. May give instruction in crafts, games, and sports.

Recreation Director: Manages recreation programs. Has overall responsibility for program planning, budget, and personnel.

Entry Requirements

A college degree with a major in parks and recreation is an increasingly important qualification for those seeking full-time career positions in the recreation field.

Job Outlook

The job outlook for group recreation workers is largely dependent upon government funding for recreation services. Job opportunities are generally expected to be more favorable in therapeutic recreation and private and commercial recreation, although competition for jobs as camp directors is expected to be very keen.

211

For More Information

National Recreation and Park Association
3101 Park Center Drive
Alexandria, Virginia 22302

American Camping Association
Bradford Woods
Bartonsville, Indiana 46151

SELLING/RETAIL BUYING

Sports-related Occupation

Sporting Goods Representative: Sells sporting goods products from a particular manufacturer to retail sporting goods stores, professional teams, college and high school teams, or other recreational groups. Often contracts with pro athletes to use the company's products as testimonials for promotional purposes.

Examples of Other Jobs in This Field

Manufacturer's Sales Worker: Sells mainly to other businesses, such as factories, banks, retailers, and wholesalers, but also to hospitals, schools, libraries, and other institutions. Visits prospective buyers to inform them about the products available, analyzes the buyer's needs, and takes orders.

Buyer: Selects the merchandise that is sold in a retail store; determines supplier and quantities of goods to keep in stock. Buyers in large retail businesses often handle only one or a few related lines of goods; those in smaller establishments may be responsible for many more types of products.

Entry Requirements

A college degree is increasingly desirable for a job as a manufacturer's salesworker. Manufacturers of nontechnical products usually prefer graduates with degrees in liberal arts or business administration. Manufacturers of technical products usually prefer graduates with degrees in science or engineering. However, many employers accept college graduates in any field of study and train them on the job.

212

Job Outlook

Overall, opportunities in manufacturing sales are expected to be good for persons with appropriate product knowledge or technical expertise plus the personal traits necessary for successful selling. Employment of buyers is expected to grow about as fast as the average for all occupations through the 1980s as the retail trade industry expands in response to a growing population and higher personal incomes.

For More Information

Manufacturers Agents National Association
P.O. Box 16878
Irvine, California 92713

National Retailers Merchants Association
100 West 31st Street
New York, New York 10001

STATISTICS

Sports-related Occupation

Sports Statistician: Compiles and analyzes team and individual performance records, game statistics, physical capabilities of players, and other numerical data to aid the manager or coach in making decisions about game strategy and choice of players. Uses statistics to evaluate players' overall contribution toward team record.

Example of Other Jobs in This Field

Statistician: Devises methods of analysis, carries out statistical procedures, and interprets the numerical results of surveys and experiments. Statisticians apply their knowledge of statistical methods to particular subject areas, such as economics, human behavior, natural sciences, and engineering.

Entry Requirements

For many beginning jobs in this field, a bachelor's degree with a major in statistics or mathematics is the minimum educational requirement. However, a bachelor's degree with a major in an applied field, such as economics or natural sciences, and a minor in statistics, is also often suitable background for entry-level positions. Opportunities for promotion are best for those with advanced degrees.

Job Outlook

For people who combine training in statistics with knowledge of a field of application, employment opportunities are especially favorable throughout the 1980s. Private industry will require increasing numbers of statisticians for quality control in manufacturing. Business firms are expected to rely more heavily than in the past on statisticians to forecast sales, analyze business conditions, and help solve management problems.

For More Information

American Statistical Association
806 Fifteenth Street, NW
Washington, D.C. 20005

WRITING AND EDITING

Sports-related Occupation

Editor of Sports Books: Reviews proposals for fiction and nonfiction sports books, selects suitable manuscripts, and manages these projects to completion. Also, often compiles and edits books of sports records and books analyzing past performances of teams and players. Usually works for a single publisher, but may contract services to several publishers at once.

Examples of Other Jobs in This Field

Writer: Develops original fiction or nonfiction prose for books, magazines, trade journals, newspapers, technical reports, company newsletters, radio and TV broadcasts, or advertisements.

Editor: Frequently does some writing, and almost always does much rewriting, but the primary duties are to plan the contents of a publication and to supervise its preparation. Editors decide what will appeal to readers; acquire manuscripts or assign topics to writers; and oversee the production of books, articles, magazines, or newspapers.

Entry Requirements

A college degree is required by many employers, but there is little agreement as to the preferred major. Some employers look for a broad liberal arts background; others prefer to hire people with degrees in communications or journalism.

Job Outlook

Throughout the 1980s, the outlook for writing and editing jobs is expected to continue to be keenly competitive. Opportunities will be best in technical writing and with firms that prepare business and trade publications.

For More Information

The Newspaper Fund
P.O. Box 300
Princeton, New Jersey 08540

American Society of Magazine Editors
575 Lexington Avenue
New York, New York 10022

PROFILE OF AN ATHLETE

Steve Hoffman

Steve Hoffman has been trying for three years to become a professional football player. As of this writing, he is one of a small group of punters attending training camp for the Washington Redskins team, after having had tryouts with several other pro teams and many months of prior training with expert tutors of the kicking game.

Steve had been a wide receiver for Dickinson College in Carlisle, Pa., home of Jim Thorpe, but a college that had not produced a pro football player in recent times. How did Steve get the idea to give it a try?

"After watching some punters on a professional team, it occurred to me that I was as good as at least three of them without even practicing, and if I practiced really hard I'd probably be as good as the other two. So I talked to my father about it, and he said that if I really thought I could do it, then I should go ahead and give it my best shot."

Whether Hoffman makes it or not in the pro ranks is beside the point. His life expectancy as a professional punter is zero to five years. Even if he succeeds gloriously, he knows another career will be necessary before too long. Two themes predominate in his thinking: (1) he is pursuing football because of his desire for excellence and his willingness to risk: "I didn't want to be 50 years old and look back and say that I didn't try," he notes; and (2) he feels confident that his liberal arts degree and the personal qualities he has worked to develop will sustain him in any career that he enters.

Hoffman is convinced that he can make a successful shift from football to a nonathletic career when the time is necessary: "I know that I apply myself well to anything I do. With my determination and my liberal education, which trained me to learn and communicate with anyone, I can be successful in whatever job I get."

14

MOBILIZING YOUR

RESOURCES FOR

THE JOB HUNT

In This Chapter . . .

The Job Market Is Chaotic

Researching Where the Jobs Are

Developing a Network of Contacts

Assessing Your Strengths

Before describing how to begin looking for a job, we want to describe the field on which you will be playing. The job market is not like an educational institution, with its typically stringent rules regulating entry. There are so many jobs and so many college graduates that people who hire often have little way of determining who are the most qualified. Looseness in the system allows you to take more initiative than you might have expected. It rewards personal initiative and the ability to persist toward your goal.

THE JOB MARKET IS CHAOTIC

Because they tend to believe that potential employers are wise and all-knowing and will "find them out," graduates fresh out of college are often quick to avoid the feared embarrassment of applying for a job in the wrong place. Those about to graduate or recently graduated may be saying to themselves:

I'm not qualified for that job; they'll laugh if I apply.

I'll blow it even if I get the job.

There are better candidates for that job.

I don't know how to break into this field.

The hiring process is a lot less scientific than you think. Scouting for athletes is, in some cases, many times more rational and systematic than job recruitment and hiring of college graduates. For one thing, the athletic variables that scouts focus on—speed, size, power—are more easily identifiable and measurable than variables that make for a productive employee. In both recruiting for college teams and drafting by professional teams, these measurable standard abilities are compared to select the best athletes available for the position. But even college and pro coaches make mistakes because they can't really measure your personal character traits and mental preparation. In the employment world at large, job interviewers are guessing at just about everything.

Unlike the pro sports drafts, hardly any research about you and your abilities or past experience is conducted. You have far more freedom in using personal initiative to make a case for yourself. And unlike sports, the best qualified are probably *not* selected for the job, strange as that may seem. Instead, the people who are best at making themselves available are often the ones who get hired.

Sounds like a terrible way to run a business, but since actual performance on the job may have a very low correlation with a person's background, employers are sometimes at a loss to predict who will turn out well and who won't. The act of hiring a college graduate to fill a job is often a wide-open process, and the following realities of the system can work to your advantage:

- Most new graduates do not have exactly the right qualifications for the job they are seeking, and it costs an employer far too much to find the ideal applicant; as a result, just being around at the right time and showing some measure of potential can be immensely important.

- Many hiring decisions are very subjective and personal; an interviewer may disregard objective criteria (absence or presence of experience, relevant course work, grades) if he or she chooses. This is because employers often unconsciously hire the applicants they like best, the ones they believe to be most motivated, and those with whom they share similar interests.

- Employees are sometimes hired on sheer potential and then taught everything they need to know about their job. In fact, some

218

employers *prefer* to provide on-the-job training so they don't have to "unteach" procedures new employees may have learned elsewhere.

• People who get hired are those who maximize their personal contact with people in places of work. This does not mean "you gotta know someone"; it means "you gotta *get to know* someone."

The hiring for technical, scientific, engineering, and many professional positions is not loose in the ways described above. For example, one cannot become an engineer, architect, doctor, lawyer, pharmacist, psychologist, minister, or biochemist without specialized training. However, in a vast number of fields, graduates are hired from a wide variety of academic backgrounds. This is largely the case in banking, retailing, radio and television, newspaper work, publishing, insurance, data processing, stock brokerage, real estate, marketing research, advertising, human services, government, politics, hotel management and tourism, and many other career areas.

The general looseness in the system of hiring that we've been describing can work to the benefit of those who understand it. The system rewards handsomely the college graduate who does not eliminate himself or herself but instead goes after a field of work with determination, and is persistent enough to be in the right place at the right time.

To arrive in the right place at the right time, an athlete must first target his or her efforts at solving three basic problems: (1) "I don't know where the jobs are or what they are about"; (2) "I don't know anyone to contact about jobs"; and (3) "I don't know what I have to offer an employer." All three problems can be handled like an unprepared opponent if you take the following initiatives in response:

1. "Where are the jobs?"   —conduct your own research
2. "I don't know anyone."   —develop a network of contacts
3. "Why would anyone hire me?"   —identify your skills and other qualifications

RESEARCHING WHERE THE JOBS ARE

Every job search begins with the task of finding where the jobs are and what they are about. "Research" refers to all those ways by which you can inform yourself of various types of occupations, employing

219

organizations, entry requirements for particular jobs, labor market conditions, and the nature of the work itself. Research sounds like it is hard and tedious work, but mostly it is enjoyable and relatively easy.

Don't worry at this point about how you will find a specific job opening. Instead, do your research for any field of work that you like. A common mistake that college graduates make in the job search is to limit their research to one or two areas of potential employment to the exclusion of all others. The next two steps in the search—establishing contacts and identifying qualifications—will be most effective if you have a wide array of options from which to choose.

You'll make progress in finding out about where the jobs are if you exercise maximum curiosity about fields of work you have never heard of before. Do not disqualify yourself before discovering what an occupation is all about. Let your personal interests be your guide, and do your research without prejudging whether you can make it in that field. Round up a long list of possibilities and then choose among them.

Research would be difficult if you had to do it alone in a painstaking manner, as you would a research paper. Fortunately, there are many sources of help available to you. Use as many of the following approaches as you possibly can:

Go to the library. Read about a field of work in whatever books you can find in the college or local library. Consult a directory that lists organizations in your field of interest and note in what geographical areas they are located. Look up a corporation to see if it has been in the news lately.

Use the career planning and placement services at your college. Often your college or university Career Planning and Placement Office will have more reference material that is relevant to your career field than the library does. You can do much research there on a field of work and find many special directories that will identify places you can apply for employment. Often this office will also have a list of alumni contacts who are willing to help you as well as information on post-graduation work internships or other types of training opportunities.

Take a course in which career research is possible. If you are wondering how you might find time to do all this research we're talking about while still in college, see if your school offers courses in which you can investigate a field of work as part of the course requirements. Such courses are frequently offered in the business, sociology, anthropology, or economics department and are usually available to upper-division students.

Attend a professional meeting. Once you have identified your target field of work, one of the best ways to obtain inside information about the nature of the field is by attending a meeting of people who are active in the profession. At professional meetings and conferences, presentations are made and information is shared informally. Admission is generally open to anyone for a registration fee, and student fees are usually lower. Regional and local meetings of a professional group may be even more useful than national meetings, in terms of information potential and the chance for personal interaction with members. Contact local branches of professional organizations in your field of interest and inquire which meetings are recommended.

Write to an organization yourself. No matter how much general information you may gather about job opportunities, at some point you are likely to find that you want to know more about particular places where you'd like to work. To do this, you can write directly to the organization—c/o its Public Information or Public Relations Office—and request that you be sent any available materials describing opportunities for college graduates. These publications are free.

Arrange information interviews on your own. Written sources will not tell you everything you'd like to know. Because much that is important about a job will not appear in print, you should supplement the above research methods by arranging informal talks with people employed in your intended field of work. In most cases, you will have to seek these informal interviews on your own; for this you will need to tap your contacts as effective sources of help.

DEVELOPING A NETWORK OF CONTACTS

Although you can obtain interviews in many ways, by far the most productive source of informal or formal job information will come from people you know, who refer you to people they know. Talking with people in person—whether they have jobs open or not—is perhaps the single most important step in the job search. By plugging into one cell of a network of contacts in any field of work, you open up your potential to meet many people because of the connections—personal, professional, or both—that exist among them. Every college student has a primary set of contacts they can tap—relatives, neighbors, faculty, friends, parents of friends—but it is your good fortune that student-athletes tend to start off with many more contacts than the average student. This is because there is a large, informal alliance of former athletes and a horde of sports fans in virtually every field of work. This alliance does not know it exists, but its members will make you feel welcome when you come knocking.

Many people who have played or followed sports feel a common bond with you and have a genuine desire to give you access to the work world—that all-important chance—that every job seeker needs. For some reason that we don't fully understand, people in this network generalize their own athletic involvement (as fan, participant, or both) to an affection for all athletes. It is as though you belong to an immense fraternity-sorority in which you hold life membership.

You may be worried that to work with contacts successfully you must have a dazzling personality. That is not true. You need only have enough social skills to meet people with some ease, even if you don't feel especially easy about it. You don't have to be highly gregarious; simply introduce yourself to an individual and then be your usual self. People even expect you to be somewhat shy or hesitant at first; this is part of any get-acquainted process. In fact, people are often turned off if you approach them like a tornado.

Questions to Ask Your Contacts

The point of developing contacts is *not* to immediately ask the person you meet for a job. Remember, this is not a job interview. The first contact should be to exchange information—you ask about the field of work, and your contact will inevitably ask information questions about you and your plans. Your information-gathering will generally be in one of the three following areas:

General nature of the work. Typical questions that you might ask include "What kind of work do you do? What kind of qualities do you look for in an employee? What are the rewards and pressures of this field?" (Every line of work has its positive and negative aspects.) Be curious about everything that a person does. As a recent (or soon-to-be) college graduate, you will be aware of only a small fraction of the jobs that exist in the marketplace. Use the information-gathering session to expand your knowledge.

Entry routes. "How might I get into this field of work? What kinds of training or experience would you recommend? How can I get an edge on the competition?" The people you talk to know their field of work from the inside. Learn from their experience.

Nature of specific jobs. "What is involved in your particular job? How does it fit with the organization? How can I work toward a job like yours?" People love to talk about themselves. Use this to your advantage. You may even find that these information-gathering sessions propel you even further into the network. It's not unusual to have the person you are talking with get on the phone and say, "I've got this guy/gal here who is interested in what you folks are doing. Why don't you two...."

Be curious. Temporarily ignore your own crying need to get a job and focus your attention squarely on your contact. Treat the meeting as if you are conducting an interview rather than trying to sell yourself. Often, if your background is suitable and you and the individual get along well, he or she may suggest to whom you might apply for a job interview. On occasion, what begins as an information exchange may even conclude as a job interview, so come prepared to talk about your capabilities and goals.

Why Work at Job Hunting If They'll Take Care of Me?

You may be translating our message so far to mean: "Good, someone will come along soon enough and find me a job." Your experience as a college athlete may have encouraged you to believe this. Let's face it. Some college athletes are pampered (although others, obviously, aren't). Coaches and other mentors may have made life easy for you, taking over some of the daily decisions in your life—where and what to eat, where and whom to room with, what to do with your time from 3 to 5 in the afternoon, etc. Your coach may have decided for you what kind of summer job to take and even have found the job for you. It's easy to get used to being taken care of and you may now be counting on coaches, fans, or others to find you a job, assuming that the loyalty they feel toward you for your athletic efforts will last forever.

Yes, a network of contacts is available to all job seekers and is potentially very large. Yes, it gives you superior access to successful people. But your contacts are not likely to find a job for you; rather, they will help you find it for yourself.

Your success in the job market may well swing on this one crucial variable—your attitude toward the network of potential helpers. If you wait for the network to produce a job for you, you will be disappointed—and out in the cold without a job. However, if you understand that people are there as vehicles for your firsthand investigation, you will reap the benefits. In short, go to them, don't wait for them to come to you.

How to Use the Network Fully

To maximize the benefits of establishing a network, use each meeting as an opportunity to practice your self-presentation skills. Because you're merely looking for information, not for a job, consider each session as a trial interview rather than the real thing.

As you repeat the information-gathering process, you will become more familiar with the questions you want to ask and more at ease in talking about yourself. Once you are accustomed to making calls, meeting people in person, and requesting additional referrals, you will discover these activities can be enjoyable. Especially if you tend to be shy, this is an excellent way to overcome your fears and move closer to an interesting career in the same stride.

How do you present yourself to people in your network? Do you just say, "Hi there, I played college hoops?" NO! If you were referred by a coach or other athletics-related person, the contact will probably already know what sport you played and will open the conversation that way. However, if he or she does not mention it, you may include this information in your introduction of yourself, but soft-pedal it from there and rapidly move on to the real focus of your meeting.

If you are not sure the person knows you have been an athlete or has any special interest in athletics, simply include the relevant information on your résumé and mention it during the general conversation in connection with job qualifications ("I learned to commit myself to a team effort in basketball and recognize that teamwork is important here in your organization"). It's OK to mention your athletic background when contacts ask you to talk about yourself, but don't try to impress them with it; let them form their own conclusions.

ASSESSING YOUR STRENGTHS

Just as the world of business is simple if you look at its core (getting a product to a consumer), so is the job hunt simple when pared to its essentials—getting yourself in touch with people who have jobs available, then offering them something they want. Analyzing what you have to offer an employer means taking stock of the unique qualities and knowledge that you have acquired in your life. To accomplish this task, review all of your capabilities and qualifications in these four categories:

Athletics. Identify the personal qualities and skills you possess as a direct result of athletics.

Academics. Review your academic program for the courses you have taken and the knowledge you have acquired that relate to your career goals.

Extracurricular activities. Consider all the nonacademic experiences

> *"We regard athletes as good candidates for highly demanding positions in industry, because they were able to fit the pressures of athletics into a busy academic schedule. Athletes are able to organize their time well, they have exceptionally high energy, and they are dedicated to accomplishing their goals. In addition, they have a lot of tenacity. We like the balance that athletes offer; they demonstrate they can handle several responsibilities at once."*
>
> —Michael Ippolito,
> Manager of Corporate Recruiting,
> International Paper Company

you have had (paid jobs, volunteer experiences, personal interests, etc.) that have given you knowledge and skills desirable in particular types of jobs.

Personal talents. Pay attention to natural talents you possess (assess whether you are a good talker, a good listener, good with numbers, good at selling, an organizer, and so on) and consider where these innate abilities can be applied.

As you review your particular strengths and unique attributes, you'll be pleased to know that athletics breeds special qualities that sports participants can use to their advantage when job hunting. Part of "selling yourself" is to recognize these assets in yourself and to talk about them as part of your total qualifications.

As we discussed in Chapter 12, competing in a college sport makes you different from most other college students in that you have already acquired work experience—as a team member—in addition to the tasks you performed as a student. In many ways, competing on a college team comes closer to mirroring the characteristics of employed life than anything else most students do during their years of higher education. When a coach says, "This player gets the job done," the reference to working life is not an accidental one. He or she means that you have trained hard, listened and learned through supervision, integrated your tasks with others (important even in individual sports), shown loyalty, and could be counted on for your ongoing participation. In short, the player has met many of the requirements of modern organizational life and has a running start on fitting into the workplace.

It is in the nature of athletics to impart the following ten qualities to team players. (Those who don't develop these qualities in the

225

course of their playing years usually end up leaving athletics, voluntarily or otherwise.) *These personal strengths are desirable in virtually all jobs, regardless of the field.* How well have you done in acquiring these qualities? How strong are you in each of them? Ask yourself these questions as you review the list.

Time management. Athletes are often outstanding in apportioning their time, because they must balance a full-time academic work load, full-time commitment to athletics, travel to other schools for games, time-out for fatigue, and possibly part-time employment or other off-campus commitments. Take a close look at the different activities you have juggled during college, and appreciate the time management skills you have developed as a result.

Teamwork. Through athletic team membership, most athletes become intimately familiar with the experience of working toward group goals. Working with a coach is a lot like working with a department manager. The dynamics of team play teaches the athlete what it means to be a role player—that it is sometimes necessary to submerge one's ego and personal goals into the goals of the organization, and that leadership is the ability to get people to work as a team.

Goal-directedness. Athletes cultivate the ability to concentrate their energies and attention over an extended period of time and to block out distractions while they proceed toward their goal. Every athlete knows that this directedness is the key to all accomplishment.

Competitiveness. The competitive spirit is the lifeblood of the athletic experience, and most athletes thrive on it. They gain experience in the rigors of winning and losing, and they relish the opportunity to fight more battles, test their abilities, and risk their self-esteem against tough opposition. This translates into a strong asset in most jobs.

Confidence. Athletes are continually in situations where they must "pump themselves up" and believe in their own powers to produce effectively under pressure. The ability to approach tough performance situations with the belief that you'll do well is crucial. Practice in maintaining self-confidence, especially under tense circumstances, can carry over to the readiness to take on stiff on-the-job challenges.

Persistence/endurance. Athletics is often characterized by long and hard work toward distant rewards and the ability to wring a maximum effort from yourself whenever necessary. This may include playing while in pain or, in general, performing under adverse circumstances. Athletics teaches intensity of effort and the belief that sufficient preparation and determination will eventually pay off.

Loyalty. Closely related to teamwork, this quality emerges from the bond that an individual athlete builds with his or her team and is expressed in the willingness to support team efforts under any circumstances. Loyalty contributes heavily to the morale of a team or work group, because it enables each team member to trust that others will work toward the same ends.

Discipline. This is a hallmark of the athletic experience. Organizing one's time, adhering to guidelines, exacting maximum effort on a regular basis, concentrating one's energies, and screening out competing priorities are all necessary for competence in athletics. The systematic application of one's energies toward a desired goal is highly valued in any work situation, especially in those that require independent effort.

Taking criticism. Athletes are accustomed to taking criticism, because their performance on the field is watched closely and any weak points seldom escape comment. Coaches recommend changes and force athletes to cope with the feeling that "I could've done it better." Athletes typically develop into good listeners when constructive criticism is offered, because they recognize its value in helping them advance toward overall goals.

Dealing with setbacks. Sports offer continued opportunities to test oneself, succeed or fail, and then come back for more. No one who competes in a sport can avoid the experience of failure, sooner or later. Athletes learn, by necessity, to face failure and bury any negative feelings as much and as soon as possible, because tomorrow's contest will require their full attention. Among the most valuable lessons of athletics are how to win, how to lose, and how to rebound after either.

We don't expect that all college athletes will have developed in great abundance all ten of the qualities we have noted. Many athletes will look at these descriptions of qualities and say: "That's not me." We would be surprised if you did not disclaim more than one of them for yourself. Nonetheless, it is likely that you have more of these qualities than most nonathletes do, and we believe you should appreciate them in yourself, the better to use them to your advantage.

Expressing Your Strengths as Skills

Employers will look at your qualifications in two ways: (1) Do you have any training or formal preparation for the job? and (2) Can you perform the tasks required by the job?

The first consideration is largely a matter of record and includes the courses you have taken, the jobs you have had, and similar evidence.

227

The second consideration is based on the skills and other capabilities you possess to perform the functions of the job you want. Why are skills particularly important? For two reasons: (a) applicants who have the appropriate formal training or preparation may not always have the skills necessary to do the job; and (b) employers generally will consider applicants who can demonstrate they possess the skills needed for a particular job regardless of the level of their formal training for it.

Every job requires two kinds of skills: job-specific skills—those that one trains for or learns on the job, and functional skills—generic skills that cut across many different jobs. The difference between the two types of skills can be illustrated in an occupational example. A radio announcer must possess the job-specific skills necessary to operate the dials at the station, but he or she must also be able to speak well, manage time carefully, and relate easily to the public. Unlike job-specific skills, functional skills transcend job titles and are applicable to a wide variety of occupations.

A Dozen of the Most Marketable Skills

The functional skills listed below are needed in a broad array of jobs across many industries and professions. In reviewing the list, consider how many of these skills you possess:

Writing: communicating clearly and persuasively in written reports, letters, and other verbal formats.

Public speaking: delivering talks, fielding questions, speaking extemporaneously, and participating in public forums with relative ease.

Supervising: overseeing the work performance of others by observing their work firsthand, making recommendations for improvements, clarifying performance goals, resolving problems, and rendering disciplinary actions when necessary.

Organizing people: coordinating projects or programs involving the efforts of others so that people work effectively together.

Organizing data: putting together quantitative and other information logically and effectively.

Research: using printed and other resources to investigate and gather information on particular topics in coherent form.

Quantitative skills: using and understanding numerical methods needed to analyze problems and suggest solutions.

Computer skills: comprehending and contributing to the design of logical systems of information flow, including a knowledge of hardware and/or an ability to write or understand software programs.

Persuading: using spoken communication, words, or media to influence the opinions and attitudes of others.

Managing: developing policies toward organizational objectives and allocating tasks to individuals so that these objectives can be accomplished.

Teaching: explaining and helping individuals or groups of people to understand concepts, procedures, and other kinds of information.

Imagination: developing and using creative, innovative approaches to the solution of problems.

Other important functional skills include planning, negotiating, relating to the public, handling detail, resolving conflicts, interviewing, counseling, selling, and delegating responsibility.

The Importance of Communication Skills

On the above list of highly potent skills in all job markets, writing and speaking stand out. Although only a small number of college graduates will take jobs as writers or be in positions that require frequent public speaking, basic competency in both writing and speaking is crucial to job success virtually across the board. If you cannot write a decent letter or cannot communicate effectively in an interview, you are likely to be eliminated from consideration for most jobs.

Communication skills are not given at birth; they are acquired. You can improve your writing and speaking skills by using them. If your friends often cannot understand you when you talk, get tutoring help. If you know you are a poor writer, take courses that require term papers (this is the most useful suffering you may ever have in school) and write letters to your friends—in short, do whatever it takes to cultivate better writing habits.

No matter how much technical knowledge you may have acquired in a particular job area, your advancement potential will depend heavily upon your ability to communicate in both your writing and your speech. Successful executives know their subject matter and can talk or write about it to anyone.

> *"If I could choose one degree for the people I hire, it would be English. I want people who can read and speak in the language we're dealing with. You can teach a group of Cub Scouts to do portfolio analysis."*
>
> —A senior vice-president of the
> First Atlanta Corporation
> ["The Money Chase," *Time*, May 4, 1981.]

Your Skills Scorecard

In any given field of work, the success of your job search may depend upon your ability to clarify your skills with respect to the particular job you are seeking. You'll state your qualifications in the résumé and cover letters you send to prospective employers. Later you'll talk about these same qualifications in job interviews. When an interviewer asks: "Why should we hire you?", you should be prepared to answer in terms of both your track record of accomplishments (your academic background and work experiences) and your skills. If your record of accomplishments is equal to that of others, skills are likely to make the difference in who gets hired.

Develop the habit of interpreting your experiences in terms of skills. By doing so, you'll be able to assess your potential for any job. The best way to convince yourself and others that you possess a particular skill is to name it and tell how you acquired it.

Example: I am good at supervising people.

I developed this skill in my job as a ranch foreman during the summers, and as cocaptain of my school's basketball team.

The following two examples, which we have called Skills Scorecards, illustrate a simple approach athletes can use to review their academic and nonacademic experiences and identify the skills they have acquired. This information can then be used to support your particular employment goals, both in discussions with interviewers and in the written materials (the résumé and cover letters) you send in your job search.

In constructing your own Skills Scorecard, you'll see that as a student-athlete you have developed certain skills in sports and others in nonathletic activities. All of these skills contribute to your overall career potential. Sports participation gives you a head start on certain skills but cannot provide the basis for all the skills you'll need for

Skills Scorecard No. 1

PLAY #1

List all your experiences on and off the field.
Sport: football
Off-field athletic activity: coaching at special education center
Academic major: history
Campus activity: fraternity officer
Off-season jobs: volunteer in political campaign, camp counselor

PLAY #2

Analyze each experience in terms of skills acquired.
determination, teamwork, self-discipline . . . . football
motivating group to action . . . football, coaching, fraternity, counselor
attention to detail . . . . .coaching, political campaign
teaching, developing patience. . . . . coaching, counselor
writing . . . . .history major
research, organizing data. . . . . .history major, political campaign
running meetings, mediating conflicts . . . . fraternity
polling and analyzing results . . . . political campaign

PLAY #3

What possible careers have you considered?
public relations
political aide
public interest group coordinator
paralegal

PLAY #4

Evaluate how the skills you have identified can be used in a given career.
public relations: writing, organizing data, research
political aide: teamwork, research, organizing data, writing, mediating
   conflicts, planning events, motivating group to action, attention to
   detail, polling and analyzing results
public interest group coordinator: research, organizing data, writing,
   determination, teamwork, running meetings, mediating conflicts,
   motivating group to action, teaching, attention to detail, polling and
   analyzing results
paralegal: research, organizing data, writing, attention to detail

231

Skills Scorecard No. 2

PLAY #1

List all your experiences on and off the field.
Sports: track, swimming
Off-field athletic activity: Players' Committee
Academic major: English
Campus activities: sports reporter for campus newspaper, sports
  commentator for campus radio station
Off-season jobs: helped set up community joggers club, summer lifeguard

PLAY #2

Analyze each experience in terms of skills acquired.
self-discipline, self-motivation . . . . .track, swimming
time budgeting . . . . track, swimming, radio commentator
concentration . . . . .track, swimming, radio commentator, lifeguard
perseverance . . . . track, swimming, Players' Committee, reporter
negotiating ability, problem solving. . . . . .Players' Committee
public speaking . . . . .Players' Committee, radio commentator
organizing . . . . .Players' Committee, setting up joggers club
writing, analytical ability . . . . English major, reporter
interviewing . . . . reporter, radio commentator

PLAY #3

What possible careers have you considered?
journalism
radio or TV commentator
advertising

PLAY #4

Evaluate how the skills you have identified can be used in a given career.
journalism: self-discipline, self-motivation, time budgeting, perseverance,
  writing, analytical ability, interviewing
radio or TV commentator: time budgeting, concentration, public speaking, writing, analytical ability, interviewing
advertising: concentration, perseverance, problem solving, organizing

your intended career. Therefore, it pays to examine the whole range of your activities, as shown in the preceding examples. Very often, even if the career you're interested in seems far removed from your background, you'll be able to identify skills in your athletic and non-athletic experiences that will support your career goal and make you a viable candidate for jobs in that field.

PROFILE OF AN ATHLETE

Jack Collins

Jack Collins is one of thousands who have tasted success in college football but who quickly discover that there is little chance of a professional career in their future. Halfback on the state championship team during high school and star offensive back for the University of Texas from 1958 until 1962, Collins had one year of professional football with the Pittsburgh Steelers and then found himself on the Dallas Cowboys taxi squad. At that point he realized he had to think of something else to do besides football.

Today Jack Collins is president of the First City Bank in Austin, Texas, a growing bank in one of the fastest-growing cities in the country. How did he prepare for such a career? Collins looks back on his years of observing Darrell Royal, one of the most successful college football coaches of all time: "I noticed how Coach Royal was a master at organizing everything, and particularly at placing people in the right roles, getting the most out of everyone. I think that I have remembered a lot of those lessons in my work as a manager and executive with the bank."

So, while Darrell Royal was putting together one of the premium organizations in collegiate sports, young Jack Collins was watching. He took his first job with Republic Bank in Dallas, worked there for ten years, and then was hired by First City Bank in Austin as a senior vice-president ten years ago. "I learned from Coach Royal the importance of letting staff do their job, whether defensive line coach or head of the loan department," Collins recalls.

Collins also cites time management and discipline as qualities that college athletes acquire which help them in their careers. Remembering his own experience, he notes, "We could not cut *any* classes without a legitimate excuse. One Wednesday morning at 6 AM I found myself running steps at the stadium because I had missed a class. I learned to take discipline, manage my time, and become a disciplinarian myself. Nowadays, when a guy comes late to our staff meetings at the bank, I feel it's important to let him know it . . . in front of everyone else."

When Collins talks about his and the bank's goals for the future, the sports metaphors fly: "We have a team goal for the bank, to become the largest bank in Austin. In order to reach this goal, we have to have a game plan, and we need the right type of people to work that plan."

Clearly, Collins relishes the competitive atmosphere that exists among banks in the area and feels comfortable in building game plans that will gain an edge on the opposition.

234

15

STRATEGIES FOR

WINNING THE JOB

YOU WANT

In This Chapter...

Rules of the Game

Key Elements in Your Career Game Plan

How You Will Know When You Are Winning

The topics discussed in the last two chapters—identifying your goals, researching jobs, making contacts, and assessing your strengths—are essential steps in the job search. However, these steps are only preparation for the game. The game itself is winning the job. This game has its own rules, which have little to do with how well you can do the job but rather with how well you can *convince the employer* that you can do the job.

While being an athlete will get you a closer look from many employers than others might receive, you cannot be careless or sloppy in how you prepare yourself for the job search. Interviewers are very keen at spotting applicants who look and act motivated and well prepared; they are even quicker to eliminate those who are not. To be as professional as possible, it is necessary to follow certain codes of behavior that are standard, accepted practices in job seeking. We shall call these the Rules of the Game and present them in five areas of the job-winning game: (1) making the initial contact, (2) dress, (3) preparing for the interview, (4) the interview, and (5) using your résumé and cover letter.

RULES OF THE GAME

1. Making the Initial Contact

(a) Call whoever in an organization is responsible for the department you'd like to work in and ask for an interview. State the specific position you desire. Be organized. Through research you should have discovered whom to call and the particular jobs he or she is responsible for.

(b) Be prepared to recount your qualifications for the job if you are asked on the phone.

(c) If the secretary of the department head refers you to the Personnel Department, call there for an interview, but ask if you may speak to the department head as well. If he or she refuses, do not persist in your request.

(d) You may precede your call by sending your résumé and a cover letter, but that is not required. Do not depend upon a résumé and letter to stimulate an employer to invite you for an interview.

(e) Precede any request for an interview with the name of the person who referred you (if any): " _____ recommended that I call you."

(f) If the organization's hiring officials cannot grant you an interview, ask where they would recommend that you apply. State your qualifications, so they can make an appropriate referral.

(g) Walk in. If other approaches frustrate you, use the most direct method of all. Go to employers without an appointment. This is sometimes inefficient, because you may get turned away or be asked to return at another time. It may work better in small organizations, where hiring procedures are often less formal. Dress appropriately wherever you go. Take an entire day's time. With persistence and some advance research, you should be able to get at least three walk-in interviews in a day.

2. Dressing Correctly

Remember that any in-person contact, no matter how informal, requires that you dress suitably. It conveys your seriousness of purpose about the work that you are seeking. In order to have your appearance count in your favor, know in advance how the people dress in your target organization, and be sure you are appropriately dressed for the position you are applying for. Be conservative but not dull. Good dress does not call attention to itself. What shows is neatness, fit with the environment of the place of work, and tastefulness. Flashiness in colors, fabric designs, jewelry, or clothing styles is out of place and distracting. If you fit in comfortably with the way people dress at your potential workplace and can match their standards easily, that will make a positive statement about your suitability for the job.

3. Preparing for the Interview

(a) Perhaps the most common job-hunting error made by college graduates is failing to prepare for job interviews. Interviewers expect you to be interested in them and well versed in their organization. You must demonstrate your knowledgeability by reading their literature closely and also by learning about how recent developments in the outside world have affected their field (check the newspaper and magazine guides in the library).

(b) Be sure you can talk about yourself clearly and concisely in terms of both your qualifications and your interest in the job and in the organization. Be fully prepared to answer why you want this particular job and believe you can do well in it.

(c) Have available a portfolio of any materials that are relevant to your past experiences. This should include a copy of your résumé and might also include brochures of programs you have organized, papers you have written relevant to the job, reference letters, job descriptions of positions you have held, and any other evidence to support your belief that you have the skills and knowledge required for the job.

4. Interviewing

(a) Be early and alert for any interview, formal or informal. Take some time to look around the workplace, if you can do so without prying.

(b) Answer questions concisely but with enough detail to be clear and accurate.

(c) Ask questions about the nature of the work, the growth potential in the position, expectations of your performance, and other questions that show you are evaluating the job as well as being evaluated.

THE ATHLETE'S GAME PLAN FOR COLLEGE AND CAREER

(d) Listen carefully to the interviewer's questions and statements, and ask for clarification whenever necessary.

(e) Don't be stiff in your behavior. Professionalism means being well organized and motivated but not artificial in your manner.

(f) Ask if you may meet with others whose work is related to the job for which you are applying.

(g) Be sure to tell the interviewer what you want him or her to know about you and your qualifications and why you believe you are a good candidate for the job, even if you are not asked directly. *This is your main agenda.*

5. Using Your Résumé and Cover Letter

Some experts believe the résumé is used primarily to eliminate candidates and should therefore not be shown until an applicant has had a chance to state his or her own case in person. However, you may be requested to submit one in advance in order to be considered at all, in which case you have no choice.

(a) Seek advice regarding the layout, content, and printing of your résumé from your college's career development or placement office before you commit yourself to its final form.

(b) Have your résumé professionally typeset or prepared on a word processor, if possible.

(c) Always have your cover letter typed as an original, not typeset or copied.

(d) Make sure that both résumé and cover letter are well written and that the grammar and spelling are correct. Poor writing is a favorite target for immediate elimination from consideration.

(e) A cover letter should always accompany a résumé that is mailed, or a letter alone can be used. Whether you send a letter or both items, be sure they are addressed to an individual by name and title. If you do not know the person's title, you may write to him or her by name, but never write to a title without a name, because this suggests you were too lazy to do the proper research.

(f) Always follow up a letter and/or résumé with a phone call, in which you request an interview.

(g) Always have a résumé available during an interview, even if you sent one in advance. It is best to have several copies available.

In the following example of a résumé and cover letter, note that Randall Athlete is a good candidate for a sales position at XYZ Corporation because of his competitiveness, sales experience, and demonstrated productivity. The jobs, activities, and experiences on his résumé support these qualities that are crucial to success in sales and marketing work. It is important that he include the skills section in his résumé, so that employers will see at a glance why he considers himself to be a good candidate. (See pages 240 and 241.)

Randall's cover letter, which will accompany the résumé he sends to his prospective employer, allows Randall to state in his own words that he believes his experiences have prepared him to do the job, even though he didn't major in business while in college. His letter is straightforward and confident, reaffirming the skills highlighted in his résumé.

While not all student-athletes will have skills and experiences as well-aligned with the job desired as Randall, it is important that you use your cover letter and résumé to state why you believe you can do the job you're applying for. In the process, be sure to refer to whatever skills you believe are relevant.

Student-athletes must hustle in the labor market like anyone else. The Rules of the Game above require hard work and attention to detail, but they offer you the maximum chance for success in job hunting. If you are as thoroughgoing and professional as possible in your approach, your efforts—and the advantages you have as an athlete—will pay off. Many employers like and respect collegiate athletes and believe that they are very capable and motivated people to hire. However, they know that not all athletes are equally good bets. Thus, you must demonstrate your worth as a potential employee by conducting your job search with the same measure of discipline and perseverance that you used to manage your athletic and nonathletic activities during college.

KEY ELEMENTS IN YOUR CAREER GAME PLAN

Although many of the steps needed for a successful job search campaign are essentially similar for anyone who is looking for a job, no two campaigns are ever the same, and each may differ greatly. Job seekers are all unique in what they want from careers and what they bring to the job marketplace. In the course of your job search, things are likely to happen that you do not expect, or you may approach the labor market in unconventional ways. There is always room for you to adjust to changing conditions and freedom for you to "call certain plays" that fit your style of looking for work.

SAMPLE RÉSUMÉ

RANDALL ATHLETE

Campus Address
University of Texas
Kinsolving Hall – 134
Austin, TX 78700
512-471-1819

Permanent Address
36 Willow Street
Dallas, TX 75200
214-234-7710

Job Objective: Sales and marketing position for a consumer goods organization

SKILLS RELEVANT TO JOB OBJECTIVE

Selling: In my summer jobs and fund-raising job on campus, I have developed my ability to sell products and ideas effectively to a wide variety of clients.

Competitiveness: My four years as member of the varsity tennis team have sharpened my natural competitiveness and motivated me to seek a position in a competitive business atmosphere.

Productivity: In four years of meeting the demands of academic and athletic schedules, concurrent with raising money and being an officer for my fraternity, I have learned how to perform at maximum capacity despite many pressures. In particular, I have learned how to manage time effectively, to deal with conflict, and to persuade and supervise others.

EXPERIENCE

Summer 1983 *Salesman, Star Hotel Corporation* —sold travel packages to companies in the Dallas area

Summer 1981–82 *Assistant Manager, John Doe Company* —managed farm equipment sales to local customers

1980–83 *Fund-raising Chairman, Alpha Beta Fraternity* —sold advertisements for fraternity yearbook; raised $10,000 in funds during a single year

CAMPUS ACTIVITIES

1980–83 Men's Varsity Tennis Team

1981–83 Vice-President, Alpha Beta Fraternity

EDUCATION
University of Texas at Austin
Bachelor of Arts, 1984
Major – History

Courses relevant to job objective

Business administration	Introduction to computer science
Marketing management	History of the corporation
Labor economics	International economics

REFERENCES Available upon request

SAMPLE COVER LETTER

May 1, 1984

Mr. James H. Johnson
Executive Vice President
XYZ Corporation
Chicago, IL 60611

Dear Mr. Johnson:

During the past month, I've had the opportunity to read a great deal about your company. I was particularly impressed with the sales growth you have achieved and with the new products you have brought to market.

I am writing this letter to you because I am interested in working for a company like XYZ. In particular, a position with your sales organization would be extremely challenging and an important step forward from my previous experience.

Most recently, I sold travel packages to corporations that use these tours to improve their business prospects. In making these sales, I had to be highly competitive, work under considerable pressure, and show confidence in my product.

Both in the travel sales job and in my previous work selling farm equipment for John Doe Company, I dealt effectively with my customers and produced results that were praised by my superiors. I enjoy selling and want to continue in this line of work, because the challenge of selling a good product appeals to me.

I feel my personal qualities of determination and resourcefulness enable me to perform well in sales and marketing work. During college I handled the responsibility of varsity tennis, part-time jobs, and a difficult course of study. I work harder than others do because I am ambitious and goal-oriented. In particular, intercollegiate athletic competition taught me how to deal successfully with pressure and challenging situations, and how to direct myself toward tangible and worthwhile goals.

I will call next week to arrange an appointment with you, so that we may discuss job opportunities with your organization. Thank you for your time and consideration.

Sincerely,

Randall Athlete

Randall Athlete

Nevertheless, every game plan for finding a job needs certain key elements—objectives, strategies for reaching them, contingency plans, tactics to be employed against likely obstacles, and so on. These are the elements you must use in order to advance in your job campaign. If you apply these faithfully, your chance of achieving success on your own terms is high.

Unlike sports contests, more than half of the contestants can win in the job market. A lot of people lose simply because they are aimless and passive. The following principles call for *initiative*, which you must have if you're going to put a career game plan into action. We've used football as a metaphor for the game plan we present here, but we're sure you can translate the ideas into the terminology of your own sport. You are going to become your own coach, so get out the Xs and Os and you're on your way.

Know Where the Goal Line Is

Imagine being in a distance run, not knowing where you are going, how much time has elapsed, or how far you have gone. What's more, the coach won't tell you when you'll get to stop. That's what working without a goal is like. Energy is always best used for a purpose. What do you want to accomplish in your life? What would you regard as a worthy objective? The more concretely you can state: "*This* is what I am aiming for," the better your entire game plan will be. Determination, persistence, drive,—all those catchwords of the motivated soul—derive from that athletic attribute of goal-directedness.

Name your goals as concretely as possible:

"I want to run a successful small business."

"I want to become a lawyer representing professional athletes."

"I intend to make $100,000 a year in the financial world."

"I want to be a successful coach for a small college."

"I hope to become a radio announcer for a big city station."

"I want to win statewide election to public office."

"I want to be a top software programmer for a leading computer company."

"I want to be a researcher developing an alternative to the internal combustion engine."

Successful career planning is the well-dressed equivalent of "taking it to the hoop." Decide what you want to do and concentrate your energies, thoughts, and movements toward that end. Even if you don't get the ball in the basket, you gamble that something else good will develop. No successful job seeker can ever predict what is going to happen. Your future will flow as much from the calculated risks you are willing to take as from the specific plans you are making. (The plans are important for the element of calculation they require; the plans are *not* intended to be tracks down which you must roll once you begin.)

Goals can be short-term and intermediate, as well:

"I want to complete my college degree."

"I want to move out of the New England area."

"I need to get out of debt before anything else."

Having one or more specific goals is absolutely essential, because they mobilize your energies, organize and direct your efforts, and give you ways to measure your progress. Just as "holding their offense to less than 150 yards," or "getting 70 percent of my first serves in," or "swimming the 200-meter breaststroke 5 seconds faster than last year" can focus your efforts, so must you have a particular job, a career goal, a rate of progress, a visible achievement, and other objectives in mind when you approach your work. A goal keeps all the cylinders in your engine functioning.

Assemble Your Arsenal

What specific weapons do you bring to the career game that will make you competitive? You may see this as a problem since, away from sports, you're not at all sure what you can offer that is marketable.

As we stressed in Chapter 14, don't be concerned at first about what the job market wants (most people believe themselves to be less qualified for jobs than they really are); just look at what you know about yourself first. Don't be looking for championship qualities or items of perfection, or ways in which you are better than everyone else. What do you do fairly *well* and wish you could do better? The job market is forgiving; it allows you to grow and improve. Look at *everything* you know about yourself. Make a list of your attributes that you regard as positive, regardless of how remote they may seem for what you imagine to be the work setting.

Example: good with my hands

          I have a lot of endurance

I laugh easily

good with children

loyal to others

fussy about getting details correct

Ask your friends to add qualities to this list, because they will know aspects of talents you possess that you either deny through modesty or are completely unaware of because they come naturally to you. This latter tactic is crucial, because the tendency to downgrade yourself or overlook important qualities is common. People think if they say they are good at something, someone will come along and make them prove it. This is not a contest, but an inventory of yourself. Be generous enough to give yourself the benefit of the doubt.

Some or all of the qualities you possess will be valued or even prized in many different careers or occupations. If you know what these qualities are and can talk easily about them, you'll have the best chance to apply your assets to what an employer might need.

Become aware of the skills and attributes you possess that will serve your stated goals. Want to be a financial wizard and you are good with numbers? That's a good start. Are there other skills you need for a particular career but do not have? (This is where talking to people who already work in that area comes in handy.) You can work toward acquiring many skills in which you might be weak. The job market encourages personal development and growth. You want to be in journalism but need help with your writing style? You hope to be a teacher but don't speak very well in front of groups? Writing and speaking skills can be *acquired* through additional study and experience; build these skills to serve your career goals. Move forward armed with skills you possess and the determination to build those you don't have.

Scout the Opposition

You are not only the coach of your game plan, you are also the scouting staff. Just as an athletic team feasts on good information about the opposition, so a well-developed career feeds off informed "intelligence gathering." Your game plan will wallow in uncertainty if you have little real knowledge about the fields of work you contemplate or fail to discover the many kinds of work suited to you and your skills. If you want to get into the film industry, get to know a good deal more about it than the bus schedule to Hollywood. Make it your business to find out about the many kinds of films that are made and the many

244

organizations that make them (such as corporations, governmental agencies, and service organizations). *Then* go out to Hollywood with some professional exposure to sell instead of just your dreams.

In career counseling terms, scouting is called job research. This research yields three basic kinds of information about a prospective job:

a) What is the nature of the work in this general category?

b) What kinds of settings do these people work in: the physical arrangements, work relationships, etc.?

c) Who are the personalities in this organization who do the work and with whom you might be working?

Answers to the first two questions can be found in printed materials; specific knowledge of the personalities can only be obtained by personal visits.

You will need research for two compelling reasons: (1) to make the best possible choice among the available alternatives; and (2) to demonstrate your motivation to an employer and therefore have a better chance of being hired.

Your game plan will surely fail without effective research. Interviewers are not impressed by unprepared job candidates. Furthermore, if you are guessing about the fields of work you are applying for, you will doubtless make a bad choice, and have to undo your decision later.

Scouting calls for using your informal network to its fullest so that you know which of your talents are most needed "out there" and where the positions are that will fit you best. Games are won by the best prepared, and jobs are no different.

Throw Long on First Down

A game plan is incomplete without a trick up your sleeve or a special play that exceeds normal caution. Take a goal of yours that others may label as unrealistic and try it anyway. Act boldly. If you see a career possibility that seems to be a long shot but that still appeals to you, find out how others got there, and then push in that direction. What is the worst that might happen to you? You are not likely to get trampled by a herd of wild buffalo or have a building fall on you for aiming at a long-shot job. Whatever the consequence of failing might be, the regret that you never tried for something you really wanted would be far worse. Besides, you can learn a lot for future tries.

Trying to become a professional athlete is one of those bold gambles. In Chapter 2, we presented figures showing how slim would be your chances of success in professional sports. This was to provide you with

245

important information, not necessarily to discourage you. If you decide to give it a shot, do so with your eyes wide open, with a termination point in mind in case things don't go as you hoped, and with a new direction to take immediately.

Just as every sports fan likes the attempted steal of home, so do those in the job market admire the guts and daring of people who set distant goals. A million bucks, a Ph.D., a screen test, a pilot's license, a business of your own, becoming manager of a skydiving club? Why not try it? The sooner you test yourself against something big, the more you will know about where your game is headed next and which abilities need more work. Even if you fail, you will wind up with an interesting experience and the satisfaction of having tried. Most important, you will gain a sharper definition of what you *really* want.

Take What the Defense Gives You

Some of those "throwing long on first down" plays will not work out as you had hoped. You don't get hired in the major corporation, the deal for a business partnership falls through, or you don't make it as a writer with a prominent magazine. What should you do when the results come in? Don't let your dreams die forever, but decide what you are going to do in the meantime. Put the dream on the shelf and adjust yourself to market realities. Even in professional sports, you may get a second chance. The difference is that in professional sports, a second chance can only come in a very few years, while your body is still young; in most other fields, your second chance for "stardom" may come a decade or more down the road.

If you miss a big opportunity, often it is not your abilities that failed. You have talent for the goals that you seek, but the market closes you off. There is too much competition for the role you want most, the product you hitch yourself to doesn't sell as well as hoped, or the market is not ready for what you have to offer. Try again later. Public preferences and needs change, *you* change, your product improves.

You must obey market pressures, even if they force you into a less thrilling line of work. In football, if the opposition denies the pass, you have to run. But in career development, if you miss an opportunity in one field or organization, there is usually something similar nearby. You may have wanted to sell stocks and bonds, but brokerage houses weren't interested. Seek out jobs in other financial institutions, such as banks or insurance companies. If you wanted to open a restaurant but it didn't work, try another small business where prospects are better. Remember, it's all right to make a mistake. Like fumbles, errors, and turnovers, they are part of the game.

246

Adjust your goals to market conditions, and try to choose something that enables you to build toward a more desirable long-range goal. If you hope to be a child psychologist one day, but cannot get into graduate school right now, then take a job that will give you experience and so improve your chances of being accepted later. Just as there are several paths to the goal line, there are many different routes to a career goal. If you make no progress at one juncture, simply look for an alternative route.

Spot the Secondary Receivers

Throwing long on first down won't often yield a touchdown. By the same token, you will probably not find your ideal long-shot career wide open to you. Taking those little gains that the defense (the job market) gives you will serve your short-run needs but won't satisfy—and shouldn't satisfy—indefinitely. What you need is a secondary mode of attack to achieve your long-range goals.

Successful game plans, like passing attacks, flow from a many-sided probing of the opposition. Understanding that many fields of work are potentially open to you is a key to your eventual success. Knowing that you have multiple possibilities helps to lower the general anxiety associated with job hunting; having alternatives seems to be a great confidence-builder.

How do you mount a multiple attack?

1. Investigate—scout many fields of work and assume there's a way into each of them for you unless and until you are *convinced* otherwise.
2. Identify key skills you possess that cut across occupational boundaries.
3. If you are closed out of one field of work, consider the entire cluster of related occupations.

Example: If you want to be in advertising, but it's too competitive at the start, try public relations, marketing research, audiovisual work, media research, and other fields directly relevant to the advertising industry.

Having multiple targets is very practical, because it means that you are seldom stuck for new ideas. The broader the areas in which you can imagine your skills being used, the more powerful your attack.

Example: If you like teaching, but a teaching job isn't available, take some of the personal attributes that led you to like teaching (enjoying interpersonal contact, being a leader, having a sense of command, being outgoing) and apply them to counseling, sales, personnel work, lobbying in government, etc.

Teachers may not always be in great demand, but the skills that go into teaching are always in demand.

Have a Secret Weapon

Let's say you've done enough scouting to have several career alternatives, you are expanding your network of good contacts, and people are showing some interest in you. You'll still have to get someone to say Yes. Because the informal network is effective and you are determined to show your numerous skills and personal qualities, you may be close to getting hired. But, you still have to close the deal. How do you make it happen?

Remember, you don't have to be the *best* candidate, because many capable people will not show enough initiative to make it to the final stage, the interview. But, when you make it that far, you still need a clincher. Let's say you want a job in a local recreation department. Did you have any relevant past experience in other recreation departments? Can you offer them something else besides your knowledge and experience in your competitive sport? Other sports? Nonsports activities, such as playing an instrument, leading square dancing? Arts and crafts? A special skill with elderly people? These extra abilities are attributes which can make you especially attractive and move you ahead of others looking for that job. It certainly helps, also, to get someone prominent to call or write you a letter of recommendation. You might even do an informal survey on your own of what nearby recreation programs have and what they seem to need. Bring the information to the person who will be deciding on who gets the job. This approach is a little gutsy, but it is likely to impress those who are hiring.

They already like you because you've taken the trouble to find them. You're probably being compared with the ten people who sent their résumés yesterday but did not have the foresight to make a personal visit. You're there and they aren't. Your informal survey of recreation departments in the area can convince them that you have exceptional motivation and are better informed about this field than other job candidates. Why should they look any further than you?

With a little effort, everyone can develop a secret weapon, something that others do not have, and emphasize it as the reason they can do more for an employer than someone else. Secret weapons come in all sizes and shapes. Yours may simply be a determination to get hired, or your cleverness in getting in to see the right person, or your ability to see potential in a job where no one else does. The ultimate secret weapon is to avoid thinking of yourself as being just like the other job candidates. Know that you are different. Know why *you* would hire *you* if you were making the final decision. In fact, that may just be one of the key questions in that final interview: "Why should we hire you above the other candidates?" *Know the answer,* and be ready to project that answer to your interviewer firmly and calmly.

The Two-Minute Drill

A two-minute drill in football practice teaches a team to be its most coordinated and to use its best plays under time pressure and with little direction from the bench. Similarly, you must be ready to perform as a job candidate at any moment. Looking for work is an unpredictable, disorderly process. You may run across a career possibility when you least expect it. You may meet a person on a train, or have dinner with a friend's mother, and discover that either of these people offers you an opportunity.

Unlike football, your two-minute drill may come unexpectedly, not just late in the game. The most unpredictable aspect of your job search is when an information session or casual encounter turns into an impromptu job interview—and you are suddenly on the spot. You cannot prepare the night before; you must be ready when a person asks:

Why do you like this field?

What makes you think you'll succeed in this line of work?

What experiences, in or out of college, best prepared you for this work?

What is it about yourself that we would like and could use?

Everyone you meet may be the person who can open the door that you want and need. Every conversation, however informal or casually it may have happened, is a potential job interview. The best way to handle the two-minute-drill scenario is to practice—talk with enough people about yourself, your aspirations, your ideas, and your abilities, that it becomes second nature. Job interviews become like ordinary, informal conversations when you have been through them enough times. Just as football teams execute well in the last two minutes when they have practiced the sequence of plays and are accustomed to the pressure, so will you do well in your "two minutes" when you have been there many times before.

HOW YOU WILL KNOW WHEN YOU ARE WINNING

What is your definition of "success" for yourself? All members of a team agree that winning the game is their immediate goal, but a win in the career arena varies according to what you regard as most important. What is so important to you that a career must provide it? What would make you choose one job over another? Money, independence, security, work environment, subject matter, social status, opportunity for achievement, creativity, advancement—all of these matter and more, but for a particular person, one or two motives will predominate. What is most important *to you*?

Winning outside of sports is seldom measurable by numbers, except with respect to money. You will recognize your career victories by an overall feeling that "This is where I want to be, I feel most like myself, and am motivated to keep doing more of what I am doing." But, such satisfaction is not automatic. It comes only when you know what motivates you, what you want from a job.

A job is just a job, a way to earn money. But a career is an expression of yourself. A job is a career only if it drives you from inside, as your sport did (or still does). What do you think will push you to do your best? Money? Fame? Contact with people? Achievement or creative expression? Responsibility for others? Challenging the marketplace? Name your own!

Career counselors call these "work values." If you are foggy about your values, you will make poor choices of work. Most people agree they want certain things in their work—security, stimulation, enjoyable people to work with—but which of these is crucial when you have to decide among alternatives? Which values are you willing to sacrifice in favor of others? Will you surrender some security in exchange for a financial challenge? Will you sacrifice a pleasurable life-style in order to have more achievement possibilities (e.g., taking a high-powered job in a location where you don't particularly want to live)? Agents for pro athletes are close to the action, but the job has pressures and a hectic life-style. How do you weigh these values against each other? Certain jobs have security, but is there enough stimulation for you? All of these are value choices, trading less of one value for more of another.

Athletes share many common values by having chosen sports for a prominent part of their lives, but they wander all over the map in terms of what they want most from a career. There is no such thing as a career an athlete would most prefer. Some want to set the business world on fire, while others prefer public service, and still others seek the creativity and independence of education, arts, and other fields. In every field of work, you will find former athletes, and you'll see them creating new fields as well.

Values are the lifeblood of any career decision. How will you know when you have "won" your game? Knowing what you want from your career will increase your chances of winning. Know your own career values and you are halfway home.

Every game plan has within it the seeds of its own success. You have a reason to believe you are going to make it and should trust your own instincts, whether you aspire to be a nuclear physicist, a professional golfer, or a real estate tycoon. If everything goes according to plan, you probably don't need our advice. However, the real trick in any game plan, the key to whether these seeds will flower, is what you do when something goes wrong, as many things probably will.

Dave wanted to start a magazine about sports teams and leagues in his local area. He is only a fair writer, has little capital to invest, and almost no experience in journalism. But he knew he wanted to do this, felt there was a need and a market for his product, and was determined to try. He got a job selling advertisements for another magazine (not sports-related) and started to meet people in the magazine trade. He looked around for partners, people with the talents he would need to start his magazine—editorial talent, organizational skills, etc.—and asked them to make their services available on a contract basis when he was ready to begin. Dave then hustled some advertising commitments for his new magazine, got advice for a marketing plan from a friend of a friend who is an expert in marketing of publications, then felt ready to put his "game" into operation. He sold enough ads to assure that the first issue would not lose money, and set out to hire the editorial talent he needed. He did not quit his present job; instead, he resolved to put out one issue and see if he could enroll a certain number of subscribers, to measure the likely future of his publication. Dave published one issue, now has 1,500 subscribers, has acquired half the ads necessary for the next issue, and feels he is six months away from quitting his job to work on the magazine full-time.

If Dave's magazine fails, will he have wasted his time? No! The lessons of a game plan are used and applied long after the original goal is sought, regardless of the results. You cannot be sure of outcomes, but you can be sure that using game plans will build your powers of self-determination and self-direction, and will make you more effective in seeking future goals, because you will have learned to channel your energies and organize your activities to obtain the things you desire.

Learning how to build success starts in your imagination and then extends to rewriting the script as necessary. Careers are "won" by first having reasons to believe you will succeed, maintaining these beliefs in the face of setbacks, and removing the obstacles to success as they occur. Until you can see, in your mind's eye, how all this will develop, it does not even exist. Once you see it, and the sequence of events forms a clear and motivating picture, you are ready to put your game plan into action.

ABOUT THE AUTHORS

STEPHEN FIGLER, associate professor at California State University–Sacramento, was a high school and college athlete and has coached at both levels. He is a member of the National Association of Academic Athletic Advisors and has helped to develop a special advising program for CSUS athletes. Dr. Figler has published a college textbook, *Sport and Play in American Life,* as well as several articles on advising college athletes. His Bachelor of Arts degree was earned at Oglethorpe University, where he won varsity letters in baseball and soccer and played junior varsity basketball. After a three-year career as a reporter and sportswriter in New York City, and later in Philadelphia, he took a master's degree at American University in physical education and educational psychology. During this period, he taught and coached in high school. His Ph.D. was earned at Stanford University in education and the social sciences.

HOWARD FIGLER is Director of the Career Center at the University of Texas at Austin. He was Director of the Counseling and Career Center at Dickinson College (Carlisle, Pennsylvania) from 1970 until 1982. Dr. Figler has written three books: *The Complete Job-Search Handbook, PATH: A Career Workbook for Liberal Arts Students,* and *Outreach in Counseling* (coauthored with David J. Drum). He earned a Bachelor of Arts degree from Emory University, where he was captain of the tennis team. He earned a master's degree in business administration from New York University and a Ph.D. in educational research and testing at Florida State University.

Have You Seen These Other Publications from Peterson's Guides?

Peterson's Annual Guides/Undergraduate Study
Guide to Four-Year Colleges 1985
FIFTEENTH EDITION
Managing Editor: Kim R. Kaye
Book Editor: Joan H. Hunter

The largest, most up-to-date guide to all 1,900 accredited four-year colleges in the United States and Canada. Contains concise college profiles, a reader guidance section, and two-page "Messages from the Colleges" that are found in no other guide. September 1984.

8½" x 11", 2,100 pages (approx.) Stock no. 2316
ISBN 0-87866-231-6   **$12.95** paperback

Peterson's Competitive Colleges
THIRD EDITION
Editor: Karen C. Hegener

The only book that determines college selectivity from objective data—and gives you the facts to work with. *Peterson's Competitive Colleges* presents a full page of comparative data for each of 302 colleges that consistently have more undergraduate applicants—with above-average abilities—than they can accept.

7" x 10", 344 pages   Stock no. 2677
ISBN 0-87866-267-7   **$7.95** paperback

**National College Databank:
The College Book of Lists**
THIRD EDITION
Editor: Karen C. Hegener

This is the updated and expanded third edition of the innovative reference book that helps college-bound students zero in on the colleges that have special features and characteristics. It groups more than 2,700 colleges by hundreds of characteristics, from size to price range to special programs. August 1984.

8½" x 11", 750 pages   Stock no. 2685
ISBN 0-87866-268-5   **$11.95** paperback

Peterson's Regional Guides to Colleges
Editor: Kim R. Kaye

Each book includes concise profiles of the four-year colleges in the region it covers. Also included are a section on financial aid and special information from admissions directors at selected colleges about the admissions philosophy, campus interviews, campus life, and special things to see on a campus visit at their college. All books are 8½" x 11" paperbacks.

Middle Atlantic Stock no. 6226 ISBN 0-87866-226-X **$6.95**
Midwest   Stock no. 2286 ISBN 0-87866-228-6 **$7.95**
New England Stock no. 6274 ISBN 0-87866-274-X **$6.95**
New York   Stock no. 2251 ISBN 0-87866-225-1 **$6.95**

**SAT Success:
Peterson's Study Guide to English and Math Skills for College Entrance Examinations:
SAT, ACT, and PSAT**
Joan Davenport Carris and Michael R. Crystal

This brand-new step-by-step text is designed as an effective self-instruction aid to build both the skills and the confidence of students preparing for college entrance examinations. Quiz-filled verbal and math sections plus mock SATs and actual questions from recent tests are included for practice.

8½" x 11", 380 pages   Stock no. 2081
ISBN 0-87866-208-1   **$8.95** paperback

**Peterson's Guide to College Admissions:
Getting into the College of Your Choice**
THIRD EDITION
R. Fred Zuker and Karen C. Hegener

This updated edition takes students behind the scenes at college admissions offices and gives current advice from admissions directors all across the country. Contains dozens of campus photos and capsule profiles of 1,700 four-year colleges.

8½" x 11", 366 pages   Stock no. 2243
ISBN 0-87866-224-3   **$9.95** paperback

College 101
Dr. Ronald T. Farrar

The first book to answer the questions college-bound students most often ask—about money, health, social life, sex, and academic concerns. Written with empathy, common sense, and knowledge, this book can serve as a springboard to frank discussions of all college-related topics. July 1984.

6" x 9", 125 pages (approx.)   Stock no. 2693
ISBN 0-87866-269-3   **$6.95** paperback

**The College Money Handbook 1985:
The Complete Guide to Expenses,
Scholarships, Loans, Jobs, and Special Aid
Programs at Four-Year Colleges**
SECOND EDITION
Editor: Karen C. Hegener

The only book that describes the complete picture of costs and financial aid at accredited four-year colleges in the United States. The book is divided into three sections: an overview of the financial aid process and ways to make it work for you; cost and aid profiles of each college, showing need-based and merit scholarship programs available; and directories listing colleges by the type of financial aid programs they offer. October 1984.

8½" x 11", 500 pages (approx.) Stock no. 2820
ISBN 0-87866-282-0   **$12.95** paperback

Winning Money for College: The High School Student's Guide to Scholarship Contests

Alan Deutschman

The first complete guide to scholarship competitions that students can enter and win on their own. It is the only compilation of facts, figures, dates, and advice pertaining to America's most prestigious—and most financially rewarding—privately offered scholarships. Includes over 50 national contests that cover public speaking, science, citizenship, and more. July 1984.

6" x 9", 190 pages (approx.)   Stock no. 2618
ISBN 0-87866-261-8   **$7.95** paperback

Peterson's College Selection Service 1985

Developed by the Staff of Peterson's Guides

This is a complete information package that will help students locate colleges with the specific characteristics they want. It includes a binder that holds two to four floppy microcomputer diskettes (depending on the brand and model of your computer), which contain information on the 1,700 accredited four-year colleges in the United States, along with programming that allows you to choose colleges from this group using nearly 600 descriptive characteristics. Includes complete instructions, a manual, and Peterson's *Guide to Four-Year Colleges 1985.* September 1984.

TRS-80 Model III, 64K with 80-column card.
Stock no. 2995   ISBN 0-87866-299-5
    $145.00

TRS-80 Model 4, 64K with 80-column card.
Stock no. 3002   ISBN 0-87866-300-2
    $145.00

Apple II Series (IIe, II+), 64K with 80-column card.
Stock no. 6288   ISBN 0-87866-288-X
    $145.00

IBM PC, 80K with 80-column card.
Stock no. 2898   ISBN 0-87866-289-8
    $145.00

How to Order

These publications are available from all good booksellers, or you may order direct from **Peterson's Guides, Dept. 4608, P.O. Box 2123, Princeton, New Jersey 08540.** Please note that prices are necessarily subject to change without notice.

- Enclose full payment for each book, plus postage and handling charges as follows:

Amount of Order	4th-Class Postage & Handling Charges
$1-$10	$1.25
$10.01-$20	$2.00
$20.01-$40	$3.00
$40.01 +	Add $1.00 shipping and handling for every additional $20 worth of books ordered.

Place your order TOLL-FREE by calling 800-225-0261 between 8:30 A.M. and 4:30 P.M. Eastern time, Monday through Friday. Telephone orders over $15 may be charged to your charge card; institutional and trade orders over $20 may be billed. From New Jersey, Alaska, Hawaii, and outside the United States, call 609-924-5338.

- For faster shipment via United Parcel Service (UPS), add $2.00 over and above the appropriate fourth-class book-rate charges listed.

- Bookstores and tax-exempt organizations should contact us for appropriate discounts.

- You may charge your order to VISA, MasterCard, or American Express. Minimum charge order: $15. Please include the name, account number, and validation and expiration dates for charge orders.

- New Jersey residents should add 6% sales tax to the cost of the books, excluding the postage and handling charge.

- Write for a free catalog describing all of our latest publications.